UNLOCKING THE HAGGADA

The Complete Haggada with In-Depth Commentary

RABBI SHMUEL GOLDIN

With illustrations by Shifra Goldin

gefen publishing house בית הוצאה לאור
JERUSALEM • NEW YORK   Est. 1981

Cover Design Concept: S. Kim Glassman
Design and Layout: Leah Ben Avraham / Noonim Graphics

ISBN: 9781675728871
1 3 5 7 9 8 6 4 2

Gefen Publishing House Ltd.
6 Hatzvi Street
Jerusalem 9438614, Israel
972-2-538-0247
orders@gefenpublishing.com

Gefen Books
140 Fieldcrest Ave.
Edison NJ, 08837
516-593-1234
orders@gefenpublishing.com

www.gefenpublishing.com
Printed in Israel

Library of Congress Cataloging-in-Publication Data

Names: Goldin, Shmuel, author, translator.
Title: Unlocking the Haggada / Rabbi Shmuel Goldin.
Other titles: Haggadah. | Haggadah. English.
Description: Jerusalem : Gefen Publishing House Ltd. ; Edison, NJ : Gefen Books, [2018]
Identifiers: LCCN 2017051981 | ISBN 9789652299376
Subjects: LCSH: Haggadah. | Haggadot--Texts. | Seder--Liturgy--Texts. |
Judaism--Liturgy--Texts.
Classification: LCC BM674.79 .G64 2018 | DDC 296.4/5371--dc23 LC record available at https://lccn.loc.gov/2017051981

We dedicate this Haggada to the memory of our beloved parents,

Shirley Margolin Parker and Dr. Joseph Parker, for whom words are inadequate to express our deep love and respect as well as the tremendous *hakarat hatov* we feel for all they have done for us. We have been blessed to have them as parents who taught us through example how to live meaningful and compassionate lives dedicated to family, community and faith. We aspire to conduct our lives and raise our children in ways that are consistent with the values they embodied.

And to our beloved grandparents,

Rose and Ben Margolin, who were instrumental in building the unique and vibrant Jewish community in Memphis, Tennessee. Their warmth, humor and wisdom, coupled with their fierce and genuine commitment to Judaism, remain as seminal influences in our lives. The many Shabbatot, *yomim tovim* and especially Sedarim we spent in their home were among the most cherished times of our lives and provide us with memories that we treasure forever.

Ethel and Abe Parker, who dedicated their lives to their three sons and who, from their modest home above a grocery store in Chattanooga, Tennessee, were able to instill in each of them an enduring love of Yiddishkeit and sense of community. These qualities endure today in their grandchildren and great-grandchildren.

May the memories of our parents and grandparents live on through their numerous acts of kindness and through the many people whose lives they enriched.

Finally, we feel fortunate to be involved in such a meaningful work produced by our teacher, spiritual leader and dear friend, Rabbi Shmuel Goldin. We are confident that this Haggada will provide insight and instruction for generations.

THE PARKER FAMILY

Michael and Toby		Jeffrey and Naava
	Julie	
Drew and Careena		Keith and Allison
	and their children	

As the children of Holocaust survivors, we are particularly appreciative of the importance of continuity – of the duty to tell and retell our story. For that reason, we are especially pleased to support Rabbi Goldin's work in creating a Pesach Haggada, a retelling of the story in Exodus and a reminder that the slavery of the Jews and their suffering is not limited to that time and that place. For us this part of the Pesach story reflects our parents' experience during the Holocaust.

For this reason and with great humility, we dedicate this Haggada to our families, Joseph Sarna of blessed memory and his wife Mania Sarna, and Jack Sarna of blessed memory and his wife Cela Sarna. We salute their bravery, their commitment to Judaism and its values, and their strength in going to a new land and creating a new life out of the ashes of their tragic childhood experience – just as their ancestors did. Everything good and valuable that we have learned in our lives, we have been taught by them. We now have a fourth generation of our beloved families. We will be together for Pesach, and we will read from Rabbi Goldin's Haggada, and we will be grateful and remember.

We thank Rabbi Goldin for what is sure to be an insightful and excellent addition to the world of Jewish letters, and we lovingly salute our parents for who they are, all they've accomplished, and for what they have given us.

Shirley Sarna and Steven Nelson
Rebecca Sarna
Mark Sarna and Anita Perkiel Sarna

Contents

To the Reader

*A*nother Haggada? I can hear the objections already...
No text in Jewish life, after all, has been published more often and with greater commentary than the Haggada text, the traditional guide to the Passover Seder service. Countless scholars, from the classical to the modern, have probed, analyzed and explained each detail of this most popular and important volume. It takes a degree of chutzpa, therefore, for any author to suggest that he has something new to add to the vast literature that has already been penned concerning the Haggada.

And yet, here I am, presenting a new Haggada, and I would like to make the case for doing so.

You see, for me, when it comes to the Haggada and the Seder experience, the issue is the *big picture* – the picture that emerges only when we consider the overall goals of the Seder evening and understand how the Haggada enables their realization. No moment on the Jewish calendar is fraught with more significance and meaning than the first evening of the Pesach festival. In home after home, country after country, generation after generation, Jewish families of all stripes and backgrounds have gathered on this evening to mark the first footfalls of their national journey.

What, however, is the Seder really all about? What are the overall goals of this richly textured service? The very title of the evening's proceedings indicates that these questions are critical. The Hebrew word *seder* means "order" or "structure." The Seder, it would seem, is designed to move its participants along a structured path from one specific "place" to another. And the Haggada? Clearly, the Haggada is the guidebook for this personal passage, outlining the steps that must be taken if each Seder is to achieve its general goals.

A fundamental problem, however, arises out of the very character of the Haggada itself. So rich is this text in wonderful detail that it is easy to lose sight of the big picture and to be captured by the nuances of the Seder service at the expense of its overall vision. When that happens, the carefully planned Seder evening becomes a series of disjointed ritual events, each beautiful and significant in its own right, but lacking a coherent flow and plan.

In order to avoid this problem, we will first view the evening from a distance, through a series of essays focusing upon the Seder's overall structure and purpose. We will only then enter the Haggada, examining the methodology of this ancient handbook as it leads each Seder participant toward fulfilling the evening's goals.

The introductory studies that follow should be read before the Seder begins. They can best be used, in fact, as preparatory material for analysis and discussion during the days leading up to the Seder.

The subsequent running commentary accompanying the Haggada text will build upon these studies through primary material and original thought selected to deepen our understanding of the evening's overall proceedings. Each section of the Seder will be prefaced with explanatory notes highlighting that section's place within the evening's general structure. The translation appearing in this volume will cleave as closely as possible to the literal meaning of the traditional text.

In this way, our Haggada will be different from most others. Notably absent will be the wide-ranging observations on minute detail that populate many Haggadot today. These observations, beautiful as they may be, tend to draw our attention away from the global flow and structure of the text. As much as possible, our focus will be on what we do and say on the Seder night, why we do and say it, and how each word and deed fits into the evening's general structure.

With excitement, I invite you to join me on a journey of discovery as together we unlock the secrets embedded within one of the most beautiful experiences in Jewish life.

Rabbi Shmuel Goldin
Jerusalem, Pesach 2019/5779

Rabbi Goldin can be reached at shmuelgoldin@rabbishmuelgoldin.com

How to Use This Haggada

As noted above, *Unlocking the Haggada* is specifically designed to lead Seder participants on a clear, guided journey through the Seder experience. To make the best use of this Haggada, therefore, please note and take advantage of its special features.

❶ Introductory essays. Meant to be read in preparation for the Seder, the five introductory essays outline the backdrop against which the Seder unfolds.

Contained within these essays is critical information concerning the Seder's overall structure, philosophical underpinnings, major mitzvot and more. Much of this information will be referenced in the ongoing commentary accompanying the Haggada text.

❷ Outline of festival preparations. The "Preparations for the Festival" section provides both practical instruction and philosophical background concerning many of the basic preparations needed for the Passover festival and for the Seder.

❸ Division into Seder units. Our Haggada divides the traditional thirteen sections of the Seder into four general units: "Setting the Stage: Preliminary Rituals," "The Past," "The Present" and "The Future." This division is clearly noted in the outline prior to the Seder's beginning (see pp. 34–35).

The division into units clarifies the overall structure of the Seder and focuses the reader on the general flow of the evening's journey. Each unit is clearly marked and color coded in the text, and is introduced by a paragraph detailing its purpose and structure. The Seder sections included in each unit are also clearly delineated from the outset.

Additional colored tabs found on the margins of the Haggada text are designed to heighten the reader's constant awareness of the Seder's flow and of the relationship of each Seder section to the others. Identifying banners at the top of each page serve a similar function.

❹ Section introductions. Each of the fourteen traditional Seder sections is prefaced by an introduction explaining that section's origin, significance and place in the overall Seder journey. Special attention is paid to the ongoing flow of the text as the connection between sections is clarified.

Additional introductions are added to the subsections and various passages of Maggid, the lengthy central section of the Haggada. In addition, a visual chart outlining the structure of Maggid and the ancient origins of that structure is inserted in the text before Maggid begins.

⑤ Food for Thought. An extensive running commentary accompanies the Haggada text. Unique to this commentary, once again, is its repeated stress on the "big picture" of the Seder, as timeless lessons rising out of each passage of the Haggada are noted and their place in the unfolding Seder journey elucidated. While the information in this commentary can prove helpful in Seder preparation, the commentary is primarily designed to be used at the Seder itself, both by the Seder leader(s) and by other participants. Its proper use at the Seder can motivate questions and discussion, thereby significantly enhancing the participatory nature of the Seder experience.

In many cases, open-ended issues will be included and labeled "For further discussion," in order to inspire continued dialogue and study as the Seder progresses.

⑥ Halachic sidebars. Titled "The Primary Mitzvot of the Seder," a number of halachic sidebars are inserted in the text as each one of the central Seder obligations first appears in the evening's ritual. This series of sidebars provides the reader with background information and practical halachic guidance concerning each of the obligatory mitzvot around which the Seder is built. The full text of each sidebar is shaded in the color of the unit in which it is found to set it apart from the ongoing text and to alert the reader to its explanatory role at the Seder.

⑦ Digressions and Insertions. The traditional Haggada text is punctuated by a set of digressions or insertions that interrupt the main flow of the proceedings. While these digressions add to the rich flavor of the evening, they can complicate the proceedings, by causing the participants to lose sight of the ongoing, structured Seder flow.

To address this issue, our Haggada clearly identifies and notes the nature of each digression or insertion and informs the readers upon their return to the main body of the text. Additionally, digressions are shaded, to further identify their character as ancillary to the Seder's main flow.

Acknowledgments

When I decided to produce a "new" Haggada, I had no idea how complicated the process would be. I quickly became aware, however, that many pieces would have to fit together in order to achieve my goal of creating a clear roadmap through the Seder. Hebrew text, translation, instructions, commentary, halachic information and more would have to coalesce into a cohesive whole, were I to succeed in taking the reader by the hand through the rich, exciting, meaningful, yet complex Pesach Eve journey.

Clearly, I needed serious help. Thankfully, it came from many sources.

Ilan Greenfield of Gefen Publishing House is an excellent partner. Throughout this project, our second major collaboration, Ilan once again demonstrated to me why Gefen has such a stellar reputation. With personal warmth and professional expertise, he oversaw every aspect of this volume's development. He remained open to new ideas as the project evolved, always with an eye toward making the finished product as meaningful and valuable as possible. I am extremely fortunate to have worked with him again.

I can't say enough about Kezia Raffel Pride, editor extraordinaire. From our previous work together, I already knew of Kezia's professionalism and patience as an editor. This time, however, she had to do much more. Her continued advice, in areas from practical format to overall vision, played a major role in the formation of this volume. And her figurative "handholding" at particularly difficult junctures kept this author on track. Without her contributions, *Unlocking the Haggadah* would never have seen the light of day.

Project manager Emily Wind is a wonderful addition to the Gefen staff. The managing of authors, editors, designers, printers and others toward the completion of their tasks in the production of disparate volumes is no easy feat. Emily does her job with excellence, equanimity, immediate responsiveness and, always, with a smile. When Emily, thank God, took time off for maternity leave, Devorah Beasley stepped right in with true professionalism and without missing a beat.

Leah Ben Avraham's talent and creativity as the volume's designer meshed with her clear understanding of our goals, enabling her to produce a finished product of which we could all be proud. Shana Cooper's excellent advice at a critical juncture in the project added an invaluable layer to the volume's structure. Thanks to Ruth Pepperman for proofreading the text with eagle eyes and catching every last thing that we all missed.

Finally, many thanks to my distinguished colleague and friend Rabbi Dr. Jacob J. Schacter for his review of the manuscript and his very helpful comments.

Our continued collaboration with OU Press is a source of deep pride to me. Affiliation with the Orthodox Union lends an invaluable layer of prestige to our efforts. I am deeply grateful to my esteemed colleagues Rabbi Menachem Genack, CEO of OU Kashrus, and

Rabbi Simon Posner, head of OU Press, for the confidence they have placed in me.

The Parkers and Sarnas, two Englewood families with whom I have enjoyed a special and treasured friendship, graciously agreed to sponsor this Haggada in memory of departed loved ones. These wonderful families share a deep commitment to Jewish values, history, tradition and continuity that makes their association with the publication of a Haggada so particularly appropriate. I thank Michael and Toby Parker, Jeffrey and Naava Parker, Julie Parker, Drew and Careena Parker, Keith and Allison Parker, Mark Sarna and Anita Perkiel Sarna, Shirley Sarna and Steven Nelson, and Rebecca Sarna for their continued cherished friendship and support.

The development of this Haggada has taken place against the backdrop of major changes in my personal and professional life. These years saw my retirement from an over forty-year career in the active pulpit rabbinate. After thirty-three years of service as Senior Rabbi of Congregation Ahavath Torah in Englewood, I transitioned to the position of that synagogue's Rabbi Emeritus and made aliya to Israel together with my dear wife, Barbara.

I will forever be grateful to the many congregants and colleagues who enriched my life over the course of my rabbinic career. The deeply meaningful journeys we shared together have shaped me in ways too numerous to mention, and I know that many of our friendships will last and deepen for years to come. The respect and love shown to me and my family as we left Congregation Ahavath Torah's active rabbinate will forever be cherished. It is but a reflection of the precious personal connections we made over the course of more than three decades in that wonderful community. I also thank the many professionals at the congregation with whom I have partnered over the years. Of particular mention are my esteemed associate of many years, Rabbi Chaim Poupko, who has appropriately succeeded me as Rabbi of Ahavath Torah, and my personal assistant, Eileen Gorlyn, whose invaluable support enabled me to accomplish what I did during my tenure in the community.

As I write these words, Barbara and I are well into our new journey as proud citizens of the State of Israel. Our first year has been filled with new experiences, opportunities and challenges. With each passing day, we become more convinced that our decision to come "home" to Israel at this point in our lives, while complicated, was the right one. I am deeply grateful to the various organizations and institutions that have provided me with teaching, lecturing and consulting opportunities since our arrival in Israel. These varied experiences have broadened my horizons and allow me to continue contributing to the Jewish community in meaningful ways.

My children, Avi and Rena, Yossi and Shifra, Yehuda and Noa, Donny and Tamara, and Rivka and Kivi; and my grandchildren, Isaac, Benjamin, Temima, Jacob, Chaim,

Rachel, Mordechai, Julia, Yehudit, Penina, Dovi, Olivia, Chana, Leo and Yonah, continue to be a source of tremendous amazement and pride. The opportunity to see your children become truly responsible adults, create their own warm homes, raise wonderful children and maintain the values that you hold dear (in their own unique ways, of course), is the greatest blessing that God can grant. Barbara and I are thankful daily for having received this blessing beyond measure.

Given the sad passing of my mother, Penina Goldin, of blessed memory, my cadre of active "family editors" was reduced to one member, my son Yossi. In spite of his extremely busy personal and professional schedule, Yossi stepped up to the plate in every sense of the word. His wise advice fills the pages of this volume. I am deeply thankful that Shifra, Yossi's "better half," agreed to further enhance this Haggada through her artistic ability. Her talent and innate understanding are readily evident in the beautiful and meaningful drawings that punctuate its pages.

Finally, thanks are due to the one person most instrumental in any and all of my accomplishments, my dear wife, Barbara. It was her wise counsel and unstinting persuasion (and I was not an easy subject) that brought us to Israel twelve years ago for our sabbatical year, a trip that launched the writing of my five-volume series *Unlocking the Torah Text*. It has been her similar wise counsel and persuasion that have brought us now to Israel as citizens (again, I was reluctant to make the move at this time – and she was 100 percent right). Barbara's role as the guiding force behind each important decision in my life is evidenced by the fact that she was the one to suggest that my next writing project be a Haggada. The list goes on and on. Simply put, personally and professionally, without her I would not be where I am today. I owe her all...

I close with an expression of deepest gratitude to Hakadosh Baruch Hu, the Creator and Sustainer of all, for the manifold blessings that He has bestowed upon me and my family over the years, and for enabling me to reach this deeply meaningful milestone. I pray that He grant us all ongoing health, strength and wisdom, and that He bless me with the continued ability to plumb the depths of His Torah and share of its beauty with others.

Before Opening the Haggada
Introductory Essays
and Festival Preparations

Making Sense of the Seder I
A Halachic Perspective

Questions

An amalgam of rituals, practices and observances populate the Seder evening. Finding a meaningful, coherent path through these experiences is often a daunting task.

What motivated the rabbis to create the Seder as we know it today? What are its critical components? Are all of the Seder rituals of equal importance? Do they all emerge from a common time and origin? Bottom line, what are the primary obligations to be fulfilled on the Seder night?

Approaches

At its most basic, the Seder serves as the vehicle for the performance of six (or seven – see below) fundamental mitzvot, all specific to the first night of Pesach. While each of these mitzvot is independent and emerges from its own unique source, the rabbis seamlessly weave their fulfillment into a coherent whole through the medium of the Seder. Many other rituals populate the evening's experience. These original six (or seven) obligations, however, remain the primary components of the Seder.

When considered as a group, the central mitzvot of the Seder reflect the rich history of the halachic process, thereby adding yet another layer of history to a "night of history." Two of the mitzvot of the Seder evening are biblically mandated to this day. The origin of another is the subject of debate, while two others are clearly of rabbinic derivation. One of the evening's requirements originates as a biblical directive, but loses its biblical character over time and is performed today as a rabbinic obligation. Finally, a last ritual is of questionable origin, with the rabbis debating whether it is an independent mitzva at all.

Outlined here, each of these mitzvot will be individually identified and more fully discussed as it is encountered at the Seder. Not included in this outline are additional mitzvot of the evening, such as Kiddush (the introductory blessings over the wine), *netilat yadayim* (the washing of the hands before eating bread – or in this case, matza), and Birkat Hamazon (the grace after meals). These mitzvot are not specific to the Seder night but are performed at meals year-round.

A. The biblical mitzvot.

1. The consumption of matza (unleavened bread). Each Jew is enjoined to consume a measure of matza on the first night of Pesach in fulfillment of the biblical commandment *"Ba'erev tochlu matzot"* (in the evening you shall eat matzot).[1]

While eating matza is, according to most authorities, obligatory only on the Seder evening, the symbol pervades the entire Passover festival. On multiple occasions, in fact, the Torah refers to Pesach as Chag Hamatzot, the festival of matzot.[2]

2. *Sippur Yetziat Mitzrayim* (the retelling of the Exodus story). The mitzva of retelling the story of the Exodus on the first night of Pesach is derived from the combination of two biblical verses: *"Zachor et hayom hazeh asher yetzatem mi'Mitzrayim"* (Remember this day on which you departed from Egypt)[3] and *"V'higgadeta l'vincha ba'yom hahu, leimor"* (And you shall relate [the Exodus narrative] to your child on this day, saying…).[4]

This obligation serves as the backbone of the entire Seder and as the backdrop against which its many rituals unfold. So central is this mitzva to the Seder that the title of the Haggada derives from the second biblical verse: *"V'higgadeta l'vincha"* (and you shall relate [the Exodus narrative] to your child…).[5]

B. The mitzva of debated origin.

Hallel (Psalms of praise). Psalms 113–118, collectively traditionally known as Hallel, or more specifically Hallel Hamitzri, the Egyptian Hallel,[6] are designated for recitation at specific festive points of the Jewish calendar year. The source of the general obligation to recite Hallel is the subject of rabbinic debate. Some authorities maintain that this obligation is biblical in origin,[7] while others view it as a rabbinical mandate.[8]

While all authorities agree that these psalms of praise should be included at the Seder, a further dispute develops as to the source of this specific mitzva.

Some scholars perceive the Hallel of the Seder to be of rabbinic origin, consistent with their opinion concerning the recitation of Hallel at other times of the year.[9] Other scholars, however, view the Seder's Hallel as uniquely biblical in derivation, emerging either as an essential element in the retelling of the Exodus story or as a natural response to the experience of personal redemption rising out of the Seder service.[10]

---

1 Shmot 12:18; Rambam, *Mishneh Torah*, Hilchot Chametz U'matza 6:1.
2 Shmot 23:15; 34:18; Vayikra 23:6.
3 Shmot 13:3.
4 Shmot 13:8, discussed in Rambam, *Mishneh Torah*, Hilchot Chametz U'matza 7:1.
5 Shmot 13:8.
6 These passages are designated by this title because of references to the Exodus contained within them.
7 Ba'al Halachot Gedolot, minyan hamitzvot; *Sefer Yere'im* 262; *Sefer Mitzvot Ketanot* 146.
8 Rambam, *Mishneh Torah*, Hilchot Chanuka 3:6.
9 *She'eilot U'tshuvot Sha'agat Aryeh*, siman 69.
10 *Mishnat Ya'abetz* 18, 19; Rabbi Joseph Soloveitchik maintains that, although the Rambam views the year-round recitation of Hallel as a rabbinical mandate, he considers the obligation on the Seder night to be of biblical origin, an essential component in the mitzva of *sippur Yetziat Mitzrayim*. See Rabbi Menachem D. Genack, ed., *The Seder Night: An Exalted Evening; The Passover Haggadah with a Commentary Based on the Teachings of Rabbi Joseph B. Soloveitchik* (New York: OU Press, 2009), p. 104.

The Seder night Hallel is augmented by the addition of Psalm 136 (known as Hallel Hagadol, the Great Hallel) and other closing prayers.

C. The rabbinic mitzvot.

1. The consumption of *arba kosot* (four cups of wine). As a symbol of freedom, the rabbis mandate the consumption of four cups of wine over the course of the Seder evening.[11] The drinking of the wine punctuates the Seder at critical moments, highlighting the transition from one section of the service to the next.

So important is the rabbinic *takana* (edict)[12] concerning the wine that charitable funds must be used to enable even the poorest in the community to meet this obligation.[13]

2. *Heseiba* (reclining while eating). The obligation to recline when seated at the Seder is mentioned in the Mishna[14] and elaborated upon in the Gemara. Like the four cups of wine, this mitzva is rabbinic in origin, designed to further cultivate the feeling of personal redemption essential to the Seder service.

While numerous authorities maintain that it is "praiseworthy" to eat the entire Seder meal while reclining,[15] *heseiba* is mandatory only at specific points in the evening's proceedings. So strong is the requirement to recline at these moments, however, that failure to do so generally necessitates repetition of the rituals involved.[16]

D. The transformed mitzva.

1. Maror (bitter herbs). With the commandment *"al matzot u'merorim yochluhu"* (with matzot and bitter herbs shall they eat it [the Passover offering]),[17] the Torah mandates the consumption of both matza and *maror* in conjunction with the Korban Pesach. As noted above, however, a second commandment to eat matza is found elsewhere in the Torah, unconnected to the Korban Pesach.[18] In contrast, no independent mandate concerning the consumption of *maror* is found in the text.

Based on this distinction in the text, the scholars conclude that a biblical obligation to eat matza on the first night of Pesach remains in force even in the absence of the Korban Pesach, while the biblical obligation to eat *maror* does not.[19] Nonetheless, the rabbis mandate that *maror* should remain at the Seder to this day, as a remembrance of the rituals performed during Temple times.[20] The mitzva of *maror* is thus transformed, at the hands of the rabbinic authorities, from a biblical to a rabbinic obligation.

---

11 Talmud Bavli Pesachim 109b.

12 Rabbinic laws can generally be divided into two fundamental categories: *gezeirot* (laws created to protect an existing Torah law) and *takanot* (laws enacted by the rabbis in response to changing need and circumstance). See my *Unlocking the Torah Text: Shmot*, Yitro 5, for a review of these and other sections of Oral Law.

13 Mishna Pesachim 10:1.

14 Ibid.

15 Rambam, *Mishneh Torah*, Hilchot Chametz U'matza 7:8; *Shulchan Aruch*, Orach Chaim, Rema 472:7.

16 *Shulchan Aruch*, Orach Chaim 472:7; Mechaber, Rema, *Mishna Berura* 472:22.

17 Bamidbar 9:11.

18 Shmot 12:18.

19 Talmud Bavli Pesachim 120a.

20 *Shulchan Aruch Harav*, Orach Chaim 475:12.

E. The questionable mitzva.

1. Charoset (a chopped mixture of apples, other fruits and wine). The Mishna records an obligation to consume *charoset* at the Seder.[21] Debate immediately ensues, however, as to the exact nature of this requirement.

The first opinion quoted in the Mishna maintains that this foodstuff must be consumed at the Seder, "even though *charoset* is not a mitzva."[22] According to this view, the Talmud explains, *charoset* is eaten at the Seder for health reasons, to counteract the deleterious effects of the *maror*.[23]

Rabbi Eliezer ben Tzadok, a second authority quoted in the Mishna, however, argues that the consumption of *charoset* at the Seder does rise to the level of an independent rabbinic mitzva.[24] Later Talmudic authorities debate the exact symbolism of this possible rabbinical edict. Some maintain that *charoset* reflects the deep dedication of the enslaved Israelites, who deliberately gave birth to their children in the wild, "under the apple tree,"[25] beyond the watchful eyes of their Egyptian taskmasters. Other authorities argue that *charoset* symbolizes the mortar used by the Israelites during their forced labor in Egypt.[26]

The rabbis continue to discuss and debate the exact parameters of this symbol across the generations. In his commentary on the Mishna, for example, the Rambam seems to indicate that the consumption of *charoset* at the Seder is not a mitzva.[27] In his codification of the law in the *Mishneh Torah*, however, this very same scholar emphatically declares, "*Charoset* is a rabbinic mitzva, a remembrance of the mortar..."[28] Attempts by later scholars to address this apparent contradiction in the Rambam's writings become part of the ongoing dialogue concerning the nature of *charoset*.

---

21 Mishna Pesachim 10:3.
22 Ibid.
23 Talmud Bavli Pesachim 116a.
24 Mishna Pesachim 10:3.
25 Shir Hashirim 8:5.
26 Talmud Bavli Pesachim 116a.
27 Rambam, *Peirush Hamishnayot*, Pesachim 10:3.
28 Rambam, *Mishneh Torah*, Hilchot Chametz U'matza 7:11; see also *Maggid Mishneh* and *Lechem Mishneh*.

Making Sense of the Seder II
A Historical Perspective

Questions

From a historical perspective, the Seder can be seen as a recreation of a powerful moment, critical to the birth of the Jewish nation. *Contrary to what we would expect, however, the moment recreated at the Pesach Seder is not that of the Exodus itself...*

The Torah narrative is clear. Pharaoh, the Egyptian king, summarily releases his Israelite slaves in the middle of the night, in the immediate aftermath of the devastating final plague of the firstborn.[1] Nonetheless, Moshe does not lead his people to freedom until the next day.[2] Based upon a midrashic tradition, the Ramban explains that the first footfalls of the nation's journey are not to be those of thieves slinking away in the darkness of night. Instead, the Israelites will leave Egypt victoriously in the middle of the day, with their heads held high, in full view of their erstwhile masters.[3]

If the Seder is designed to be a recreation of the actual Exodus from Egypt, therefore, it should be marked at high noon on the fifteenth day of Nisan, the first day of Pesach. Instead, across the generations, Jews have gathered in their homes on Pesach Eve to reexperience *the night before the Exodus*.

Historically, the Israelites in Egypt marked that night, at God's command, by retreating to the safety of their homes in extended family groups. There, each group consumed a Korban Pesach while, outside their doors, the final plague rained down upon the Egyptians. Centuries later, we mirror their actions. We join in family groups for the Seder, commemorating the moment when our ancestors prepared for an unknown future through the consumption of their first ritual family meal. The question, however, is obvious. Why is the moment of the Korban Pesach memorialized each year through the Seder, while the actual moment of the Exodus, midday of the following day, passes unmarked? Wouldn't it be logical to celebrate the moment of the Exodus itself on the festival clearly designed to commemorate that event?

---

1 Shmot 12:31.
2 Shmot 12:41, 51.
3 Ramban, Shmot 12:31, based upon *Mechilta*, Shmot 12:31, and *Midrash Tehillim* 113:2.

Approaches

The answers to our question may well lie in a series of powerful lessons that emerge from the rituals of the first Korban Pesach – lessons that we are meant to remember and commemorate each year...[4]

I. Between Liberty and Freedom

Most immediately, the first Korban Pesach draws our attention to the two different dimensions of freedom that exist in Jewish thought: *dror* and *cherut*.

A. *Dror* (liberty) – the removal of external constraints, physical or otherwise, that impede upon an individual's personal choice and independent action. *Dror* is either conferred upon an individual by an outside force or attained by an individual through severance from that force.

B. *Cherut* (freedom) – the injection of positive purpose and value into one's life. The individual who enjoys *cherut*, by choosing to pursue a higher goal, actively frees himself from servitude to the surrounding world and its potentially enslaving influences. *Cherut* is not granted by another but must be attained by an individual alone.

One can be free even when not at liberty. One can be at liberty yet not be free.

While still enveloped in the darkness of Egyptian servitude, the Israelites are commanded to declare their *cherut*. By setting aside a lamb, the god of Egypt, on the tenth day of Nisan; by publicly waiting four days and then slaughtering and consuming that lamb on Pesach Eve, the Israelites demonstrate that they are already free from Egypt and the Egyptians. *Although physical liberty will only be achieved on the morrow, the Israelites attain their spiritual freedom while still in Egypt, on the night of the Korban Pesach.*

How appropriate, then, that we mark this night each year at the Seder. How many times through a long and arduous history have we, the descendants of those first Israelites, been forced to relive the scene of the Korban Pesach in actual life? How many times has our nation been called upon, against the backdrop of physical darkness and persecution, to declare spiritual and philosophical freedom from its oppressors? How many times will we be forced to do so again, before the dawn of the messianic age?

As we sit in the comfort of our homes, we recall Sedarim courageously observed under very different circumstances; from basements in Catholic Spain to prisons in Arab lands, from Nazi labor camps to the Soviet Gulag. And, through these collective memories, a sobering message of the Seder becomes abundantly clear. The ability to achieve freedom, even in the absence of liberty, has always been and continues to be a talent crucial to the survival of the Jewish nation.

At the same time, reliving the night of the Korban Pesach also reminds us of the emptiness of liberty without freedom. Had the Israelites left Egypt without first

---

4 Many of these ideas appear in my *Unlocking the Torah Text: Shmot*, Bo 4.

experiencing the rituals of the previous night, their emancipation would have been incomplete. *Dror* only has meaning when it is accompanied by *cherut*, when the removal of external constraints is accompanied by the injection of positive purpose.

Why do so many citizens of the United States and other democratic countries remain deeply unhappy in spite of the liberties they possess – liberties unimaginable in other times and places?[5] How many of us and those around us, living at liberty in free societies, nonetheless feel enslaved to the pressures of an outside world? The ancient formula proposed by the Talmudic sages rings true to our day: *"Ein lecha ben chorin ela mi she'oseik b'talmud Torah"* (No one is free except for he who involves himself in the study of Torah).[6] Meaning in life is attained through the recognition of a purpose beyond oneself. Only through belief in and pursuit of such a higher cause can a human being truly be "free."

II. A Societal Blueprint

Digging a bit deeper, another critical layer of meaning can be uncovered in the rituals surrounding the first Korban Pesach.

A careful reading of the text reveals that the instructions concerning the first Korban Pesach unfold in three stages, ritualistically outlining a *three-stage societal blueprint* by which the emerging Israelite nation is to be built:

> Speak to the entire assembly of Israel, saying: On the tenth of this month they shall take for themselves, each man, a lamb for each father's house, a lamb for the household. And if the household shall be too small for a lamb, then he and his neighbor who is near to his home shall take according to the number of people; each man according to his ability to eat shall be counted for the lamb.[7]

A. "A lamb for each father's house, a lamb for the household." The first and foremost pillar of Jewish society is the family unit.

God deliberately refrains from marking the birth of the Jewish nation with constitutional conventions, mass rallies or declarations of independence. Each Israelite is, instead, commanded to return to the privacy of his home, where he is to participate in the family meal that is the Korban Pesach.

By insisting upon a retreat to the home as a prelude to our nation's birth, God delivers a simple yet powerful message: As you prepare to begin your historical journey, stop and mark this evening within the societal unit most critical to your success. Remember always that your survival will depend upon the health of the family. If the family is strong, if the home fulfills its educational role, your people will be strong and your nation will endure.

---

5   According to a 2016 Harris Poll, fewer than one in three Americans self-identifies as happy. Lily Rothman, "Exclusive: New 'Happiness Index' Number Reveals How Americans Feel Right Now," *Time*, July 1, 2016.

6   Pirkei Avot 6:2.

7   Shmot 12:3–4.

The Jewish home is and always has been the single most important educational unit in the perpetuation of our people. What our children learn at home, more than what they learn in any other setting, indelibly shapes both their knowledge of and attitude toward Jewish tradition and practice.

Furthermore, Jewish experience will be enriched across the centuries, not only by the nuclear family, but by the extended family, as well. God, therefore, insists that the Korban Pesach shall be "for each father's home" as well as "for the household."

B. "And if the household shall be too small for a lamb, then he and his neighbor who is near to his home shall take..." Moving beyond the family unit, the text arrives at the second foundation of Jewish society: the community.

The family unit, as important as it is, cannot operate in a vacuum. Each household will be required, at times, to reach beyond its walls, either to ask for or to offer assistance and support. God, therefore, instructs any family that cannot perform the Pesach rituals on its own to turn outward. If neighbors work together, creating communal institutions of mutual support, the nation they build will survive and thrive.

An apparent redundancy in the text underscores the mindset that must characterize these shared communal endeavors. A neighbor is, by definition, an individual who lives in close proximity to another. Why, then, does the Torah state that the Korban Pesach should be shared with "his neighbor who is *near to his home*"?

Perhaps the text stresses that we should adopt an attitude toward our neighbors that defines them as "near to our home." By recognizing the vulnerabilities, rights and dreams that we and our neighbors all share, we will be moved to assist those around us to reach their goals, even as we strive to achieve our own.

C. "Each man according to his ability to eat shall be counted for the lamb." Finally, the Torah reminds us that no individual can escape the obligations raised by the third societal foundation: personal responsibility.

Strong families and communities can, at times, serve as a refuge for those who wish to escape the burdens of their own obligations. After all, if there are others to "do the job," why should we?

Such an attitude clearly robs our people of essential human resources. Each and every individual has a unique and invaluable contribution to make to our nation's story – a contribution that is solely his or her own. God therefore symbolically demands that the computation concerning the size of each Korban Pesach be based upon the full participation of all involved in that *korban*. Our national aspirations will be fully met only if "each man" performs "according to his ability."

Gathering in their homes on the first Pesach Eve of our nation's history, our ancestors ritually underscored the three societal foundations that would make their nation's journey enduring. Centuries later, we commemorate that moment by underscoring the very same foundations. *We gather in extended family units* in the comfort of our homes; *we invite others to join us*, even formalizing our invitation through the recitation of a special paragraph (*Ha lachma anya*); and *we encourage the personal participation of each and every individual* at the Seder, young and old alike.

III. Hurry Up and Wait

A third lesson emerges from the notion of ritualized haste and urgency that seems so central to the observance of the Korban Pesach: "And so shall you consume it: your loins girded, your shoes on your feet and your staff in your hand. *And you shall eat it in haste*; it is a Passover offering to God."[8]

At face value, this sense of haste seems totally unnecessary.

The Exodus is not a sudden, unexpected event. The conclusion of Egyptian exile was clearly predicted as far back as the days of Avraham (see my *Unlocking the Torah Text: Bereishit*, Lech Lecha 4; Vayeishev 3). The Israelites themselves have been waiting and hoping for this moment over centuries of servitude. To further complicate matters, as explained above, when Pharaoh finally urges the Israelites to leave Egypt during the night, Moshe insists that the departure take place in broad daylight, midday of the following day.

Why introduce a sense of urgency into the Korban Pesach when the departure from Egypt could well have been experienced in a calm, ordered fashion?

Once again, through ritual, the Torah conveys an idea that cannot be ignored: *Great opportunities are often presented in swiftly fleeting moments.* While it is true that the moment of the Exodus had been predicted and anticipated for centuries, when that moment finally arrives, an instantaneous decision on the part of each Israelite is required. Hesitation will prove fatal. Only those individuals decisive and courageous enough to leave a known existence for the unknown will merit becoming part of the glorious story of their people. Those who miss this small temporal window of opportunity will be too late and will disappear into the mists of history. The difficulties inherent in the choice to leave Egypt are reflected in the rabbinic tradition that only a small percentage of the Israelites ultimately depart.[9]

(As we will note in our further studies, the challenge presented by fleeting opportunities is further ritualized in another Seder symbol: matza, unleavened bread – see pp.136–38).

Finally, we consider one strikingly strange instruction associated with the ritualized haste surrounding the Korban Pesach. "And so shall you consume [the Korban Pesach]: your loins girded, your shoes on your feet and your staff in your hand."[10]

Why must the Israelites eat the Korban Pesach already prepared for a journey that will only begin on the morrow? Certainly there will be time to dress appropriately and

---

8   Shmot 12:11.
9   *Mechilta*, Shmot 13:17.
10 Shmot 12:11.

pick up staffs after the ritual is concluded. Is this detail simply a further demonstration of symbolic speed, or is there an even deeper lesson to be learned?

Commenting on this extraordinary scene, the rabbis only seem to muddy the waters further: "Rabbi Yossi Haglili stated: 'Here the text comes to provide good advice for travelers, that they should be energetic.'"[11]

What, exactly, is Rabbi Yossi adding to the mix? Are the rituals of the first Korban Pesach to be reduced to "good advice for travelers," conveying a lesson that is already clearly self-evident?

Upon consideration, however, Rabbi Yossi's observation emerges as a brilliant example of rabbinic methodology, which often couches complex, critical lessons in easily remembered tales and pictures. According to Rabbi Yossi, the Torah proposes that, from the moment of the Korban Pesach, all Jews become "travelers" in the journey of our people across the face of history. As we travel along that long and arduous road, one talent becomes critical to our survival – a talent captured in the image of the Israelites dressed for tomorrow's journey the night before. *Somehow, we have to learn to be prepared for tomorrow's challenges today.*

In generation after generation, in society after society, the descendants of the Israelites will confront ever-changing circumstances and challenges. At times, change may occur so rapidly and so totally as to seem impossible to predict. Most often, however, the seeds of these transformations will be visible in advance to those perceptive and energetic enough to notice.

At the dawn of their national history, in the darkness of the night, a people gather in groups to eat a family meal while fully prepared for a journey that will only begin on the morrow. From that time on, that people's ability to determine and prepare for changes before they emerge full-blown will be central to their success and survival.

"Who is truly wise? He who sees that which is a-borning."[12]

The story is told of the Jewish optician who lives in Berlin in the 1930s. Noting the events taking place around him, he decides to emigrate to Israel. To inform his patients of his departure, he places a sign outside his office: "For all of you who are nearsighted, there is a doctor around the corner. For all of you who are farsighted, follow me."

While the story is poignant, it is also, of course, simplistic. How can we judge, from the safety of our own environment, the issues that must have confronted the Jewish community of Europe in the years leading up to World War II? Had we been there, would we have believed that countries such as Germany – representing the height of civilization at the time – could possibly commit the unspeakable atrocities that were to come? Are we so certain that, ensconced comfortably in homes that had been ours for decades, we would have been able to pick up and leave?

---

11 *Mechilta*, Shmot 12:11.
12 Talmud Bavli Tamid 32a.

And yet...the facts remain. Had we been more intuitive, had we listened to what was being said by the Nazis, had we mobilized in the face of impending danger – who knows how many would have been saved?

We must also ask: Are we any better equipped today? Would we see the danger signs looming on the horizon of our own exiles in time to make a difference? Are some of those signs already appearing? Are we sensitive not only to the open physical threats against us but also to the subliminal philosophical dangers that so often lie beneath our radar screen?

We would do well to keep the image of the first Pesach table before us as we continue our travels. The lessons learned around it continue to inform our journey to this day.

Making Sense of the Seder III
An Experiential Perspective

Questions

The third and final level of the Seder emerges from the evening's familiar yet puzzling tripartite structure: the rituals preceding the meal; the meal; the rituals following the meal.

Logic, one might argue, would have dictated a different flow for the evening's proceedings. Why not conclude the evening's ceremonies and then sit down to eat? Or – a suggestion certain to garner popular support – why not eat the meal and then conduct the rituals? *Ma nishtana*; why is this night different? Why is a meal embedded in the middle of a structured ceremonial service?

Our question concerning the Seder's overall configuration is compounded when we recognize that the meal is not only placed in the middle of the Seder, but in the middle of Hallel! Some of Hallel's passages of praise are recited immediately before we eat our meal, while others are recited directly thereafter. Even if a case can be made for embedding the meal in the middle of the Seder – to highlight, perhaps, the recreation of the first Pesach feast (see above) – the decision to disrupt Hallel in progress is difficult to understand.

Certainly we could manage to finish our praises of God before we sit down to eat. Or, conversely, we could easily delay the starting of Hallel until after the meal has ended. Why do we deliberately interrupt this liturgical composition midstream?[1]

Approaches

When we step back far enough to view the Seder on a global level, a striking answer emerges from the Haggada text. After a series of preliminary rituals, all of the passages in the Haggada that are recited before the meal focus primarily on *the past*. All of the passages recited following the meal, until the Seder's end, focus on *the future*.[2] And the

---

1   Some authorities trace the splitting of Hallel to Temple times, when an obligation existed to recite Hallel in conjunction with the Korban Pesach (Mishna Pesachim 9:3). In this view, in order to demonstrate the connection between the offering and the prayers, Hallel was divided to surround the offering (Maharal, *Gevurot Hashem* 62).

2   As an example of this phenomenon, the division of the Hallel can prove instructive. The focus of the passages preceding the meal is summed up in the proclamation "When Israel came forth from Egypt, the House of Yaakov from a people of a strange language; Yehuda became His holy one, Israel His dominion" (Tehillim 114:1–2). The passages following the meal, on the other hand, are peppered with phrases reflecting the future, such as: "The Lord has been mindful of us: He will bless us, He will bless the House of Israel,

meal itself? Apparently, the meal is meant to reflect *the present*. On the Seder night, we sit down to a meal like no other in our experience. With the past and future flow of our people's history literally surrounding us, in the company of family and friends, we attempt to sense and understand our own singular place in the unfolding story of the Jewish nation.

The Seder thus captures the three dimensions of "time-awareness" identified by the influential twentieth-century scholar Rabbi Joseph Soloveitchik (the Rav) as essential to the life of each Jew: *retrospection, anticipation* and *appreciation*:

> *Retrospection* [my italics] refers to man's ability to re-experience the past, to feel deeply that which is only a memory, to transport an event of the distant past into a "creative living experience" of the present.... The Seder itself is a recreation and a reliving of the past as a present reality. History becomes part of our present time-awareness. Memory is more than a storehouse; it can become a present-day experience, a part of the "I" awareness.
>
> *Anticipation* [my italics] is man's projection of visions and aspirations into the future.... In *anticipation*, man moves from reminiscing to expectation, from memories to visions. To live fulfillingly in time requires both a worthy past and a promising future. Time awareness is not only for dreaming.... We derive from retrospection the moral imperative to act now in order to realize our visions for the future. The Haggada opens with "*Avadim hayinu*, we were once slaves (retrospection)" and it concludes with "*Nishmat kol Chai*, the soul of every living thing," which is an anticipatory vision of the future, moving from hindsight to foresight.
>
> The third time-awareness dimension is *appreciation* [my italics], which means valuing the present and prizing each moment as a precious gift. Retrospection and anticipation are significant only insofar as they transform the present. In every fraction of a second, visions can be realized or destroyed.[3]

---

he will bless the House of Aharon, he will bless those who fear the Lord, both small and great" (Tehillim 115:12–13); "I will raise the cup of salvation and call upon the name of the Lord. I will pay my vows to the Lord in the presence of all His people.... I will bring an offering of thanksgiving, and I will call upon the name of the Lord. I will pay my vows to the Lord in the presence of His people, in the courts of the Lord's house, in the midst of you, O' Yerushalayim, Hallelu-ya" (Tehillim 116:14–19); "O' praise the Lord, all you nations; praise Him, all you peoples. For His kindness is great; and the truth of the Lord endures forever, Hallelu-ya" (Tehillim 117:1–2).

3   Abraham R. Besdin, *Reflections of the Rav*, vol. 1, *Lessons in Jewish Thought – Adapted from the Lectures of Rabbi Joseph B. Soloveitchik* (Jerusalem: Jewish Agency, Alpha Press, 1979), pp. 200–201.

Time awareness, the Rav concludes, is the "unique singular faculty of the free man, who can use or abuse it."[4] Only one who is free has the capacity to control his time. A slave's time is controlled by others.

The Seder moves its participants beyond a celebration of freedom, toward recognition of the responsibilities that such freedom entails. The evening opens with *retrospection*, as before the Seder meal we trace the origins of our people from the patriarchal era through the launching of the national era with the Exodus from Egypt. After the meal, we *anticipate*, envisioning our glorious march toward messianic days. And during the meal, we should strive to *appreciate*; to capture – through our discussions around the table – an understanding of our own unique place in the unfolding drama of Jewish history. The Seder teaches us that past, present and future must become one for the Jew, investing each moment with eternal significance. Only by injecting ourselves into the flow of our nation's history can we each hope to fully realize our personal and communal responsibilities.

Here, then, is the third, and arguably the most important, level of the Seder experience. On this night, we do not simply perform a series of critical mitzvot, nor do we limit ourselves to the commemoration of one historical moment alone.

The ultimate goal of the Seder is much greater. On this night we celebrate *Jewish history in its totality* and commit ourselves to determining and fulfilling *the role that we must play* in its continued unfolding.

The Seder is, therefore, unique to Pesach. On the festival when our national history began in earnest, we gather to understand *what that history means to us* and *what we can mean to that history*.

The third level of the Seder experience, however, cannot be reached in a vacuum. We cannot be expected to move abruptly from our preoccupation with "everyday lives" toward a real encounter with our place in Jewish history. The Haggada thus serves as our guide. Step by step, within this text, the rabbis craft an ingenious experiential journey into the heart of Jewish history. The key to that journey, as we will now see, is the concrete rabbinic formulation of the central mitzva of *sippur Yetziat Mitzrayim*, the retelling of the Exodus story.

---

4   Ibid., p. 201.

More Than a Mitzva
Sippur Yetziat Mitzrayim

Questions

No mitzva is more central to the Seder experience than the mitzva of *sippur Yetziat Mitzrayim*, the retelling of the Exodus story. The Maggid section of the Haggada, within which this obligation is codified into text, is the largest segment of the Haggada and the centerpiece around which the entire evening revolves.

As found within our Haggada, however, Maggid seems unnecessarily complicated and confusing. In place of a straightforward review of the Exodus story, this section contains a wide array of elements, including the *Ma nishtana* (the four questions preferably asked by a child), comments concerning the Exodus, allusions to earlier Jewish history, numerous digressions and asides, halachic analysis, an examination of the biblical formula recited by Israelite farmers on the festival of Shavuot in Temple times, and more. To complicate matters further, the components of Maggid are seemingly presented in something of a "jumble," without a readily discernible general structure or pattern. It seems inconceivable that this most significant section of Seder night text would unfold haphazardly, without clear rhyme or reason.

Is there a basic structure to the Maggid section of the Haggada, the section through which we fulfill the central mitzva of *sippur Yetziat Mitzrayim*? If so, how and when did this formal structure unfold? What were the driving forces in the development of the Maggid text before us? What does the structure of Maggid teach us concerning the rabbinic understanding of the biblical mitzva of *sippur Yetziat Mitzrayim*?

Approaches

In the arena of biblical law, the rabbis are charged with the essential task of "quantifying" what is written in the Torah. The Torah text is generally terse in its presentation of the law; essential practical details are often omitted. It remains for the rabbis to quantify Torah observance, to determine – through a combination of received tradition, biblical exegesis and logical analysis – exactly how the Torah's divine commandments are to be executed.[1] In other words: When God says, "Jump!" the rabbis ask and answer the question, "How high?"

The mitzva of *sippur Yetziat Mitzrayim*, the retelling of the story of the Exodus, is a clear example of this process. Two terse verses in the book of Shmot serve as the source

---

1   For an overview of this process, see my *Unlocking the Torah Text: Shmot*, Yitro 5.

of the biblical obligation to tell the story of the Exodus on Pesach Eve: *"Zachor et hayom hazeh asher yetzasem mi'Mitzrayim"* (Remember this day on which you departed from Egypt)[2] and *"V'higgadeta l'vincha ba'yom hahu, leimor"* (And you shall relate [the Exodus narrative] to your child on this day, saying...).[3] It remains for the rabbis, however, to define the parameters of this divine commandment, including:

1. When the mitzva is to be performed: on the Seder night, in the presence of the matza and *maror.*[4]

2. Who is obligated to perform the mitzva: both men and women.[5]

3. How this mitzva differs from the year-round, daily mitzva to remember the Exodus.[6] Rabbi Chaim of Brisk lists four distinctions between this mitzva and the year-round commandment:

   a. The Seder night mitzva must be performed in question-and-answer form.

   b. The Seder night mitzva must include a lengthy discussion of the events leading to and surrounding the Exodus.

   c. The Seder night mitzva must include a discussion of the reasons for the other mitzvot of the evening.

   d. The year-round mitzva is connected to the recitation of the Shma, while the Seder night mitzva is a stand-alone obligation.[7]

Rabbinic involvement in the mitzva of *sippur Yetziat Mitzrayim,* however, is not limited to the delineation of its technical parameters. Intent upon ensuring the inclusion of specific elements in the story's "retelling," the rabbis, early on, begin to suggest formal text for the Haggada.

According to many authorities, the first version of a standardized Haggada text is authored by the Anshei Knesset Hagedola (the Men of the Great Assembly). Convened during the pivotal period from the end of the prophetic era until the beginning of the Hellenistic period (fourth to third centuries BCE), this scholarly congress sets the course for much of Jewish law and liturgy.[8]

By the time of the codification of the Mishna (circa 200 CE), a clearly structured blueprint for Maggid, the section of the Haggada into which the retelling of the Exodus story is incorporated, has been fashioned by the rabbis. Consistent with their

---

2 Shmot 13:3.
3 Shmot 13:8; Rambam, *Mishneh Torah,* Hilchot Chametz U'matza 7:1.
4 Rambam, *Mishneh Torah,* Hilchot Chametz U'matza 7:1.
5 *Shulchan Aruch,* Orach Chaim 472:14. Note: Although the Talmud states that women are exempt from positive time-bound biblical commandments, there are many exceptions to that rule. In this case, for a variety of possible reasons, the authorities insist that women are obligated in all the mitzvot specific to the Seder night.
6 Devarim 16:3, fulfilled through the recitation of the third paragraph of the Shma.
7 *Haggada Shel Pesach Mi'Beit Levi.*
8 Talmud Bavli Brachot 33a; Menachem Kasher, *Haggada Shleima* (Jerusalem: Machon Torah Shleima, 1956).

understanding that the story should be told in the form of a parent teaching a child, the rabbis mandate *a three-step response* to a set of introductory questions (the famous *Ma nishtana*). This tripartite response shapes the text of Maggid to this day and provides a powerful insight into the rabbinic vision for the Seder night:

1. ***Matchil b'genut u'mesayeim b'shevach***: One opens with shame and closes with praise.

2. ***V'doresh mei'Arami oved avi ad she'yigmor kol haparasha kula***: And one studies the passage beginning with the words "An Aramean tried to destroy my father..." until he finishes the entire passage.

3. ***Rabban Gamliel haya omer, kol she'lo amar shelosha devarim eilu b'Pesach lo yatza yedei chovato***...: Rabban Gamliel was wont to say: Anyone who has not said [spoken of] these words on Pesach has not fulfilled his obligation: Pesach (the Korban Pesach), matza (unleavened bread), and *maror* (bitter herbs).[9]

A full understanding of the three steps outlined in the Mishna rests, I believe, upon acceptance of a critical postulate presented in our previous study. From the rabbinic perspective, the biblical mitzva of *sippur Yetziat Mitzrayim* does not simply obligate the retelling of the Exodus story. Instead, the mitzva strikes deeper, to a much more fundamental obligation. On the holiday of Pesach, as the Jewish nation annually celebrates the first footfalls of its national journey, the Torah enjoins each Jew to reconnect with his or her role as a participant in that journey.

Charged with the quantification of this overarching mitzva, the rabbis delineate a process carefully designed to move each Seder participant toward a full appreciation of his or her own place in Jewish history. They consciously divide Maggid into three parts, mirroring what they see as the three essential stages of this personal Seder night journey: historical awareness, historical personalization/participation, and historical perpetuation.

I. *Matchil B'genut U'mesayeim B'shevach*: **Historical Awareness**

The first step of the mitzva of *sippur Yetziat Mitzrayim*, the rabbis explain, consists of "open[ing] with shame and clos[ing] with praise."

On a practical level, this instruction becomes the subject of a debate in the Talmud that shapes our practice to this day. Rav and Shmuel, the leading rabbinic figures during the transition from the Mishnaic period to the period of the Gemara (early third century), each suggest a different path toward the fulfillment of the Mishna's mandate.

Rav argues for a *global approach* to the narrative of *sippur Yetziat Mitzrayim*. A proper retelling of the Exodus story, Rav maintains, must begin centuries before the Exodus, with a statement reflecting the negative origins of the Jewish people: "In the beginning, our fathers were idol worshipers." Shmuel, in contrast, argues for a *narrower approach*. This scholar maintains that the narrative should focus on the Exodus itself and should

---

9 Mishna Pesachim 10:4–5.

thus open with the negative statement "We were once slaves to Pharaoh in Egypt."[10]

Following a tradition that may have developed as early as the Geonic period (seventh to eleventh centuries CE),[11] our Haggada incorporates the positions of both authorities. As a direct answer to the *Ma nishtana*, the text offers Shmuel's response: "We were once slaves to Pharaoh in Egypt, but the Lord, our God, brought us out of there." Later, in the form of further context to the story, the Haggada presents Rav's reply: "In the beginning our fathers were idol worshipers, and now God has brought us near to serve Him."

No matter the text(s) chosen, however, the Mishna's general instruction " One opens with shame and closes with praise" seems superfluous. Isn't it abundantly obvious that any retelling of the Exodus story will begin with "shame" and proceed to "praise"? The historical transition from the negative to the positive is, after all, the whole point of the Exodus narrative. Why do the rabbis feel compelled to instruct us to do something that should be self-understood?

The key to this directive lies in understanding that, from the rabbinic perspective, the Maggid journey must begin with the attainment of *historical awareness*. At this initial stage of the process, the rabbis address the fundamental question "How does the Jew view history?" Their answer is powerful and succinct: *Matchil b'genut u'mesayeim b'shevach*, "One opens with shame and closes with praise."

The authors of the Mishna are not referring to the Exodus story alone. They are instead issuing a global statement concerning Jewish history as a whole. That is why later scholars are not content with the inclusion of Shmuel's "we were once slaves…" The story must hearken back to the dawn of Jewish history, to Rav's "in the beginning our fathers were idol worshipers…" The Jewish journey in its entirety, the rabbis explain, is structured and purposeful. It is a journey effectively summed up in the declaration *Matchil b'genut u'mesayeim b'shevach*. The path along which we travel is not haphazard, but moves from a fixed point to a fixed goal, *from humble beginnings to a glorious end*.

This first stage of Maggid thus captures what is, according to Rabbi Joseph Soloveitchik, Judaism's central contribution toward man's understanding of history: the concept of a *destiny-driven history*:

> While universal (non-Jewish) history is *governed by causality*, by what preceded, covenantal (Jewish) history is *shaped by destiny* [my italics], by a goal set in the future.… Jewish history is pulled, as by a magnet, toward a glorious destiny; it is not pushed by antecedent causes. This is the meaning of the Patriarchic Covenant; it is a goal projected, a purpose pursued, a destination to be reached.[12]

---

10 Talmud Bavli Pesachim 116a.

11 Quoted in Rabbeinu Chananel, Talmud Bavli Pesachim 116a. It should be noted that debate develops among the early scholars as to whether Rav and Shmuel are actually disagreeing with each other or whether their views were always meant to be seen as complementary. See Kasher, *Haggada Shleima*, introduction and chapters 3–4, for a review of the opinions on the matter.

12 Abraham R. Besdin, *Reflections of the Rav*, vol. 2, *Man of Faith in the Modern World* (Hoboken, NJ: Ktav

Centuries earlier, the towering sixteenth-century scholar Rabbi Yehuda Loew (the Maharal) ingeniously conveys this same idea by reinterpreting the very title afforded to the entire Pesach evening ritual: *Seder* (order). The evening is called the Seder, the Maharal insists, not only because of the ordered, ritualized structure of the proceedings. Instead, the title testifies, on this night of history, to the existence of *historical seder* – to the fact that there is "order" to Jewish history itself.[13]

The journey of each participant in the Seder must begin with the attainment of "historical awareness," with the realization that there is a pattern and purpose to Jewish history. We are traveling from *genut* to *shevach*: from humble beginnings to a glorious future.

Not by accident, this first section of Maggid closes with the paragraph of *V'hi she'amda*, "And this has stood," delineating God's protection of the Jewish nation from its enemies, over and over again, across time.

II. *V'doresh Mei'Arami Oved Avi Ad She'yigmor Kol Haparasha Kula*: Historical Personalization/Participation

In this second stage of Maggid, the Mishna mandates: "And one studies the biblical passage beginning with the words *Arami oved avi* (An Aramean tried to destroy my father) until he finishes the entire passage." In fulfillment of this mandate, the referenced biblical section is incorporated into the Haggada in the form of Torah study, with the original text quoted, dissected and analyzed in the light of the Oral Law.

The biblical passage chosen by the rabbis for study during the Seder is found at the beginning of Parashat Ki Tavo in the book of Devarim. Originally conveyed by Moshe to the Israelites toward the end of their desert wanderings, this text constitutes the majority of the *vidui bikkurim*, the formula to be recited yearly by an Israelite farmer upon bringing his first fruits to the Temple. Within this formula, the farmer offers a brief overview of early Jewish history, from the descent into Egyptian slavery through the Exodus and entry into the Land:

> An Aramean sought to destroy my forefather, and he descended to Egypt and dwelt there, few in number, and he became there a nation, great, strong and numerous.
>
> And the Egyptians mistreated us and afflicted us, and they placed upon us hard work.
>
> And we cried out to the Lord, the God of our fathers, and the Lord heard our cries, and He saw our affliction and our travail and our oppression.
>
> And the Lord took us out of Egypt with a strong hand and an outstretched arm and with great awesomeness and with signs and with wonders.[14]

Publishing House, 1989), p. 70; see also my *Unlocking the Torah Text: Bamidbar*, Bamidbar 2a, Approaches B.

13 Chidushei Harim, quoting the Maharal, *Haggada Ma'ayana shel Torah*.

14 Devarim 26:5–7.

The selection of this portion of the *vidui bikkurim* as the centerpiece of the mitzva of *sippur Yetziat Mitzrayim* seems abundantly strange.

Given the host of primary sources in the Torah concerning the Passover story – sources from the book of Shmot that record the details of the Exodus as they unfold – why do the rabbis deliberately choose a secondary textual source that refers to these events only in retrospect? The *vidui bikkurim* is designed, after all, to be recited by Israelite farmers only after the land of Canaan is conquered and settled, long after the events surrounding the Exodus have occurred.

To complicate matters further, the *vidui bikkurim* is clearly associated in the Torah with a festival other than Pesach. The first fruits are to be brought to the Temple each year on the festival of Shavuot. Why designate a passage associated with Shavuot as the "Torah study" centerpiece of the Pesach ritual?

The answer to our question may well lie in an easily missed yet powerfully profound internal transition in the text of the *vidui bikkurim* itself.

The farmer opens his proclamation in the third person: "An Aramean tried to destroy my father, and *he descended* to Egypt and dwelt there, few in number, and *he became* there a nation, great, strong and numerous."

When, however, the farmer begins to discuss the birthing pangs of the Jewish nation in the cauldron of Egyptian slavery, a remarkable change occurs. Suddenly this man, speaking centuries after the Exodus, begins to speak of these historical events *in the first person*:

> And the Egyptians *mistreated us* and *afflicted us*, and they *placed upon us* hard work.
>
> And *we cried out* to the Lord, the God of our fathers, and the Lord *heard our cries*, and He *saw our affliction and our travail and our oppression*. And the Lord *took us out* of Egypt with a strong hand and an outstretched arm and with great awesomeness and with signs and with wonders.

As the *vidui* progresses, the farmer is transformed from an observer to a personal participant. He no longer objectively reports on events that happened to others; he now describes events as if they happened to him. Past, present and future merge for the Jew, once the Jewish nation is born. *An event that happens to any Jew at any time happens to all Jews at all times.*

The rabbis, therefore, could not have chosen a more appropriate textual centerpiece for the mitzva of *sippur Yetziat Mitzrayim* than the passage of *vidui bikkurim*.

No other passage of the Torah can aid us more directly in reaching the second stage of the carefully orchestrated Maggid journey: the stage of *historical personalization/participation*. As we channel the words of that long-ago farmer bringing his first fruits to the Temple, we join him in his temporal journey as well. Together we become one with our forefathers in the land of Egypt, experiencing the Exodus as if it happened to us.

Another question, however, remains. The manner in which this text is presented in the Haggada is puzzling. As we have noted, the *vidui* is quoted, dissected and analyzed in what can best be described as a ritualized exercise in Torah study. While the study of Torah text is always appropriate, why is this formalized, somewhat stilted biblical analysis so critical to the mitzva of *sippur Yetziat Mitzrayim*? The story can clearly be told without the far-ranging rabbinical exegesis contained in our Haggada.

The answer to this question lies in recognizing that no single act in Jewish experience injects a participant more personally into the flow of Jewish history than the act of Torah study. The rabbis therefore make a conscious decision to teach the critical lesson of *historical personalization/participation* not only through the selection of the *vidui* text, but also through its mode of presentation in the Haggada. The challenge of personalizing history is met in this section of the Haggada *both through the text chosen to be studied and through the act of Torah study itself.*

A number of years ago, an acquaintance who became Jewishly observant later in life shared with me the following observation: "Do you know what I find most amazing about the experience of Talmud study? It is that when I study Talmud, the boundaries of time fall away. I sit at my study table and the Tannaim of the Mishna – Rabbi Akiva, Rabbi Meir and their colleagues (32 BCE–200 CE) – speak to me. Suddenly the Amoraim of the Gemara – Rav Papa, Rav Huna and their contemporaries (200–500 CE) – enter the discussion. Then Rashi (1040–1105) chimes in to explain a difficulty. Strikingly, Rashi's descendants and their colleagues (the Tosafists, 1105–1290 CE) object to Rashi's comments. Other voices emerge from multiple eras. And, in my struggle to understand, I become part of the conversation, as well – a conversation that stretches from the dawn of our history and that will continue to the end of time."[15]

During the second stage of Maggid, we thus move beyond historical awareness to personalization/participation in multiple dimensions at once. Both the chosen text of this section and the very act of shared Torah study inject us into the historical flow of our people, enabling us to become personal participants in the unfolding drama.

The second stage of Maggid, like the first, closes with a statement delineating our newfound realizations. *"Al achat kama v'kama..."* (How much more so should we be grateful...), we recite, as we personally thank God for a series of historical events that are as current to us as if they happened today.

III. *Rabban Gamliel Haya Omer, Kol She'lo Amar Shelosha Devarim Eilu B'Pesach Lo Yatza Yedei Chovato:* Historical Perpetuation

The final, third stage of Maggid opens with a declaration in the name of the Mishnaic sage Rabban Gamliel: "Anyone who has not said [spoken of] these three things on Pesach has not fulfilled his obligation, namely: Pesach (the Korban Pesach), matza (unleavened

---

15 Rabbi Joseph Soloveitchik's eloquently expressed similar sentiments can be found in Besdin, *Reflections of the Rav*, vol. 2, *Man of Faith in the Modern World*, pp. 21–23.

bread), and *maror* (bitter herbs)." The text continues with Rabban Gamliel's elucidation of these three symbols.

Rabban Gamliel maintains that a failure to "say" the symbols of the Seder – Pesach, matza and *maror* – prevents the participant from "fulfilling his obligation." To what halachic obligation does Rabban Gamliel refer? Some authorities maintain that at issue are the obligations incorporated in the symbols themselves.[16] According to this approach, for example, Rabban Gamliel argues that an individual who consumes matza during the Seder but fails to discuss the significance of this act has not properly fulfilled the mitzva of *achilat matza* (consuming matza on the Seder night). Many other sages, however, disagree and maintain that Rabban Gamliel refers to the mitzva of *sippur Yetziat Mitzrayim*.[17] According to these scholars, Rabban Gamliel argues that an individual cannot properly fulfill the obligation to retell the Exodus story on the Seder night without verbally mentioning the Korban Pesach, the matza and the *maror* in the process.

This second position seems baffling. Isn't Rabban Gamliel turning the medium into the message? Logically, the symbols of the Seder night are tools designed to aid in the reexperiencing of the Exodus story. Why would Rabban Gamliel transform them into essential features of the narrative itself? Surely, the story of the Exodus can be told without a verbal mention of these three symbols.

Rabban Gamliel's position becomes clear when we recognize that the most elusive and important step of Maggid yet remains: *historical perpetuation*.

Upon arriving at this point of the seder, Rabban Gamliel confronts a formidable challenge. We have gained an awareness of and a sense of personal participation in the flow of Jewish history. Our task, however, is far from complete. To become full participants in history, on this night of history, we must ensure the future participation of our progeny. Not by accident, the very formulation of the mitzva of *sippur Yetziat Mitzrayim* emerges, in part, from the biblical statement "*V'higgadeta l'vincha*" (and you shall relate to your child).[18]

Within this context, Rabban Gamliel recognizes and reminds us that *concrete mitzvot* are essential to the perpetuation of Jewish tradition. Ideas, concepts and values, as important as they may be to any faith tradition, are personal and varied. An individual's understanding of Jewish thought is bound to be different from that of his ancestors, and different, as well, from that of his children and grandchildren. Religious perspective is greatly shaped, after all, by personality, environment and experience.

In contrast, physical symbols and ritual worship possess the power of constancy. The tefillin that an individual puts on each morning are fundamentally the same as those that were worn by his great-great-grandfather and the same as those that will be worn, with God's help, one day by his great-great-grandsons. Concrete, physical, symbolic

---

16 Commentary of the Abudarham and Maharsha as explained in Rabbi Shlomo Wahrman, *Sefer Orot HaPesach* (North Bergen: independently published, 1992), chapter 54.

17 Rambam, *Mishneh Torah*, Hilchot Chametz U'matza 7:5.

18 Shmot 13:8; Rambam, *Mishneh Torah*, Hilchot Chametz U'matza 7:1.

mitzvot are critical to the uniform transmission of Jewish tradition, thought and law. Without such mitzvot, the Jewish nation would have long ago faded into oblivion.

Rabban Gamliel reaches, therefore, a critical conclusion: *To become full participants in history, on this night of history, we must ensure the future participation of our progeny.* He therefore insists that we have not accomplished the mitzva of *sippur Yetziat Mitzrayim* until the narrative includes a discussion of the concrete mitzvot of the Seder evening. While these obligations are independent mitzvot, Rabban Gamliel believes them also to be essential components of the narrative itself. These mitzvot, and mitzvot like them, will guarantee the perpetuation of Jewish tradition. They must therefore be spoken of as we journey toward a full understanding of our personal place in history.

Thus, with Rabban Gamliel's assistance, we arrive at the third and final stage of the Maggid: *historical perpetuation.* We recognize that to become full participants in our nation's journey, we must actively enable that journey to continue. Only upon reaching that realization and making that commitment do we fully rise to the challenge of the Seder night.

Once again, this section of the Maggid closes with a paragraph reflecting our accomplishment. Having coursed through the stages of historical awareness, personalization/participation and perpetuation, we can now fully state: *"B'chol dor va'dor chayav adam lirot et atzmo k'ilu hu yatza mi'Mitzrayim"* (In each generation, a person must see himself/herself as if he/she came out of Egypt). The Haggada then automatically moves to the section of Hallel (praise) that precedes the meal, as the Seder participants express gratitude to God for the gifts that He has bestowed upon them and upon the entire Jewish people.

And so, as we each complete the mitzva of *sippur Yetziat Mitzrayim*, we also conclude our own personal Maggid journey, mandated by the rabbis centuries ago – a journey designed to help each of us realize, on the night that celebrates Jewish history, our own personal, active and essential role in the story of our people.

Preparations for the Festival

Bedikat Chametz, *Biur Chametz*, and *Bitul Chametz*: Searching for, Burning and Nullifying *Chametz*

hametz is defined as any product containing leaven produced by one or more of five species of grain: wheat, spelt, barley, oats or rye.[1] A series of six biblical commandments – five negative and one positive – define our fundamental relationship with this material over the Pesach festival. The five negative commandments prohibit consumption of, benefit from and ownership of *chametz* over the holiday.[2] The one positive biblical commandment mandates ridding one's domain of *chametz* before the festival begins.[3]

The Talmud outlines two procedures through which individuals can rid their domains of actual *chametz* before the onset of Pesach.

1. ***Bedika* and *biur*: search and destroy.** In order to rid ourselves of any *chametz* in our possession, we thoroughly clean our homes before the Pesach festival. This general cleaning is followed by a formal search for *chametz* by candlelight on the evening of the fourteenth day of Nissan (the night before the festival begins)[4] and a burning of the *chametz* the next morning[5] (see below).

2. ***Bitul* (nullification): the verbal nullification of our *chametz*.** Through the process of *bitul*, we "nullify" the *chametz* in our possession. The rabbis debate, however, the actual mechanism through which *bitul* works.

Some authorities view the procedure as a literal act of "mind over matter." By verbally declaring any remaining *chametz* to be valueless, these scholars maintain, we effectively destroy it, thereby fulfilling the biblical commandment to "rid our homes of *chametz*"[6] before the festival.[7] Other scholars see *bitul* as a formal relinquishment of ownership over the *chametz*. By declaring the *chametz* to be *hefker* (ownerless), these authorities argue, we avoid the obligation to physically rid our property of it.[8] As we will see below, *bitul* is accomplished through the recitation of a formula recited twice with variations:

---

1   Talmud Bavli Pesachim 35a.
2   Shmot 12:19, 20; 13:3, 7; Devarim 17:3.
3   Shmot 12:15.
4   Mishna Pesachim 1:1.
5   Ibid., 1:4.
6   Shmot 12:15.
7   Rashi, Pesachim 4b, s.v. "B'vitul b'alma."
8   Tosafot, Pesachim 4b, s.v. "Mi'd'Orayta."

in the evening after the search and in the morning after the burning.

For various reasons, Talmudic scholars mandate that both the *bedika/biur* and the *bitul* must be performed in the preparation of our homes for the Pesach festival.[9]

Bedikat Chametz and Bitul Chametz

The formal search for *chametz* takes place by candlelight on the eve of the fourteenth of Nissan, the night before the festival of Pesach begins.[10] When Pesach begins on Saturday night, the search takes place on the previous Thursday night, the eve of the thirteenth of Nissan.

An individual leaving home before the evening of the fourteenth of Nissan, but within thirty days of the holiday, performs the search on the evening before departure. In this case, however, no blessing is recited.[11] A second search, with the blessing, is performed on the fourteenth in the new location.

> The search should begin as soon as possible after nightfall and should include a genuine investigation of all areas where *chametz* might be found. A candle is lit, the following blessing is recited and the search commences. Once the blessing is recited, extraneous conversation is prohibited until after the completion of the search.

בָּרוּךְ אַתָּה יי אֱלֹהֵינוּ מֶלֶךְ הָעוֹלָם, אֲשֶׁר קִדְּשָׁנוּ בְּמִצְוֹתָיו וְצִוָּנוּ עַל בְּעוּר חָמֵץ.

Blessed are You, Lord, our God, Who has sanctified us with His commandments and commanded us concerning the removal of *chametz*.

> After the search is completed, the following formula of *bitul chametz* (the nullification of *chametz*) is recited:

כָּל חֲמִירָא וַחֲמִיעָא דְּאִכָּא בִרְשׁוּתִי, דְּלָא חֲמִתֵּה וּדְלָא חֲמִתֵּה בִּעַרְתֵּה וּדְלָא יְדַעֲנָא לֵיהּ, לִבָּטֵל וְלֶהֱוֵי הֶפְקֵר כְּעַפְרָא דְאַרְעָא.

Any manner of leaven that may still be in my possession, that I have not observed or not removed, or of which I have no knowledge, let it be nullified and considered ownerless, like the dust of the earth.

Biur Chametz

On the morning[12] of the fourteenth of Nisan, the day before Pesach, all remaining

---

9 Talmud Bavli Pesachim 2a; Tosafot, ibid., s.v. "Ohr l'arba assar"; Talmud Bavli Pesachim 6b. It should be noted, of course, that much more is actually entailed in properly preparing our homes for Pesach. In addition to a thorough cleaning throughout the house, kitchens must be kashered in order to ensure that we do not consume any *chametz* material that may have been absorbed in our utensils. Finally, in addition to removing *chametz* from our possession through *bedika*, *biur* and *bitul*, the practice has developed to sell any remaining *chametz* to a non-Jew before the festival. The laws involved in all these procedures are numerous and detailed and should be fulfilled under rabbinic guidance.

10 *Shulchan Aruch*, Orach Chaim 433:1, 444:1.

11 Ibid., 436:1; Rema, ibid.

12 The exact time by which *chametz* must be burned is dependent upon when Pesach falls in the solar calendar

chametz that has not been destroyed or sold is burned. If Pesach begins on Saturday night, the burning takes place on the previous Friday morning.[13]

At the time of the burning, the formula of *bitul* is again recited, with variations.

כָּל חֲמִירָא וַחֲמִיעָא דְּאִכָּא בִרְשׁוּתִי, דַּחֲזִתֵּהּ וּדְלָא חֲזִתֵּהּ, דַּחֲמִתֵּהּ וּדְלָא חֲמִתֵּהּ, דְּבִעַרְתֵּהּ וּדְלָא בִעַרְתֵּהּ, לִבָּטֵל וְלֶהֱוֵי הֶפְקֵר כְּעַפְרָא דְאַרְעָא.

Any manner of leaven that may still be in my possession, that I have seen or not seen, that I have observed or not observed, that I have removed or not removed, let it be nullified and considered ownerless, like the dust of the earth.

Eruv Tavshilin: The Mixing of Foods

The laws governing physical activity on *yom tov* (a festival) are generally similar to those governing such activity on Shabbat. One glaring distinction, however, does exist: according to biblical law, cooking and other food preparations that are prohibited on Shabbat are permissible on *yom tov*, as long as the food involved is intended for use on that festival or on Shabbat immediately following the festival.[14]

By the time of the Mishna, however, the rabbis become concerned that the biblical allowance for food preparation on *yom tov* for the Shabbat that follows could lead individuals to err and cook on *yom tov* for weekdays that follow, as well. The Mishnaic authorities, therefore, establish an edict prohibiting food preparation on *yom tov* even for a Shabbat immediately following the holiday.[15]

This new limitation, however, creates its own obvious problem: in years when *yom tov* immediately precedes Shabbat, the ability to properly prepare for the Sabbath day is now severely curtailed. To address this problem, the Talmudic scholars institute the ritual of *eruv tavshilin*. Consisting of the setting aside of two types of food for Shabbat before the onset of the festival, this procedure formally intertwines the ongoing preparations for *yom tov* with the ongoing preparations for Shabbat.[16] By insisting that only those who set aside an *eruv tavshilin* may prepare on *yom tov* for Shabbat,[17] the rabbis allow for Shabbat readiness while maintaining their mandate against possible error. Shabbat preparation on *yom tov* is now presented as a unique allowance, requiring special dispensation. Individuals will therefore not be misled by this allowance into assuming that all cooking is automatically allowed on festivals, including cooking for a weekday.[18]

---

of that year. A rabbinic authority should be consulted for the determination of the particular time.

13 *Shulchan Aruch*, Orach Chaim 444:1, 445:1; Rema, ibid.

14 Talmud Bavli Pesachim 46b; Rambam, *Mishneh Torah*, Hilchot *Yom Tov* 1:9; 6:1.

15 Talmud Bavli Pesachim 46b; Rambam, *Mishneh Torah* 6:1.

16 Hasagot Hara'avad on Rambam, *Mishneh Torah*, Hilchot *Yom Tov* 6:2.

17 Mishna Beitza 2:1.

18 Rava maintains that the ritual is designed to preserve the honor of Shabbat as one remembers to set aside proper foodstuffs for Shabbat in the midst of festival preparations. Rav Ashi, in contrast, argues that the eruv is to honor the festival: by insisting that only after performing *eruv tavshilin* may one prepare on *yom tov* for

Eruv Tavshilin

When Shabbat immediately follows Pesach, a matza and a portion of another cooked food are selected, on the day before the festival, for Shabbat use. The following blessing and formula are recited:

בָּרוּךְ אַתָּה יי אֱלֹהֵינוּ מֶלֶךְ הָעוֹלָם, אֲשֶׁר קִדְּשָׁנוּ בְּמִצְוֹתָיו, וְצִוָּנוּ עַל מִצְוַת עֵרוּב.

Blessed are You, Lord, our God, Who has sanctified us with His commandments and commanded us concerning the mitzva of *eruv* .

בַּהֲדֵין עֵרוּבָא יְהֵא שָׁרֵא לָנָא לַאֲפוּיֵי וּלְבַשּׁוּלֵי וּלְאַטְמוּנֵי וּלְאַדְלוּקֵי שְׁרָגָא וּלְתַקָּנָא וּלְמֶעְבַּד כָּל צָרְכָנָא, מִיּוֹמָא טָבָא לְשַׁבַּתָּא לָנוּ וּלְכָל יִשְׂרָאֵל הַדָּרִים בָּעִיר הַזֹּאת.

With this *eruv* it shall be permitted for us to bake, cook, keep [food] warm, kindle fire, and perform all other necessary [food] preparations on the holiday for the Sabbath; for us and for all other Jews who live in this city.

The foods are set aside and must be consumed on Shabbat.

Hadlakat Neirot: The Kindling of Lights

In order to ensure safety, tranquility and a dignified atmosphere within each Jewish home, the rabbis mandate the kindling of lights before sunset on the eve of each Shabbat and festival.[19] "Where there is no light," Rashi declares in his explanation of this law, "there is no peace."[20] This mandate is so significant in the eyes of the early scholars that an entire chapter of the Mishna is dedicated to its proper observance.[21]

The obligation of *hadlakat neirot* is primarily reserved for women. When no women are present, however, the lights should be kindled by a man.[22] A minimum of two candles are generally lit per household, representing the biblical commandments of *shamor* and *zachor*, to "remember" and "guard" the Sabbath day.[23] Many have the custom of adding an additional light with the birth of each child in the family.

As a rule, a blessing over a mitzva is recited immediately before the performance of that mitzva (see pp. 148–49). In the case of the Shabbat candles, the prevalent custom is to light the candles, cover one's eyes, recite the blessing and uncover the eyes. This procedure allows the blessing to immediately precede the benefit derived from the Shabbat lights.[24]

Many individuals add a prayerful request, immediately following the blessing over the candles, for children and for the opportunity to raise those children toward

---

Shabbat, the rabbis teach the populace not to treat the sanctity of the festival lightly. Talmud Bavli Beitza 15b.

19 Talmud Bavli Shabbat 23b.
20 Rashi, ibid.
21 Mishna Shabbat, chapter 2.
22 *Shulchan Aruch*, Orach Chaim 263: 1, 3.
23 Ibid., 263:1.
24 Rema, ibid., 263:5.

meaningful Torah scholarship and observance. This tradition is based upon the Talmudic contention that "those scrupulous in [the kindling of Sabbath and festival] candles will be blessed with children who are Torah scholars."[25]

Hadlakat Neirot

Candles are kindled in the home before sunset on the festival eve (on the eve of the second day of *yom tov* in the diaspora and on the eve of a festival immediately following Shabbat, the candles are kindled after nightfall).

> When the festival coincides with Shabbat, the candles are kindled, the eyes are covered and the following blessing is recited.[26] When the festival does not fall on Shabbat, some maintain the same procedure, while others kindle the candles from an existing flame, after the blessing's recitation, without covering the eyes (on Shabbat the words in parentheses are added):

בָּרוּךְ אַתָּה יי אֱלֹהֵינוּ מֶלֶךְ הָעוֹלָם, אֲשֶׁר קִדְּשָׁנוּ בְּמִצְוֹתָיו וְצִוָּנוּ לְהַדְלִיק נֵר שֶׁל (שַׁבָּת וְ)שֶׁל יוֹם טוֹב.

Blessed are You, Lord, our God, Who has sanctified us with His commandments and commanded us to light the candles of (the Sabbath and) the festival.

> The eyes are uncovered and the following blessing and meditation are recited:

בָּרוּךְ אַתָּה יי אֱלֹהֵינוּ מֶלֶךְ הָעוֹלָם, שֶׁהֶחֱיָנוּ וְקִיְּמָנוּ וְהִגִּיעָנוּ לַזְּמַן הַזֶּה.

Blessed are You, Lord, our God, King of the universe, Who has granted us life, sustained us and enabled us to reach this occasion.

יְהִי רָצוֹן מִלְפָנֶיךָ יי אֱלֹהַי וֵאלֹהֵי יִשְׂרָאֵל, שֶׁתְּחוֹנֵן אוֹתִי (וְאֶת אִישִׁי וּבָנַי וּבְנוֹתַי וְאָבִי וְאִמִּי) וְאֶת כָּל קְרוֹבַי, וְתִתֶּן לָנוּ וּלְכָל יִשְׂרָאֵל חַיִּים טוֹבִים וַאֲרֻכִּים, וְתִזְכְּרֵנוּ בְּזִכָּרוֹן טוֹבָה וּבְרָכָה, וְתִפְקְדֵנוּ בִּפְקֻדַּת יְשׁוּעָה וְרַחֲמִים, וּתְבָרְכֵנוּ בְּרָכוֹת גְּדוֹלוֹת, וְתַשְׁלֵם בָּתֵּינוּ, וְתַשְׁכֵּן שְׁכִינָתְךָ בֵּינֵינוּ. וְזַכֵּנוּ לְגַדֵּל בָּנִים וּבְנֵי בָנִים חֲכָמִים וּנְבוֹנִים, אוֹהֲבֵי יי, אַנְשֵׁי אֱמֶת, זֶרַע קֹדֶשׁ בַּיי דְּבֵקִים, וּמְאִירִים אֶת הָעוֹלָם בַּתּוֹרָה וּבְמַעֲשִׂים טוֹבִים וּבְכָל מְלֶאכֶת עֲבוֹדַת הַבּוֹרֵא. אָנָּא, שְׁמַע בָּעֵת הַזֹּאת אֶת תְּחִנָּתִי בִּזְכוּת שָׂרָה, רִבְקָה, רָחֵל וְלֵאָה אִמּוֹתֵינוּ, וְהָאֵר נֵרֵנוּ שֶׁלֹּא יִכְבֶּה לְעוֹלָם וָעֶד, וְהָאֵר פָּנֶיךָ וְנִוָּשֵׁעָה, אָמֵן.

May it be Your will, Lord, my God and God of my forefathers, that You show favor to me (and to my husband | my sons | my daughters | my father | my mother) and to all of my relatives. Grant us and all of Israel lives that are good and long; remember us with beneficent memory and blessing; consider us with a consideration of salvation and mercy; bless us and rest Your Presence among us. Privilege us to raise children and grandchildren who are wise and understanding, lovers of the Lord, people of truth, holy offspring who cleave to the Lord. And [may they] illuminate the world with Torah and good deeds and with all labor in the service of the Creator. Please, at this time, hear my supplication, in the merit of Sarah, Rebecca, Rachel and Leah, our Mothers. And shine our light, that it be not extinguished forever. And cause Your countenance to shine; and we will be redeemed. Amen!

---

25 Talmud Bavli Shabbat 23b.

26 On Shabbat, the kindling of a flame is totally prohibited. The candles are thus lit before Shabbat is accepted through the recitation of the blessing. The eyes are covered and uncovered, so that the light of the candles will be enjoyed immediately following the blessing. On a *yom tov* that does not coincide with Shabbat, a flame may be kindled from an existing flame. The blessing may therefore be recited before kindling the candles from such a flame, and the eyes need not be covered. Some authorities advocate this unique *yom tov* procedure, while others prefer the maintenance of consistency in the kindling of Shabbat and *yom tov* candles.

Seder Preparations

The Seder Plate

Ideally all preparations for the Seder should be completed before the festival begins so that the Seder can start promptly (it is also recommended to check with your local rabbi, in particular when the Seder is on Friday night, concerning certain preparations that may be subject to restrictions once the holiday begins). The following items are set on a Seder plate, which is then placed before the leader of the Seder. If numerous families are sharing in a Seder, a separate Seder plate may be set before the head of each household.

a. *Maror* – bitter herbs (see pp. 154–59)

b. *Karpas* – a vegetable to be used for dipping (see pp. 48–49)

c. *Charoset* – a mixture of chopped apples, other fruits and wine (see p. 158)

d. *Zero'a* and *beitza* – two cooked foods representing the Pesach and Chagiga offerings (a roasted shank bone or if not available, another roasted meat dish and a roasted egg are often used due to their additional symbolism)

Some traditions also include one or more of these items on the Seder plate:

a. Salt water into which the *karpas* is to be dipped

b. The matzot (see below)

c. *Chazeret* – *maror* to be used in the Korech sandwich (see pp. 158–59)

Traditions vary concerning the exact placement of the items on the plate. If there is no family tradition to the contrary, the most widespread practice is as follows:

The Matzot

Three matzot are placed before the leader(s) of the Seder (some have the custom of placing them on the Seder plate, while others place them separately at the table). These matzot will be used at a number of points during the evening's proceedings. Additional matzot will also be used, as necessary, to provide all participants with the required amounts over the course of the Seder. (For halachic information on matza, see pp. 152–53.)

The *Maror*

While various vegetables are acceptable for use as maror at the Seder, the preferred choice is romaine lettuce. The lettuce should be carefully washed and inspected for insects. Again, enough lettuce should be prepared to provide all Seder participants with the required amounts. (For halachic information on maror, see pp. 156–57.)

The Wine

Wine glasses are placed before each Seder participant to be used for the four cups of wine consumed over the course of the Seder. Enough wine should be purchased to enable all in attendance to drink the required amount for each of four cups. Under certain circumstances, grape juice may be used in place of wine. (For halachic information on the four cups of wine, see pp. 41–43.)

The Seder

The Structure and Sections of the Seder

In order to emphasize the structured nature of the Seder night, the Haggada introduces the evening's proceedings through a listing of the sections of the Seder. In many homes it is customary to sing this list as an introduction to the evening's proceedings.

On the facing page, we have further categorized the established list into *four overall units*, corresponding to the Seder's philosophical timeline.[1] These four units will be highlighted, along with the traditional sections of the Seder, in our running commentary on the Haggada text. Also indicated are the three subdivisions of Maggid, corresponding to Maggid's three primary goals.[2] These subdivisions will also be highlighted in our running commentary on the text.

קַדֵּשׁ
וּרְחַץ
כַּרְפַּס
יַחַץ
מַגִּיד
רָחְצָה
מוֹצִיא מַצָּה
מָרוֹר
כּוֹרֵךְ
שֻׁלְחָן עוֹרֵךְ
צָפוּן
בָּרֵךְ
הַלֵּל
נִרְצָה

---

1 See "Making Sense of the Seder III: An Experiential Perspective," pp. 12–14.
2 See "More Than a Mitzva: *Sippur Yetziat Mitzrayim*," pp. 15–23.

קַדֵּשׁ

וּרְחַץ

כַּרְפַּס

יַחַץ

Seder Unit I
SETTING THE STAGE
Preliminary Rituals

Seder Sections:
Kadesh, Urchatz, Karpas, Yachatz

The Seder opens with the recitation of the festival Kiddush.

Three introductory rituals are then performed: Urchatz, the first washing of hands; Karpas, the eating of a vegetable dipped in salt water; and Yachatz, the breaking of the middle matza. While these three ceremonies certainly have intrinsic symbolic value, they are primarily placed at the beginning of the Seder to encourage questioning on the part of any children present. Questions are integral to the retelling of the Exodus story, which should optimally unfold *derech haggada l'ben* (as a parent would teach a child).[1]

Thematically, the three preliminary rituals following Kiddush thus directly connect to the *Ma nishtana*, the four questions that will formally launch the Maggid section of the Haggada.

---

1   *Minchat Chinuch*, mitzva 21.

Seder Section 1 • KADESH
The Recitation of Kiddush

The Pesach Seder begins in recognizable territory, with Kiddush, the set of blessings over wine that introduces Shabbat and festival evening meals throughout the Jewish year (for halachic information on the four cups of wine, see pp. 41–43). On Friday evenings, Kiddush opens with an introductory paragraph referencing the Shabbat of creation. The festival Kiddush then follows, consisting of a blessing over wine and a blessing referencing the unique sanctity of the day. On Saturday evenings, Kiddush is followed by Havdala, a blessing that speaks of divinely ordained distinctions, including that between the sanctity of Shabbat and the sanctity of the Pesach festival. Finally, the *shehecheyanu* blessing is recited, thanking God for allowing the Seder participants to reach this wonderful occasion.

The first cup of wine is raised.
When the festival occurs on Shabbat, begin here:

וַיְהִי עֶרֶב וַיְהִי בֹקֶר יוֹם הַשִּׁשִּׁי. וַיְכֻלּוּ הַשָּׁמַיִם וְהָאָרֶץ וְכָל צְבָאָם. וַיְכַל אֱלֹהִים בַּיּוֹם הַשְּׁבִיעִי, מְלַאכְתּוֹ אֲשֶׁר עָשָׂה, וַיִּשְׁבֹּת בַּיּוֹם הַשְּׁבִיעִי, מִכָּל מְלַאכְתּוֹ אֲשֶׁר עָשָׂה. וַיְבָרֶךְ אֱלֹהִים אֶת יוֹם הַשְּׁבִיעִי, וַיְקַדֵּשׁ אֹתוֹ, כִּי בוֹ שָׁבַת מִכָּל מְלַאכְתּוֹ, אֲשֶׁר בָּרָא אֱלֹהִים לַעֲשׂוֹת.

When the festival begins on a weekday, begin here (on Shabbat, add the words in parentheses):

סַבְרִי מָרָנָן וְרַבָּנָן וְרַבּוֹתַי: **בָּרוּךְ אַתָּה יי אֱלֹהֵינוּ מֶלֶךְ הָעוֹלָם, בּוֹרֵא פְּרִי הַגָּפֶן.** בָּרוּךְ אַתָּה יי אֱלֹהֵינוּ מֶלֶךְ הָעוֹלָם, אֲשֶׁר בָּחַר בָּנוּ מִכָּל עָם, וְרוֹמְמָנוּ מִכָּל לָשׁוֹן, וְקִדְּשָׁנוּ בְּמִצְוֹתָיו, וַתִּתֶּן לָנוּ יי אֱלֹהֵינוּ בְּאַהֲבָה (שַׁבָּתוֹת לִמְנוּחָה וּ)מוֹעֲדִים לְשִׂמְחָה, חַגִּים וּזְמַנִּים לְשָׂשׂוֹן; (אֶת יוֹם הַשַּׁבָּת הַזֶּה וְ)אֶת יוֹם חַג הַמַּצוֹת הַזֶּה, זְמַן חֵרוּתֵנוּ, (בְּאַהֲבָה), מִקְרָא קֹדֶשׁ, זֵכֶר לִיצִיאַת מִצְרָיִם. כִּי בָנוּ בָחַרְתָּ וְאוֹתָנוּ קִדַּשְׁתָּ מִכָּל הָעַמִּים. וְ(שַׁבָּת וּ)מוֹעֲדֵי קָדְשֶׁךָ (בְּאַהֲבָה וּבְרָצוֹן) בְּשִׂמְחָה וּבְשָׂשׂוֹן הִנְחַלְתָּנוּ: בָּרוּךְ אַתָּה יי מְקַדֵּשׁ (הַשַּׁבָּת וְ)יִשְׂרָאֵל וְהַזְּמַנִּים.

When the festival falls on Saturday night, add the following paragraph:

בָּרוּךְ אַתָּה יי אֱלֹהֵינוּ מֶלֶךְ הָעוֹלָם, בּוֹרֵא מְאוֹרֵי הָאֵשׁ: בָּרוּךְ אַתָּה יי אֱלֹהֵינוּ מֶלֶךְ הָעוֹלָם, הַמַּבְדִּיל בֵּין קֹדֶשׁ לְחֹל בֵּין אוֹר לְחֹשֶׁךְ, בֵּין יִשְׂרָאֵל לָעַמִּים, בֵּין יוֹם הַשְּׁבִיעִי לְשֵׁשֶׁת יְמֵי הַמַּעֲשֶׂה. בֵּין קְדֻשַּׁת שַׁבָּת לִקְדֻשַּׁת יוֹם טוֹב הִבְדַּלְתָּ. וְאֶת יוֹם הַשְּׁבִיעִי מִשֵּׁשֶׁת יְמֵי הַמַּעֲשֶׂה קִדַּשְׁתָּ. הִבְדַּלְתָּ וְקִדַּשְׁתָּ אֶת־עַמְּךָ יִשְׂרָאֵל בִּקְדֻשָּׁתֶךָ. בָּרוּךְ אַתָּה יי הַמַּבְדִּיל בֵּין קֹדֶשׁ לְקֹדֶשׁ.

On all nights recite:

בָּרוּךְ אַתָּה יי אֱלֹהֵינוּ מֶלֶךְ הָעוֹלָם, שֶׁהֶחֱיָנוּ וְקִיְּמָנוּ וְהִגִּיעָנוּ לַזְּמַן הַזֶּה.

The first cup of wine is consumed, while leaning to the left (see pp. 44–45).

When the festival occurs on Shabbat, begin here:

(In an undertone – And it was evening and it was morning,)
The sixth day. And the heavens and the earth and all their hosts were completed. And God completed on the seventh day His work which He had done; and He rested on the seventh day from all His work which He had done. And God blessed the seventh day and made it holy, for on it He rested from all His work, that He, God, created to [continue to] do.

On Shabbat, add the words in parentheses:

With your permission: gentlemen, my masters and teachers.

Blessed are You, Lord, our God, King of the universe,
Who creates the fruit of the vine.

Blessed are You, Lord, our God, King of the universe, Who has chosen us from among all people, and raised us above all tongues, and sanctified us through His commandments. And in love, You, Lord, our God, have given us (Sabbaths for rest and) appointed times for happiness, festivals and seasons for joy; this (Sabbath day, and) this festival of matzot, the time of our freedom, in love, a holy convocation, in remembrance of the Exodus from Egypt. For You have chosen us and sanctified us from all the nations, and You have given us as a heritage (Your holy Sabbath and) appointed times in love and in favor, in happiness and in joy. Blessed are You, Lord, Who sanctifies (the Sabbath and) Israel and the festive seasons.

When the festival falls on Saturday night, add the following paragraph:

Blessed are You, Lord, our God, King of the universe, Who creates the lights of fire. Blessed are You, Lord, our God, King of the universe, Who makes a distinction between sacred and profane, between light and darkness, between Israel and the nations, between the seventh day and the six workdays. You have made a distinction between the holiness of the Sabbath and the holiness of a festival, and you have sanctified the seventh day above the six workdays. You have distinguished and sanctified Your people, Israel, with Your own sanctity. Blessed are You, Lord, Who makes a distinction between holy and holy.

On all nights recite:

Blessed are You, Lord, our God, King of the universe, Who has granted us life, sustained us and enabled us to reach this occasion.

The first cup of wine is consumed, while leaning to the left (see pp. 44–45).

Food for Thought

A. By opening with the familiar, the Haggada reminds us that the Seder, while unique, is also a standard festival meal and part of a regular ongoing calendar cycle. Ultimately, continuing observance – and not participation in one-time events – will guarantee the perpetuation of Jewish tradition.

B. While Kiddush is well known to us from its year-round recitation, this familiar ritual acquires deeper layers of significance on the Seder night. The Kiddush cup is the first of the four cups of wine rabbinically mandated for the Seder night. Furthermore, by serving as the introduction to the Seder, Kiddush enables us to mirror the historical events that introduce the Exodus itself.

Kiddush opens the Seder through a mitzva that deals with the sanctification of time. With the recitation of these blessings, we fulfill the biblical obligation to verbally "remember" the sanctity of each Shabbat and festival,[1] at its opening and, according to many, at its close.[2] Historically, the Exodus is also launched through a mitzva that deals with the sanctification of time. Fifteen days before their release from Egyptian bondage, the Israelites receive their first mitzva as a nation, the divine directive of Kiddush Hachodesh, the sanctification of the new moon.[3] The transmission of this edict is a critical first step in the redemption process, marking the moment when the nation's allegiance to divine law begins.

C. By selecting the mitzva of Kiddush Hachodesh as the introduction to His body of law, God turns the Israelites' attention toward the precious commodity that will immediately become theirs as free people – the commodity of time. As we have already noted (see p. 14), no less a scholar than Rabbi Joseph Soloveitchik maintains that the fundamental distinction separating the free person from the slave is *control of time*: "Time-awareness is the singular faculty of the free man, who can use or abuse it. To a slave, it is a curse or a matter of indifference. It is not an instrument which he can harness to his purposes. The free man wants time to move slowly because, presumably, it is being employed for his purposes."[4]

On the eve of their release from physical bondage, God prepares the Israelites for their spiritual transition to freedom: *I grant you control over time itself. Your time will now be your own, to be used as you wish. Recognize the responsibility that such newfound control brings. As free people, endeavor to use your time wisely, filling your lives with meaning.*

D. Through the recitation of Kiddush, we thus introduce our Seder journey as God introduced the Exodus to his nation. We ritually sanctify the moment before us and silently commit to the sanctification of all our moments, through the wise use of time in the fulfillment of God's will.

---

1   Talmud Bavli Pesachim 106a.
2   Rambam, *Mishneh Torah*, Hilchot Shabbat 29:1.
3   Shmot 12:1–2.
4   Besdin, *Reflections of the Rav*, vol. 1, pp. 201–2.

The Primary Mitzvot of the Seder
ARBA KOSOT: The Four Cups of Wine

A. The rabbinic obligation to consume four cups of wine over the course of the Seder evening emerges abruptly in the Mishna without introduction or clear explanation: "Even the poorest man in Israel shall not eat until he reclines, *and he shall have no fewer than four cups of wine*, even [if this wine must be provided for] from the communal coffer."[5]

B. Centuries later the Talmud classifies the four-cup requirement as a *takana* (rabbinic edict) enacted to promote a sense of freedom during the Seder.[6]

C. Later halachic authorities, citing Talmudic support, identify the four cups as signposts in the unfolding Seder ritual, each cup heralding the fulfillment of a specific segment of the evening's proceedings.[7]

D. The mysterious origin of the Seder's four cups warrants explanation. What exactly motivates the rabbis to add these cups of wine to the already existing edicts of the night (matza, *sippur Yetziat Mitzrayim*, etc.)?

The hint of an answer can be found in the way the rabbis introduce this requirement in the Mishna: "even the poorest man..."

Apparently, as the rabbis begin to structure the disparate obligations of the Seder into a cohesive whole, they encounter a problem. In a perfect world, with the Jewish nation safely ensconced in its homeland, and with each Jew comfortably ensconced in his home, the existing edicts of the Seder would suffice to convey the Exodus experience. Confronting a less-than-perfect world, however, the rabbis recognize that something more is needed to create the atmosphere of freedom essential to the Seder. "Even the poorest man in Israel...": each Jew, no matter how desperate his personal or national condition, is obligated to "feel free" on this night of historical freedom. To help create this sense of freedom, the rabbis mandate four cups of wine as celebratory signposts marking the sections of the Seder and drawing these sections into an overall structure. Within the bosom of his family, reclining comfortably with four cups of wine, even "the poorest man in Israel" is made to feel master of his destiny.

E. Once the four cups of wine are established, scholars across the ages offer various suggestions concerning their symbolism. One early, well-known interpretation connects the four cups of wine to the "four redemptions" referenced by God in His prediction of the impending Exodus:[8] *"V'hotzeiti etchem"* (and I will take you out [from

---

5   Mishna Pesachim 10:1.
6   Talmud Bavli Pesachim 109b.
7   Rambam, *Mishneh Torah*, Hilchot Chametz U'matza 7:10.
8   Talmud Yerushalmi Pesachim 10:1. While some later scholars substitute the phrase "four languages of redemption," this early version citing "four redemptions" seems more authentic (see Moshe Yaakov

under the burdens of Egypt]); *"v'hitzalti etchem"* (and I will rescue you [from their service]); *"v'ga'alti etchem"* (and I will redeem you [with an outstretched arm and with great judgments]); *"v'lakachti etchem"* (and I will take you [to Me for a people])."[9]

Many authorities maintain that the four terms employed in this passage represent four distinct stages in the Israelites' difficult transition from slavery to freedom, each stage a self-contained "redemption."[10] With each cup of wine, Seder participants symbolically journey with their forefathers from one redemptive stage to the next. The nineteenth-century scholar Rabbi Naftali Tzvi Yehuda Berlin (the Netziv) actually suggests that wine is chosen for this rabbinic mitzva because of the beverage's cumulative effect. Like successive cups of wine, each stage of redemption builds upon the preceding steps, with increasing impact.[11]

The four cups of wine thus help make the Exodus story "real" by reminding us that freedom could not have been achieved in one fell swoop. The transition from slavery to responsible autonomy is filled with pitfalls and challenges. As the Exodus unfolds, God systematically lays waste to all that has held the Israelites in thrall to their Egyptian taskmasters. Nonetheless, the generation of the Exodus never fully succeeds in separating itself from Egypt. At the very border of their promised land, the erstwhile slaves fail through the sin of the spies.[12] Only their children, the generation that has not known slavery as adults, can enter the land in their stead.[13]

F. Other scholars trace the symbolism of the four cups to alternative sources, including the following.

1. Four cups[14] mentioned during Yosef's conversation with Pharaoh's butler in an Egyptian prison, centuries before the Exodus.[15] Yosef's correct interpretation of the butler's dream, predicting that servant's release from prison, directly leads to Yosef's own ascension to power. These seminal events set the stage for the descent of the Israelites into Egypt, their subsequent enslavement and, ultimately, their exodus from that land.

2. Four decrees[16] leveled by Pharaoh against the Israelites during the initial course of their enslavement.[17]

3. Four "cups of calamity"[18] destined to be leveled against the enemies of the Jewish nation

---

Weinberg, *Haseder Ha'aruch* [Jerusalem: Machon Otzer Hamoadim] 2:118:1) and supports the idea of a staged redemptive process.

9   Shmot 6:6–7.
10 Sforno, Shmot 6:6; *Ha'amek Davar*, Shmot 6:6.
11 *Ha'amek Davar*, Shmot 6:6.
12 See my *Unlocking the Torah Text: Bamidbar*, Shelach 1, 2, 3.
13 Bamidbar 14:28–33.
14 Bereishit 40:11–13.
15 Talmud Yerushalmi Pesachim 10:1; Midrash Rabba Shmot 6:5.
16 Shmot 1:14, 16, 22; 5:16.
17 Midrash Rabba Shmot 6:5.
18 Yirmiyahu 25:15, 51:7; Tehillim 11:6, 75:9.

and four corresponding "cups of redemption"[19] destined to be experienced by the Jews.[20]

4. Four regimes who subjugate the Jewish nation across the course of its historical journey: the Kasdim, the Medeans, the Greeks and the Edomites (Romans).[21] According to some authorities, the consumption of the four cups of wine at the Seder reflects our belief that God will redeem us from our current exile (which began at the hands of the Romans), as He redeemed our ancestors in the past.[22]

5. The four categories of individuals who are halachically required to offer thanks to God upon their safe passage through danger: travelers across the seas, travelers through wilderness, released prisoners and survivors of illness.[23] The generation of the Exodus experienced each of these "salvations." They crossed the Reed Sea, they successfully traversed the Wilderness of Sinai, they were released from Egyptian bondage and the ill among them were miraculously healed at Mount Sinai prior to Revelation.[24]

G. Several halachic notes.

1. Both men and women are obligated in the mitzva of the four cups (and in all other mitzvot of the Seder night).[25]

2. Each cup of wine must minimally hold the halachic measurement known as a *revi'it*. Numerous positions are advanced as to the exact size of this measurement. According to Rabbi Moshe Feinstein, 3.3 fluid ounces suffices for each of the four cups. When the first night of Pesach falls on Shabbat, however, he maintains that the first cup should contain at least 4.42 ounces.[26]

3. Preferably one should drink the entire contents of each cup, or at least a majority of its contents. In cases of difficulty, the requirement is fulfilled by drinking the majority of a *revi'it*.[27]

4. Each cup of wine should be consumed while reclining to the left (see *heseiba*).[28]

5. Wine should preferably be used for the four cups. If one is unable to consume four cups of wine, the wine may be diluted with grape juice. If even diluted wine cannot be consumed, grape juice alone may be used.[29]

---

19 Tehillim 16:5, 23:5, 116:13 (written in the plural, designating two cups).
20 Talmud Yerushalmi Pesachim 10:1.
21 Midrash Rabba Shmot 6:26.
22 Bnei Yissaschar, Nisan 4:3.
23 Talmud Bavli Brachot 54b.
24 Vilna Gaon, commentary on the Haggada. This great sage employs this symbolism to explain the other appearances of sets of four throughout the Seder, as well: the four questions, the four children, etc.
25 Talmud Bavli Pesachim 43b, 108b.
26 Rabbi David Feinstein, *The Kol Dodi Haggada* (New York: Mesorah, 1990), pp. 12–13.
27 *Mishna Berura*, Orach Chaim 472:32, 33.
28 Rambam, *Mishneh Torah*, Hilchot Chametz U'matza 7:8; *Shulchan Aruch*, Orach Chaim 472:7.
29 Rabbi Shimon Eider, *Laws of the Seder* (Jerusalem: Feldheim, 1985), section 2, pp. 7–8.

The Primary Mitzvot of the Seder
HESEIBA: Reclining

A. The rabbinic obligation to recline on the Seder night emerges from the same Mishnaic source as the four cups of wine: "Even the poorest man in Israel *shall not eat until he reclines*, and he shall have no fewer than four cups of wine, even [if this wine must be provided for] from the communal coffer."[30]

B. The act of reclining at the Seder is mandated by the rabbis as yet another symbol of freedom.[31]

C. While numerous authorities maintain that it is "praiseworthy" to recline during the entire Seder,[32] *heseiba* is only obligatory during those particular points when the sense of freedom is essential. These points include the drinking of each of the four cups of wine; the consumption of the matza at the beginning and at the end of the meal (the afikomen); and, according to many authorities, the consumption of the Korech sandwich containing matza and *maror* (some include *charoset*).[33]

D. In general, failure to recline at the mandatory points listed above necessitates repetition of the rituals involved, without the accompanying blessing.[34] Many authorities argue, however, that if an individual drank the third or fourth cup of wine[35] or consumed the afikomen without reclining, he need not repeat the process.[36]

E. Some authorities maintain that one should recline upon the consumption of the *karpas* (the vegetable dipped in salt water and consumed at the beginning of the Seder; see pp. 48–49).[37] Others argue that one should not.[38] All agree, however, that the ritual need not be repeated if one fails to recline.

---

30 Mishna Pesachim 10:1.
31 Rambam, *Mishneh Torah*, Hilchot Chametz U'matza 7:7.
32 Ibid., 7:8.
33 Ibid., 7:8; *Shulchan Aruch*, Orach Chaim, 472:7; 475:1, 477:1.
34 Rema, *Shulchan Aruch*, Orach Chaim 472:7.
35 Ibid.
36 *Mishna Berura*, Orach Chaim 472:22.
37 *Kitzur Shulchan Aruch* 119:3; Abudarham, commentary on the Haggada.
38 *Shibbolei Haleket*, commentary on the Haggada; Maharal, commentary on the Haggada.

Seder Section 2 • URCHATZ
The First Washing of Hands

In preparation for the consumption of *karpas*, a vegetable dipped in salt water, the Seder participants wash their hands. Unlike the washing of hands before the consumption of bread, however, this ritual is not accompanied by a blessing.

Urchatz is the first in a series of three rituals performed at the beginning of the Seder in order to stimulate questioning on the part of children present.

Other than the omission of the *bracha*, the hands are washed as they are usually washed before the consumption of bread.

> The washing cup is taken in the right hand and passed to the left hand. Water is poured twice over the right hand. The cup is then passed to the right hand, and water is poured twice over the left hand.

Food for Thought

A. The ritual of Urchatz is rooted in the Talmudic mandate obligating an individual to wash hands before consuming foods dipped in water or other specific liquids.[1]

B. This requirement, like the more well-known obligation of handwashing prior to the consumption of bread, traces back to the days of the Temple. At that time, a state of ritual purity was required for the handling and consumption of *teruma*, foodstuffs designated for the Kohanim, the priestly caste. In order to ensure that the populace would grow accustomed to maintaining the laws of purity when necessary, the rabbis decreed handwashing for other foodstuffs such as bread and dipped foods, as well.[2]

C. A review of the sources, however, reveals that the obligation of handwashing before bread carries a significant overlay – unrelated to the Temple period – that is not present in connection with dipped foods.

Bread occupies a unique place in halacha as man's most basic and central foodstuff. The law, therefore, mandates that the consumption of bread, at any time by every Jew, mirror the dignified comportment that God generally requires from His people. The Talmud, in fact, connects the obligation of handwashing before bread to the biblical declaration "and you shall sanctify yourselves."[3] Through this regular ritual practice, the nineteenth-century scholar Rabbi Yechiel Michel Epstein explains, each

---

1   Talmud Bavli Pesachim 115a.
2   Talmud Bavli Chullin 106a.
3   Vayikra 20:7, cited in Talmud Bavli Brachot 53b.

46

Jew is reminded of God's overall desire "that His people demonstrate cleanliness, sanctity and purity."[4]

D. The philosophical distinction between the two handwashing rituals results in a concrete distinction in practice. Jews continue to wash their hands before eating bread to this day. The handwashing ritual prior to the consumption of dipped foods, however, is not universally observed. This leniency traces to the opinion of those authorities who maintain that the obligation of handwashing before dipped foods, which is solely based on the issue of ritual purity, no longer applies after the destruction of the Temple.[5] Because the status of the obligation to wash before a dipped food is uncertain in our time, therefore, no blessing is recited when we wash our hands before Karpas at this point in the Seder.

E. A basic question, however, remains. Given that handwashing before dipped food is hardly practiced in our day, why must it be scrupulously observed at the Seder? The answers proposed by the scholars include the following.

1. Urchatz is primarily performed at this point of the Seder in order to encourage questioning on the part of the children present.[6]

2. As noted above, the obligation of handwashing before dipped foods was universally observed when the Temple stood. Urchatz is, therefore, one of the many rituals performed on the Seder night as a remembrance of Temple times.[7]

3. A Kabbalistic tradition maintains that all mitzvot must be practiced more scrupulously than usual on the festival of Pesach. The practice of washing before dipped foods, therefore, becomes universally mandated on the Seder night.[8]

4. We wash our hands at this point not only because of the dipped *karpas*, but out of respect for the central mitzvot of *sippur Yetziat Mitzrayim* and Hallel that are soon to follow.[9]

---

4   *Aruch Hashulchan*, Orach Chaim 158:3.

5   Tosafot Pesachim 115 a–b; Rabbi Meier of Rotenberg quoted in the Tur, Orach Chaim 473.

6   *Chayei Adam* 130, Haseder b'ketzara.

7   Netziv in his introduction to his Haggada, Imrei Shefer.

8   *Chazon Ovadia, chelek* 2, amud 138.

9   *Mishna Berura* 432:2; see also 473:6.

Seder Section 3 • KARPAS
The Eating of a Vegetable Dipped in Salt Water

Karpas is the second in the series of three rituals performed at the beginning of the Seder in order to stimulate questioning on the part of the children present. The blessing over vegetables should be recited at this point with the intention that it apply not only to the *karpas*, but also to the *maror* that will be eaten later, directly before the meal.

> Each Seder participant dips a piece of vegetable smaller than the size of an olive in salt water. The blessing recorded below is recited, and the vegetable is consumed. Various opinions are suggested among the commentaries as to whether one should lean to the left upon the consumption of *karpas*. Absent a preexisting family custom, the accepted practice is not to lean.

בָּרוּךְ אַתָּה יי אֱלֹהֵינוּ מֶלֶךְ הָעוֹלָם, בּוֹרֵא פְּרִי הָאֲדָמָה.

Blessed are You, Lord, our God, King of the universe,
Who creates the produce of the earth.

The karpas is consumed.

Food for Thought

A. The classical scholars debate the mechanism by which *karpas* serves its function as a catalyst for children's queries at the Seder. Some authorities suggest that the unusual act of eating a vegetable before the meal will prompt the children to ask questions.[1] Other scholars focus on the act of dipping itself as the stimulus for questioning.[2]

B. Although a number of early halachic authorities maintain that the *karpas* should be dipped into *charoset*,[3] the law is codified according to the opinion that the dipping should be into salt water or vinegar.[4]

C. The Karpas ritual thus becomes a jarring study in contrast. Generally, the act of dipping food into liquid is seen as a sign of luxury and indulgence. In this case, however, we specifically dip the *karpas* into salt water to mark the bitterness of bondage. A shadow is cast over our sense of freedom, as the salt water reminds us of the tears and sweat that marked our ancestors' years of enslavement.

D. Because the consumption of the dipped *karpas* is ultimately a reminder of slavery, most authorities maintain that the vegetable should be consumed without *heseiba* (leaning to the left).[5]

---

1 Rashi, Talmud Bavli Pesachim 114a; Rashbam, ibid.
2 Arba Turim, Orach Chaim 173.
3 Rashi, Talmud Bavli Pesachim 114a; Rambam, *Mishneh Torah*, Hilchot Chametz U'matza 8:2; Arba Turim, Orach Chaim 173, in the name of Rav Amram.
4 Tosafot, Talmud Bavli Pesachim 114a, in the name of Rabbeinu Tam; *Shulchan Aruch*, Orach Chaim 173:6; *Chayei Adam* 130; Haggada of the Maharal; *Kitzur Shulchan Aruch* 119:3.
5 *Haggada shel Pesach Torat Chaim* (Jerusalem: Mosad Harav Kook, 1998); *Haseder Ha'aruch*, vol. 3, Haggada shel Pesach, Yachatz.

Seder Section 4 • Yachatz
The Breaking of the Middle Matza

Yachatz is the final introductory ritual in the series of three designed to encourage questioning from children as the Seder opens. (Note: In many households, the afikomen serves as a continuing source of children's involvement and interest. Children will often "steal" and hide this piece of matza, only to "barter" for its return, at the end of the meal.)

Many allegorical explanations are offered for the use of three matzot on the Seder evening. From a halachic standpoint, however, each of these matzot serves the necessary function(s) elucidated below.

> The leader of the Seder takes the middle matza and breaks it into two.
> The smaller of the two pieces is put back between the two whole matzot. This broken piece will serve as the primary matza over which the Maggid is read, and, ultimately, as the portion over which the blessing of eating matza will be recited before the meal.[1] The two whole, surrounding matzot serve as the *lechem mishneh* (double portion of bread) required at every Shabbat and *yom tov* meal.
> The larger of the two matza pieces created by Yachatz is set aside for even later use, as the afikomen, at the meal's end.

Food for Thought

A. Numerous authorities trace the ritual of Yachatz to the Torah's description of matza as *"lechem oni,"*[2] translated by some as "a poor man's bread."

A poor man, these scholars explain, is often forced to subsist on a piece of bread, rather than upon a whole loaf.[3] As a symbol central to the remembrance of slavery, the matza must mirror this difficult level of subsistence. The middle matza is therefore broken to create the piece over which the Haggada will be read and the *bracha* of matza recited.

B. Later authorities explain the "setting aside" of the afikomen as also mirroring the actions of the poor. A poor man, these authorities maintain, is always concerned over the source of his next meal. As a hedge against hunger, therefore, he will often "set aside" a portion of any food that he currently possesses for later use.[4]

---

1 Talmud Bavli Pesachim 115b; see Rashi and Rashbam there; *Shulchan Aruch Harav.*
2 Devarim 16:3.
3 Beit Yosef, Orach Chaim 473.
4 Rabbi Shlomo Kahn, quoted in David Derovan, Moshe Berliner, eds., *Haggada shel Pesach* (New York: Student Organization of Yeshiva University, 1974); Shlomo Riskin, *The Passover Haggada* (New York: Ktav, 1983).

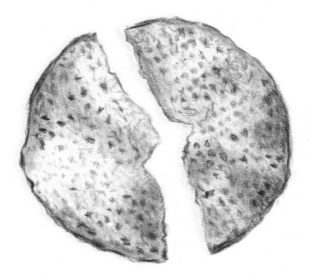

C. The contemporary Israeli scholar Rabbi Yosef Zvi Rimon offers a beautiful additional insight into the ritual of Yachatz. The breaking of the matza at this point in the Seder, Rabbi Rimon explains, represents a moment of rupture and crisis when all seems dark and beyond repair. The Jewish nation has survived such moments throughout its arduous history by maintaining faith in the principle that "disruption will eventually lead to progress and renewal."

"Already at Yachatz," Rabbi Rimon continues, "we await afikomen. At the moment of crisis, as the 'bread of affliction' is broken into two, we recognize this rupture as a stage in the redemption process, and we anticipate eating the matza of freedom."[5]

---

5   Rabbi Yosef Zvi Rimon, *Pesach Haggadah Shirat Miriam* (Jerusalem: Mossad Harav Kook, 2015), p. 119.

מַגִּיד

Seder Unit II
THE PAST

Seder Sections: Maggid

The introductory rituals behind us, we are now poised to enter the second unit of the Seder, and with it, begin the central Seder experience.

This second unit of the Seder consists solely of Maggid,[1] the formal retelling and reexperiencing of the Exodus story.

After opening with a brief invitation to others to join us at the Seder, Maggid presents a series of questions (the famous *Ma nishtana*); leads the Seder participants on a three-stage historical/philosophical journey (see pp. 15–23), "More Than a Mitzva: *Sippur Yetziat Mitzrayim*," and notes below); and closes with the first portions of Hallel, psalms of praise and thanksgiving.

---

1   We base this contention on the premise, accepted by many scholars, that the Hallel contained in this section of the Haggada is intrinsic to the fulfillment of the mitzva of *sippur Yetziat Mitzrayim*.

Seder Section 5 • MAGGID
The Retelling, Reexperiencing and Celebration of the Exodus Story

The following chart provides an introductory overview of the structure of the central Maggid section of the Haggada. As we have repeatedly stressed, a clear understanding of the structure of Maggid is essential to the entire Seder experience.

THE STRUCTURE OF MAGGID

Introductory passages	1. *Ha lachma anya*	A preliminary invitation	Pages 58–60
	2. *Ma nishtana*	Opening questions	Pages 61–63
MAGGID'S FIRST GOAL **(5A) Historical Awareness**	1. *Avadim hayinu*	The first answer to the *Ma nishtana*	Pages 64–67
	2. *Ma'aseh b'Rebbi Eliezer; Amar Rebbe Eliezer ben Azarya; Baruch Hamakom; K'neged arba'a banim; Yachol mei'rosh chodesh*	A major digression; consisting of a series of halachic asides quantifying the mitzva of *sippur Yetziat Mitzrayim*	Pages 68–82
MISHNAIC DIRECTIVE: *Matchil b'genut u'mesayeim b'shevach* (One opens with shame and closes with praise).	3. *Mi'tchila ovdei avoda zara hayu avoteinu*	The second answer to the *Ma nishtana*	Pages 83–84
	4. *Baruch Shomer havtachato*	Blessing, perspective and gratitude	Pages 85–90
	5. *V'hi she'amda*	Closing declaration	Page 91

MAGGID'S SECOND GOAL (5B) Historical Personalization/ Participation MISHNAIC DIRECTIVE: *V'doresh mei'Arami oved avi ad she'yigmor kol haparasha kula* (And one studies the passage beginning with the words "An Aramean tried to destroy my father..." until he finishes the entire passage).	1. *Tzei u'lemad*	Shared Torah study	Pages 92–128
	2. *Dayenu*	Perspective and gratitude	Pages 129–31
	3. *Al achat kama v'kama*	Closing declaration	Page 132
MAGGID'S THIRD GOAL (5C) Historical Perpetuation MISHNAIC DIRECTIVES: *Rabban Gamliel haya omer, kol she'lo amar shelosha devarim eilu b'Pesach lo yatza yedei chovato* (Rabban Gamliel was wont to say: Anyone who has not said [spoken of] these words on Pesach has not fulfilled his obligation: Pesach [the Korban Pesach], matza [unleavened bread], and *maror* [bitter herbs]).	1. *Rabban Gamliel haya omer*	Discussion of three Seder symbols	Pages 133–38
B'chol dor va'dor chayav adam lir'ot et atzmo k'ilu hu yatza mi'Mitzrayim (In each generation a person must see himself as if he left the land of Egypt).	2. *B'chol dor va'dor*	Closing declaration	Pages 139–40
L'fichach anachnu chayavim l'hodot (Therefore we are required to thank).	3. *L'fichach anachnu chayavim l'hodot*	Expressions of gratitude: the first sections of Hallel	Pages 141–45

The Primary Mitzvot of the Seder
SIPPUR YETZIAT MITZRAYIM: Retelling the Story of the Exodus

A. As detailed in our introductory essay (see "Making Sense of the Seder I: A Halachic Perspective"), the biblical obligation to retell the Exodus story emerges from two Torah passages: *"Zachor et hayom hazeh asher yatzatem mi'Mitzrayim"* (Remember this day on which you departed from Egypt)[1] and *"V'higgadeta l'vincha ba'yom hahu, leimor, ba'avur zeh asa Hashem li b'tzeiti mi'Mitzrayim"* (And you shall relate [the Exodus narrative] to your child on this day, saying, it is because of this that Hashem did for me for when I left Egypt).[2]

Both passages are needed to properly delineate the mitzva.

The statement "And you shall relate to your child on this day, saying..." indicates that the Exodus story should be directed to children on the Seder night.[3] If children are not present, the narrative should nonetheless unfold in question-and-answer form, as a parent would teach a child.[4]

The continuation of this sentence, *"it is because of this* that Hashem did for me for when I left Egypt," indicates that the mitzva should be performed in the presence of symbolic mitzvot, specifically on the first night(s) of Pesach, "when the matza and *maror* are lying before us."[5]

The broader Torah mandate "Remember this day on which you departed Egypt" specifies that although the Exodus narrative should be told as a parent would teach a child, the story must be recited even if an individual is alone, albeit still in question-and-answer form.[6]

B. The mitzva of *sippur Yetziat Mitzrayim* differs from the year-round obligation to remember the Exodus[7] in a number of significant ways (see p. 16). Uniquely, the Seder night mitzva should:

1. Unfold in question-and-answer form (see above).

2. Include lengthy discussion not only of the Exodus, but also of the events leading to the enslavement and redemption of the Israelites.

3. Feature a discussion and explanation of the symbolic mitzvot of the evening.[8]

C. A puzzling anomaly is noted by the commentaries regarding this critical mitzva. Rabbinic dictate generally requires the recitation of a *birkat hamitzva*, a blessing immediately prior to the performance of a mitzva. Yet no such *bracha* is found in our Haggadot in connection with the biblical mitzva of *sippur Yetziat Mitzrayim*.

---

1 Shmot 13:3.

2 Shmot 13:8.

3 Rambam, *Mishneh Torah*, Hilchot Chametz U'matza 7:2.

4 Ibid.; Talmud Bavli, Pesachim 117a.

5 *Mechilta D'bei Rebbi Yishmael*, Mesechta D'pischa 17:5.

6 *Minchat Chinuch*, mitzva 21.

7 Talmud Bavli Brachot 12b; Rambam, *Mishneh Torah*, Hilchot Kriat Shma 1:3.

8 Menachem Mendel Gerlitz, ed., *Haggada shel Pesach Mi'beit Halevi* (Jerusalem: Oraita Publishing, 1983), p. 110, in the name of Harav Chaim Soloveitchik of Brisk.

Two general approaches are suggested by the scholars to explain the absence of this blessing.

1. Some authorities maintain that the requirement for a *bracha* is actually fulfilled through the recitation of other blessings over the course of the day. Their suggestions include the blessings mentioning the Exodus in the evening prayers,[9] the blessings of Kiddush,[10] the blessing "He who redeemed us..." found at the end of the Maggid section[11] and the blessing over the daily study of Torah recited each morning.[12]

2. Other scholars explain that the amorphous character of the mitzva of *sippur Yetziat Mitzrayim* precludes the requirement for the recitation of a blessing in the first place. The unique characteristics to which they point include the lack of concrete parameters to the mitzva,[13] the fact that the mitzva's primary fulfillment is through thought and understanding as opposed to action[14] and the logical nature of the mitzva that would have mandated its fulfillment even had it not been divinely commanded.[15]

Finally, an additional, particularly beautiful explanation for the blessing's absence is offered by the eighteenth–nineteenth-century scholar Rabbi Moshe Schreiber, the Chatam Sofer. As the Maggid opens, the Chatam Sofer explains, each Seder participant must literally view him- or herself as a Hebrew slave in Egypt prior to the Exodus. *There is, as of yet, no Israelite nation; there is, as of yet, no Torah law; there can be, as of yet, no recited blessing.*

The situation can be compared, the Chatam Sofer suggests, to a convert standing in the mikva immediately prior to conversion. The convert is unable to recite a blessing at this moment while bearing the status of a non-Jew. Only after an initial immersion – marking the convert's entry into the Jewish faith – can the *bracha* be recited, after which a second immersion is performed.

Similarly, only after each Seder participant courses through Maggid, only after reexperiencing a personal "conversion to Judaism" through the Exodus and the Revelation at Sinai can that participant begin to perform mitzvot (including the recitation of *brachot*). The usual *birkat hamitzva*, therefore, cannot be recited in conjunction with the performance of the mitzva of *sippur Yetziat Mitzrayim*.[16]

D. As noted in our introductory essay concerning the mitzva of *sippur Yetziat Mitzrayim*, a three-stage structure for the performance of the mitzva, clearly delineated by the time of the Mishna, is followed in our Haggadot to this day. This format, consciously designed to move each Seder participant along a step-by-step journey into the heart of Jewish history, will be referenced in our running commentary on the text.

---

9   Meiri, Brachot 12; *Shibbolei Haleket* 218.
10 Rabbeinu Yerucham 5:4 in the name of Rabbeinu Peretz; Abudarham in the name of the Rif.
11 *Shibbolei Haleket* 218.
12 *Rivevot Ephraim, chelek* 2:129:23.
13 *Orchot Chaim* 18; Abudarham quoting the Rashba.
14 Maharal, *Gevurot Hashem* 62.
15 *Sefat Emet*, vol. 3, Pesach 5647.
16 Chatam Sofer, Haggada shel Pesach.

Ha Lachma Anya: A Preliminary Invitation

The matzot are uncovered, the Seder plate is raised
and the following paragraph is recited:

הָא לַחְמָא עַנְיָא דִי אֲכָלוּ אַבְהָתָנָא בְּאַרְעָא דְמִצְרָיִם. כָּל דִכְפִין יֵיתֵי
וְיֵכֻל, כָּל דִצְרִיךְ יֵיתֵי וְיִפְסַח. הָשַׁתָּא הָכָא, לְשָׁנָה הַבָּאָה בְּאַרְעָא דְיִשְׂרָאֵל.
הָשַׁתָּא עַבְדֵי, לְשָׁנָה הַבָּאָה בְּנֵי חוֹרִין.

This is the bread of affliction that our forefathers ate in the land of Egypt.
Whoever is hungry, let him come and eat; whoever is in need, let him come and
observe the Passover rituals. This year we are here; next year may we be in the
Land of Israel! This year we are slaves; next year may we be free people!

Food for Thought

A. Many authorities maintain that the passage of *Ha lachma anya* was recorded in Aramaic, the common vernacular in Talmudic times, because of its importance. This paragraph, openly inviting others to join in the Seder proceedings, was clearly meant to be understood by all.[17] While this passage appears neither in the Talmud nor the Midrash, it is already found in works of the Geonic period (589–1038 CE).[18]

B. The issuance of an invitation to others at this point in the Seder, however, seems gratuitous. A genuine invitation would obviously have been extended during the weeks before the Seder. At the very least, we should have invited any potential guests before reciting Kiddush and performing the introductory rituals. At this point, the Seder has already begun, our doors are closed and no one can hear us. Why extend an invitation now, specifically as we open the section of Maggid?

C. Numerous commentaries view the phrase *"Kol ditzrich yeisei v'yifsach"* (Let all who are in need come and conduct [the Pesach ritual]) as evidence that *Ha lachma anya* is not really a practical invitation to our Seder, at all. It is instead, they argue, a formula recited on the Seder night in remembrance of the Korban Pesach.

These authorities note that concerning the Korban Pesach, the Torah declares, *"They shall* perform it."[19] The plural conjugation of this commandment indicates that, although an individual could legally consume the Korban Pesach alone, every effort had to be made to join with others in the performance of this ritual.[20] Additional

---

17 Eliezer Ben Yoel HaLevi (Ra'avya) 525:162; Rashbatz (Shimon ben Tzemach), *Yavin Sh'mua* 39:3.

18 *Seder Rav Amram Gaon; Siddur Rav Sa'adia Gaon.*

19 Shmot 12:47.

20 Rambam, *Mishneh Torah,* Hilchot Korban Pesach 2:2.

textual passages[21] led the rabbis to place great emphasis upon the advance establishment of *chaburot*, discreet groups of individuals designated for the consumption of each Korban Pesach.[22] Clearly, the ritual celebrating the moment of the Jewish nation's birth was meant to be a shared rather than a solitary experience.

To remember and mark this aspect of the Korban Pesach, we now symbolically invite others to join us in the Pesach rituals.[23]

D. The question remains, however: Why issue this invitation now, specifically as an introduction to the Maggid section of the Haggada?

Perhaps, from an entirely different perspective, the paragraph of *Ha lachma anya* can be viewed less as an invitation and more as a statement of purpose. Through a beautiful formula that consciously weaves together references to the past, present and future, the Haggada bids those present to pause and openly consider the goals of the timeless adventure before them.

Over the course of Maggid, we will journey along a path from slavery to freedom. Before that journey begins, *Ha lachma anya* reminds us that our own yearly Seder passage is designed, at least in part, to sensitize us to the arduous journeys of others and to our ability to assist them in their travails.

This approach is supported by the observations of Rabbi Yosef Dov Soloveitchik on the relationship between *chesed* (acts of kindness) and freedom: "*Chesed* is the characteristic mark of the free man. The bondsman is not spiritually capable of joining the *chesed* community, because he is too much concerned with himself. Only free and proud people think of others and share with others."[24]

Each year, as we prepare to reexperience the birth of our nation, we proclaim what is, in part, the purpose of this transformative journey. Through the yearly exploration of our own transition from slavery to freedom, we hope to become that "free and proud people" who will recite *Ha lachma anya* as a matter of course, a nation of individuals who will naturally and instinctively welcome others into our lives and homes.

E. For continued discussion.

Living in a *Ha lachma anya* world can be exceedingly complex. As I write these words, the global community struggles with the exploding number of refugees fleeing civil war in Syria and strife in other lands. The humanitarian call for open borders is tempered, in country after country, by a fear of terrorist infiltration – a fear fed by the growth of radical groups such as the Islamic State and their ever-increasing attacks upon civilian populations.

Caught in the middle of this debate, the Jewish community stands in a particularly sensitive position. Will we, haunted by the memory of the world's silent acquiescence to the Holocaust, stand up for the rights of today's refugees? Can we, many of whose families were so recently refugees, remain

---

21 Shmot 12:3, 4.
22 Rambam, *Mishneh Torah*, Hilchot Korban Pesach 2:2.
23 *Shibbolei Haleket.*
24 Rabbi Joseph B. Soloveitchik, *Festival of Freedom: Essays on Pesah and the Haggadah* (Jersey City, NJ: Ktav, 2006), p. 22.

silent as we witness the plight of others?

Or is this situation different? Can the world let down its guard in the midst of a global war against Islamic fundamentalism? Should the safety of potential host countries trump their compassion for others? And can we, an ever-vulnerable global Jewish community, ignore the open anti-Semitism emerging from so many quarters of the Muslim world? How will we be affected by increasing Muslim populations in the countries of our own residence?

Even in the State of Israel, the problem has reached crisis proportions. An influx of illegal immigrants from various countries in distress has posed a critical dilemma for the Jewish state. How are these immigrants to be treated? How many of them classify as refugees, deserving of a safe haven in the storm? How many are seeking economic opportunity alone? What number can and should the small Jewish state safely absorb without causing havoc to its own social structure?

Similarly, today's raging struggle over immigration policy in the United States can be framed by Hillel's dialectic, "If I am not for myself, who is for me; and if I am [only] for myself, what am I?"[25]

When and how should our own particular concerns play a role in delineating the parameters of compassion toward others? And if we allow those concerns to enter into our computations, will our stance against the world's repeated indifference to the plight of Jewish victims be weakened? Even

more fundamentally, will our own moral code be eroded?

By the time of this Seder, these specific events and concerns may have passed. Other, similar concerns, however, are certain to arise in their stead. In a complex world, the issues are never black and white, but they cannot be ignored. It's one thing to preach *Ha lachma anya*; it's quite another to live it...

F. Finally, a word about the mystery of matza.

The symbol of matza is discussed twice during the retelling of the Exodus narrative: first here, in the paragraph of *Ha lachma anya*, and again as the section of Maggid draws to a close. The two references to the symbol, however, could not be more different. At this point, we refer to the matzot as *lachma anya*, the "bread of affliction" or a "poor man's bread." The matza appears here as a symbol of bondage and oppression. Later, in contrast, we will describe matza as emerging from the moment of redemption: "Because our fathers' dough did not have the opportunity to ferment before the Supreme King of Kings revealed Himself to them and redeemed them...."

Unlike the other static symbols of the Seder, matza is, apparently, a symbol of *both slavery and redemption*. The basis for and significance of this seemingly contradictory identity will be discussed when we arrive at the second mention of matza, toward the close of Maggid.

---

25 Pirkei Avot 1:14.

Ma Nishtana: Opening Questions

The second cup of wine is poured, the Seder plate is moved to the side (again to encourage questioning) and the following four questions are recited, usually by the youngest child or children present:

מַה נִּשְׁתַּנָּה הַלַּיְלָה הַזֶּה מִכָּל הַלֵּילוֹת?

שֶׁבְּכָל הַלֵּילוֹת אָנוּ אוֹכְלִין חָמֵץ וּמַצָּה. הַלַּיְלָה הַזֶּה כֻּלּוֹ מַצָּה.

שֶׁבְּכָל הַלֵּילוֹת אָנוּ אוֹכְלִין שְׁאָר יְרָקוֹת. הַלַּיְלָה הַזֶּה מָרוֹר.

שֶׁבְּכָל הַלֵּילוֹת אֵין אָנוּ מַטְבִּילִין אֲפִילוּ פַּעַם אֶחָת. הַלַּיְלָה הַזֶּה שְׁתֵּי פְעָמִים.

שֶׁבְּכָל הַלֵּילוֹת אָנוּ אוֹכְלִין בֵּין יוֹשְׁבִין וּבֵין מְסֻבִּין. הַלַּיְלָה הַזֶּה כֻּלָּנוּ מְסֻבִּין.

How different this night is from all [other] nights!

For on all other nights we eat *chametz* or matza; on this night only matza!

For on all other nights we eat other kinds of vegetables; on this night *maror*!

For on all other nights we do not dip even once; on this night we do so twice!

For on all other nights we eat sitting upright or reclining; on this night we all recline!

Food for Thought

A. While often perceived as a simple device for the involvement of children in the Seder proceedings, the *Ma nishtana* is really much more.

"At this juncture," the Mishna states, "the son asks his father [the *Ma nishtana*]."[26]

The Talmud explains, however, that these questions should be asked and answered even if no child is present.[27] In this way, the Exodus narrative will unfold at each Seder according to the mandated format: *As a parent would teach a child.* The reasons for maintaining this format, even in the absence of children, will become clear by the time we reach the final stages of Maggid.

Rabbi Joseph Soloveitchik (the Rav)

maintains that the deeper significance of the *Ma nishtana* is reflected in an apparent inconsistency in the Rambam's comments on the Seder.

In his halachic review of the Seder proceedings, the Rambam states: "The second cup is poured and at this point the child asks. *And the reader recites* the *Ma nishtana...*"[28]

Noting the Rambam's apparent distinction between the questions raised by the "child" and the *Ma nishtana* recited by the "reader," the Rav explains that, according to the Rambam, "the *Ma nishtana* was not designed for the child; it is too difficult a text."[29] The formulaic questions of the *Ma nishtana* are, instead, meant to be recited by the Seder leader and are separate and

---

26 Mishna Pesachim 10:4.
27 Talmud Bavli Pesachim 116a.
28 Rambam, *Mishneh Torah*, Hilchot Chametz U'matza 8:2.
29 Genack, *The Seder Night: An Exalted Evening*, p. 29.

apart from the spontaneous questions to be raised by the children themselves.

The Rav goes on to cite the practice of his famed grandfather, Rabbi Chaim Soloveitchik, at whose Seder each participant recited the *Ma nishtana*.[30]

Even the majority of us, who maintain the popular practice of relegating the *Ma nishtana* to children, should not dismiss these questions as "child's play." The questions of the *Ma nishtana*, as well as those raised spontaneously around the Seder table, are integral to our fulfillment of the mitzva of *sippur Yetziat Mitzrayim*, as they set the tone for our discussions throughout the night.

B. While the basic text of the *Ma nishtana* emerges from the Mishna,[31] variations have developed due to historical circumstance. Given the absence of the Korban Pesach, our Haggadot follow the lead of the Rambam, who, in his version of the Haggada, replaces the Mishnaic question concerning the Korban Pesach with a query concerning the rabbinic mitzva of *heseiba* (reclining).[32]

C. Various approaches are offered by authorities as to why the *Ma nishtana* consists specifically of these four questions, and not others. The Abravanel, for example, suggests that the questioner is not probing the rituals themselves, but their inherently contradictory nature. *How*, the questioner asks, *are we to understand the opposing practices of the evening? We eat matza, a poor man's bread, but we recline as free men. We consume the bitter herb, but we dip our foods as a symbol of luxury.*[33]

D. For continued discussion.

By opening the Seder with rituals designed to encourage questioning and by introducing the Maggid with *Ma nishtana*, the Haggada conveys a significant pedagogical lesson: *questions are essential to the process of learning.*

My years as an educator have convinced me that we often forget this truth. Jewish education is not geared enough toward the development of critical thinking. So intent are we upon the communication of information to those in our charge that we neglect to encourage questioning and exploration on their part. As a result, our students' questions frequently go not only unanswered, but unasked, with unfortunate results.

I have often found that when we encourage exploration on the part of even our younger students, the results can be astonishing. Ideas, concepts and concerns that we would never expect children to consider naturally emerge from their lips. And unfortunately, I have also found the opposite to be true as well. When we fail to encourage our younger students to ask

---

30 Ibid.

31 Mishna Pesachim 10:4.

32 Rambam, *Mishneh Torah*, Hilchot Chametz U'matza, Nusach Hahaggada. Interestingly, in his review of the laws of the Seder, the Rambam records five questions, including both the question concerning the Korban Pesach and the question concerning *heseiba*; *Mishneh Torah*, Hilchot Chametz U'matza 8:2. The version of the Mishna in the Talmud Yerushalmi Pesachim 10:4 records only three questions, including the question concerning the Korban Pesach, but omitting the questions on both *maror* and *heseiba*.

33 *Zevach Pesach*, commentary of the Abravanel on the Haggada.

and to think, they often fail to become truly involved in the learning process.

Years ago, upon the passing of my teacher, Rabbi Joseph Soloveitchik, I attempted to convey his greatness to the members of my community. I told them that in a world in which many mentors say to their students, "I want you to think like I think," the Rav insisted, "I want you to think, like I think." He demanded that we think for ourselves.

A similar sentiment was expressed by the renowned scientist Dr. Isidore Rabi, awarded the Nobel Prize for physics in 1944. He credited his mother's encouragement for his scientific accomplishments. Apparently every day when he came home from school as a child, rather than asking what he learned that day, as other mothers did, she greeted him with the words "Izzy, did you ask a good question today?" The focus on asking good questions, said Rabi, "made me become a scientist!"[34]

The Seder reminds us to encourage our children to question, explore, and to think for themselves. This lesson is well worth remembering.

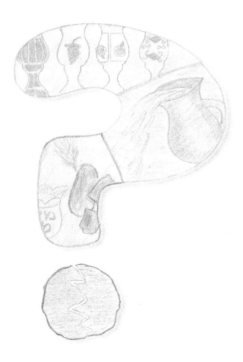

---

34 Donald Sheff, letter to the editor, "Izzy, Did You Ask a Good Question Today?" *New York Times*, January 19, 1988; "Great Minds Start with Questions," *Parents Magazine*, September 1993.

Seder Section 5a • MAGGID's First Goal
Historical Awareness

Having recited both the opening invitation of *Ha lachma anya* and the questions of *Ma nishtana*, we now enter the first major stage of Maggid.

As indicated in our introductory essay (see pp. 15–23), the Maggid section of our Haggada unfolds in three distinct stages as it leads us through the mitzva of *sippur Yetziat Mitzrayim*. This tripartite structure was clearly delineated by the time of the Mishna, in which it is recorded.

The Mishna sums up the first of these stages with the enigmatic directive *"Matchil b'genut u'mesayeim b'shevach"* (One opens with shame and closes with praise). On a practical level, this Mishnaic directive determines the textual flow at this opening stage of the Seder. We have suggested, however, that the rabbis are actually addressing the broad, fundamental question "How does the Jew view history?" Their powerful and succinct response, "One opens with shame and closes with praise," shapes the first section of Maggid into a vehicle that moves each Seder participant toward a state of overall historical awareness.

Just as the Exodus from Egypt inexorably moved our ancestors from "shame" to "praise," the Jewish journey, in its entirety, follows a *seder* (order). For the Jew, history is destiny driven, structured and purposeful. The path along which we travel is not haphazard, but moves from a fixed point to a fixed goal, from humble beginnings to a glorious end.

Gaining awareness of the purposeful character of Jewish history is the first requisite step in the journey shaped by Maggid.

Structurally, this first section of Maggid opens with an immediate response to the *Ma nishtana*, digresses for a series of seemingly disparate observations, and then returns to a second response to the *Ma nishtana*.

If you have not yet read the full introductory essay on *sippur Yetziat Mitzrayim*, it will be helpful to do so now (see pp. 15–23). Our running commentary on the text will be referencing numerous points that are discussed in detail in that essay.

Avadim Hayinu: The First Answer to the *Ma Nishtana*

This passage, the first direct answer to the *Ma nishtana*, summarizes the transition from slavery to freedom and begins to establish parameters for the mitzva of retelling the Exodus narrative.

The Seder plate is returned to the table, the matzot are uncovered,
and the following paragraph is recited:

עֲבָדִים הָיִינוּ לְפַרְעֹה בְּמִצְרָיִם. וַיּוֹצִיאֵנוּ יי אֱלֹהֵינוּ מִשָּׁם בְּיָד חֲזָקָה
וּבִזְרֹעַ נְטוּיָה. וְאִלּוּ לֹא הוֹצִיא הַקָּדוֹשׁ בָּרוּךְ הוּא אֶת אֲבוֹתֵינוּ מִמִּצְרַיִם, הֲרֵי
אָנוּ וּבָנֵינוּ וּבְנֵי בָנֵינוּ מְשֻׁעְבָּדִים הָיִינוּ לְפַרְעֹה בְּמִצְרָיִם. וַאֲפִילוּ כֻּלָּנוּ חֲכָמִים,
כֻּלָּנוּ נְבוֹנִים, כֻּלָּנוּ זְקֵנִים, כֻּלָּנוּ יוֹדְעִים אֶת הַתּוֹרָה, מִצְוָה עָלֵינוּ לְסַפֵּר
בִּיצִיאַת מִצְרָיִם. וְכָל הַמַּרְבֶּה לְסַפֵּר בִּיצִיאַת מִצְרַיִם, הֲרֵי זֶה מְשֻׁבָּח.

We were slaves to Pharaoh in Egypt, and the Lord, our God, took us out from there with a strong hand and with an outstretched arm. And had the Holy One, Blessed Be He, not taken our fathers out of Egypt, then we, our children and our children's children would have remained subjugated to Pharaoh in Egypt.

And even if all of us were wise, all of us understanding, all of us elders, all of us versed in the knowledge of the Torah, we would still be obligated to discuss the Exodus from Egypt. And every individual who elaborates in the retelling of the Exodus narrative is to be considered praiseworthy.

Food for Thought

A. The paragraph of *Avadim hayinu* (we were once slaves) is incorporated into the Haggada at the suggestion of the Talmudic sage Shmuel.

As we have noted (see pp. 17–18), Shmuel interprets the Mishnaic directive "One opens with shame and closes with praise" narrowly. He therefore offers a limited response to the *Ma nishtana*, restricting the narrative to the story of the Exodus itself.[1]

Shmuel's colleague, Rav, argues for a broader response. The Maggid narrative, Rav maintains, should begin centuries before the Exodus, with a statement reflecting the negative spiritual origins of the Jewish people: "In the beginning, our fathers were idol worshipers" (see pp. 17–18).[2]

Following a tradition that may have developed as early as the Geonic period (seventh to eleventh centuries CE),[3] our

---

1 Talmud Bavli Pesachim 116a.
2 Ibid.
3 Quoted in Rabbeinu Chananel, Talmud Bavli Pesachim 116a. It should be noted that debate develops among the early scholars as to whether Rav and Shmuel are actually disagreeing with each other or whether their views were always meant to be seen as complementary. See Kasher, *Haggada Shleima*, introduction, chapters 3–4, for a review of the opinions on the matter.

SEDER UNIT II : The Past

Haggada incorporates the positions of both authorities. Shmuel's response to the *Ma nishtana* is recorded here, while Rav's response appears later in the text.

The order in which these two responses are recorded in the Haggada, however, seems counterintuitive. The historical events cited by Rav begin well before those cited by Shmuel. Why then does the text quote Shmuel's response before Rav's? Why not proceed in chronological order?

The answer lies in the Haggada's sound pedagogical technique. When a child (or an adult, for that matter) asks a question, that question should be answered directly. Afterwards, additional background material can be added for clearer perspective.

The immediate answers to the *Ma nishtana* are to be found in the story of slavery and redemption. Shmuel's response, limited to that narrative, is therefore offered first. Only later do we turn to the questioner and say: *We have answered your questions directly. If you really want to understand the story, however, we have to go back further in time, to the beginning.* We then offer Rav's response.

B. Two telling observations on the phrase "We were once slaves to Pharaoh in Egypt" are offered by Rabbi Joseph Soloveitchik.

1. Pharaoh's Egyptian slaves are referred to in the Torah as "*avdei Paro*" (Pharaoh's slaves).[4] In contrast, the Haggada informs us that our ancestors were "*avadim l'Paro*" (slaves to Pharaoh).

The Israelites remained a spiritually free people armed with their own heritage, inner personality and perception of reality. Had they become "Pharaoh's slaves" – had they lost their independent identity completely – the Exodus could never have occurred.[5]

2. Our ancestors were "slaves to Pharaoh *in Egypt*."

A slave who is "owned" by an individual can earn the trust of his master. Like Yosef in the house of Potiphar, such a slave can achieve personal success and even rise to a position of power within the household.

When a slave is owned by a cruel corporate state, however, he loses his individuality. He becomes a nameless, faceless entity for whom any advancement is impossible. Robbed of the opportunity for friendship or trust, he exists in a world in which the same impersonal, indifferent relationship persists from day to day, week to week, year to year. The Israelites were slaves not only to Pharaoh, but to "Pharaoh in Egypt." They were slaves to a corporate state. This made their experience of bondage even more difficult to bear.[6]

C. Numerous scholars question the statement "And if the Holy One, Blessed Be He, had not brought our fathers out from Egypt, then we, and our children, and our children's children would still be subjugated to Pharaoh in Egypt."

How can we be so certain, these scholars ask, that we would "still be subjugated to Pharaoh in Egypt"? Given the vagaries of

---

4   Bereishit 50:7; Shmot 10:7, 11:3.
5   Genack, *The Seder Night: An Exalted Evening*, pp. 33–36. Support for the Rav's contention can be gleaned from the well-known midrashic claim that the Israelites ultimately merited redemption from Egypt due to their loyal preservation of their unique names, language and moral code (Midrash Rabba Bamidbar 13:20).
6   Ibid.

history, we might well have been eventually freed from Egyptian bondage even without divine intervention.

Some authorities answer this question by noting that the Hebrew word *meshubad* (enslaved) can also be translated as "beholden." Had God not redeemed us from bondage, these scholars admit, we indeed might have eventually been set free by the Egyptians or by another political power. Under those circumstances, however, we would have remained "beholden" to our erstwhile masters or to others for granting us our freedom. By redeeming us through divine intervention, God ensures that we are in no way indebted to other human beings. We come into our national existence as the servants of God alone, not as the servants of man.[7]

Another solution perhaps lies in the obvious effect that centuries of immersion in Egyptian culture must have had upon the Israelites. By the time of the Exodus, only radical events could wean the nation away from the ideas, beliefs and mores of their Egyptian masters. Had God not redeemed us through divine intervention, had we not witnessed the ten plagues laying waste to all elements of the powerful society around us, we would have emerged a very different people. We would have remained, culturally and philosophically, "subjugated to Pharaoh in Egypt."

D. As the paragraph of *Avadim hayinu* draws to a close, the text quietly shifts focus from the substance of the Exodus story to the structure of the mitzva of its retelling.

What are the parameters of the mitzva of sippur Yetziat Mitzrayim? the text effectively asks, and responds, "Even if we were all wise, even if we were all understanding..." No matter who we are, no matter how scholarly or learned we may be, we are obligated to tell this tale and share it with each other. And the more we delve into the story, the more deserving we will be.

By taking this first step toward defining the boundaries of the mitzva of *sippur Yetziat Mitzrayim*, the passage of *Avadim hayinu* subtly introduces the next series of paragraphs in the text.

---

7   Rabbi Eliyahu Dessler, *Michtav Me'Eliyahu*.

A Sudden Digression

At this point in the Seder, the Haggada does something abundantly strange.

After offering the Talmud's first answer to the *Ma nishtana*, the text does not immediately proceed to the second response to these questions. Instead, the Haggada breaks the flow of the Exodus narrative by inserting a series of seemingly unrelated paragraphs. Included in this startling digression are a scholarly conversation recorded in Bnei Brak, an observation in the name of Rabbi Elazar ben Azarya, a comment concerning the timing of the mitzva of *sippur Yetziat Mitzrayim* and a discussion regarding four (imaginary) sons.

Why are these paragraphs included here, in the middle of our responses to the *Ma nishtana*? What connects these seemingly disparate passages to the Exodus narrative or, for that matter, to each other?

A careful review of the paragraphs involved reveals an easily missed overall theme. Seen as a group, these passages deal with the "quantification" of the mitzva of *sippur Yetziat Mitzrayim* – the fixing of practical parameters for the performance of the mitzva. When can this mitzva be performed? How exactly should it unfold? To whom must this story be told? How should we craft an appropriate narrative for each listener? These are among the questions addressed during this lengthy digression.

We can now understand the logic behind this textual detour. As we begin to fulfill the Seder's central mitzva of *sippur Yetziat Mitzrayim*, the rabbis resolve to teach us a critical general lesson: *how we perform a mitzva is as important as performing it in the first place.* Our individual fulfilment of any halachic obligation, even one as personal as retelling the Exodus with our family and friends, must adhere to technical standards set forth by the law itself.

To drive this lesson home, the rabbis temporarily halt the main flow of the Seder and force us to do something uniquely Jewish: to assess the quality of our actions as we act. They set forth a series of paragraphs, focusing on various technical aspects of the mitzva of *sippur Yetziat Mitzrayim*. In keeping with the Haggada's narrative style, these passages unfold as stories, parables and maxims, with numerous lessons and internal digressions of their own. They become, in time, some of the most popular segments of the Haggada.

The intriguing nature of these passages, however, should not blind us to their fundamental purpose. "You have begun to do a mitzva," the rabbis assert. "Now stop for a moment and make sure that you are doing it right!"

Only after we review the halachic requirements presented – only after we assess our proposed performance of the mitzva of *sippur Yetziat Mitzrayim* against the objective standards of Jewish law – will the rabbis allow us to return to the Exodus narrative.

As the Seder's historical journey begins in earnest, the rabbis thus remind us of the critical role that uniform mitzva observance has played throughout our history. Exactitude in the performance of mitzvot has kept us connected across the centuries, not only to the rich world of biblical and rabbinic law, but to each other, as well. Uniformity of ritual practice unites us with our God and with our people, across space and time.

Aside #1: *Ma'aseh b'Rebbe Eliezer:*
A Scholarly Discussion in Bnei Brak

The series of asides incorporated at this point in the Haggada begins with a reference to a scholarly discussion between the great Mishnaic sages: Rabbi Eliezer, Rabbi Yehoshua, Rabbi Elazar ben Azarya, Rabbi Akiva and Rabbi Tarfon.

מַעֲשֶׂה בְּרַבִּי אֱלִיעֶזֶר, וְרַבִּי יְהוֹשֻׁעַ, וְרַבִּי אֶלְעָזָר בֶּן עֲזַרְיָה, וְרַבִּי עֲקִיבָא, וְרַבִּי טַרְפוֹן, שֶׁהָיוּ מְסֻבִּין בִּבְנֵי בְרַק, וְהָיוּ מְסַפְּרִים בִּיצִיאַת מִצְרַיִם כָּל אוֹתוֹ הַלַּיְלָה, עַד שֶׁבָּאוּ תַלְמִידֵיהֶם וְאָמְרוּ לָהֶם: רַבּוֹתֵינוּ, הִגִּיעַ זְמַן קְרִיאַת שְׁמַע שֶׁל שַׁחֲרִית.

It happened that Rabbi Eliezer, Rabbi Yehoshua, Rabbi Elazar ben Azarya, Rabbi Akiva and Rabbi Tarfon were reclining [at a Seder] in Bnei Brak and were discussing the Exodus from Egypt all that night, until their students came and told them: "Our Masters! The time has come for the recitation of the morning Shma!"

Food for Thought

A. According to the Vilna Gaon, the dialogue in Bnei Brak is chosen to open this section of the Haggada because of its connection to the immediately preceding paragraph of *Avadim hayinu*. Two components of the mitzva of *sippur Yetziat Mitzrayim* first mentioned in *Avadim hayinu* are concretely demonstrated in the conversation before us.

1. *Even if all of us were wise…it is a mitzva upon us to tell the story of the Exodus from Egypt.* The sages who participate in the discussion in Bnei Brak are all towering scholars of great renown, clearly familiar with the Exodus narrative in all its details. Nevertheless, they all actively engage in the retelling of the narrative on the Seder night.

2. *And any individual who discusses the Exodus from Egypt at length is praiseworthy.* The sages examine the Exodus narrative all through the night, until the time arrives for the recitation of the morning Shma.[8]

B. A fascinating puzzle, however, arises regarding the presence of one of the participants in Bnei Brak. To understand this difficulty, a brief halachic review is required.

The Talmud in Pesachim records a debate between Rabbi Elazar ben Azarya and Rabbi Akiva concerning the time by which the Korban Pesach was to be consumed on the Seder night. Rabbi Elazar ben Azarya maintains that it had to be completed by midnight, while Rabbi Akiva argues that the Korban Pesach may be eaten until dawn.[9]

---

8 *Vilna Gaon Haggadah: The Passover Haggadah with Commentaries by the Vilna Gaon and His Son R' Avraham* (Brooklyn: Mesorah, 1993).

9 Talmud Bavli Pesachim 120b.

This disagreement carries practical implications to this day, even absent the Korban Pesach. The Talmudic scholar Rava contends, based upon a textual connection drawn in the Torah,[10] that matza consumption on the Seder night is subject to the same time constraints as the Korban Pesach.[11] Rabbi Yosef Karo, therefore, rules in the *Shulchan Aruch* that the afikomen, should be consumed by midnight.[12]

Finally, some scholars go one step further, arguing that *sippur Yetziat Mitzrayim* is subject to the same time restrictions as the consumption of the Korban Pesach and of matza. *Rabbi Elazar ben Azarya*, they maintain, *would insist upon concluding the narrative by midnight on Seder night.*[13]

If this analysis is correct, however, how could Rabbi Elazar ben Azarya have participated in a Seder discussion lasting the entire night? Wouldn't he have insisted upon ending the conversation by midnight?

Perhaps the episode before us reflects the great respect that the rabbis of the Talmud showed for each other. Bnei Brak was, at the time, Rabbi Akiva's residence and the city for which he was the halachic decisor. Out of deference to Rabbi Akiva's authority, therefore, all present, including Rabbi Elazar ben Azarya, followed Rabbi Akiva's ruling that the Korban Pesach, and consequently the mitzva of *sippur Yetziat Mitzrayim*, could be performed throughout the night.

C. Other commentaries open the door to less literal interpretations of the scholarly conversation on that fateful Pesach evening.

The sages mentioned in this episode all lived during the time of the Bar Kochba revolt against Rome and/or during the years of horrific persecution that followed. Rabbi Akiva himself was a major supporter of Bar Kochba, for a time believing this great warrior to be the promised Mashiach.[14]

Might this gathering in the darkness of the night actually be a clandestine meeting prior to the Bar Kochba revolt? Are the rabbis discussing the current evils of Roman rule even as they recall past persecutions in Egypt? Are they debating the wisdom of armed rebellion against the might of Rome? Or, having already decided upon the perilous path of war, are they now carefully laying out plans for the military campaign?

Perhaps, on an allegorical level, the "night" during which this discussion ensues is not only the night of Pesach, but the "night of our persecution" across time. If so, the Haggada references a scene destined to be repeated time and again. Surrounded by the encroaching darkness of a hostile world, fearful of a knock on the door, Jewish leaders converge in secret to discuss, debate, plan and share ways to ensure the survival of their people and tradition.[15]

D. For continued discussion.

Over time, we naturally come to view the events and figures of Jewish history one-dimensionally. The personalities of

---

10 Shmot 12:8.

11 Talmud Bavli Pesachim 120b.

12 *Shulchan Aruch*, Orach Chaim 477:1. It remains unclear, however, whether Rabbi Yosef Karo, the author of the *Shulchan Aruch*, actually determines the halacha according to Rabbi Elazar ben Azarya or whether he is arguing for an extra stringency (see *Haseder Ha'aruch* 1:78:3).

13 See *Haseder Ha'aruch* 1:62 for a discussion of the issue.

14 Talmud Yerushalmi Ta'anit 4:5.

15 Various versions of this approach can be found in a multitude of Haggadot.

the past loom larger than life, the choices before them seem less complex than our own, distinctions between right and wrong seem clearer and easier to discern.

Such a fantasized view of history is not only wrong, but dangerous, robbing us of critical lessons to be learned from the past.

The dramatic periods directly before and after the destruction of the Second Temple serve as a perfect case in point.

During the years preceding the destruction of the Temple in 70 CE, debate rages among the leaders of Judea as to whether rebellion against Rome is warranted, or even wise. No less a figure than Rabbi Yochanan ben Zakai, the scholar who eventually orchestrates Jewish survival after the Temple's destruction, initially advocates for compromise and conciliation with Rome.[16]

When war does break out, Judea remains rife with internal conflict. So deep is this tragic discord that internecine battles spill out into the streets of Yerushalayim even as the city is under enemy siege. Inexorably, the Judean revolt is smothered by the Romans, the Temple is destroyed and thousands of Jews are exiled from the land.

The Jews rebel against Rome twice in the years that follow. The second of these insurrections garners the support of Rabbi Akiva, arguably the greatest sage of his day. So taken is Rabbi Akiva with the charismatic leader of the rebellion, Shimon bar Kosiba, that he dubs him Bar Kochba, "son of a star."[17] This act reflects Rabbi Akiva's hope, shared by many at the time, that Shimon might be the messianic figure referred to in the biblical verse "there shall come a star out of Yaakov."[18] Rabbi Akiva's support for the rebellion, however, is far from uniformly accepted, even within the rabbinic community.[19]

After initial dramatic victories, the Bar Kochba revolt is cruelly suppressed by the Romans, with devastating consequences. In the rebellion's aftermath, the Romans kill, exile, or sell into slavery the majority of the population of Judea. The Roman emperor, Hadrian, moves to erase Jewish national identity by prohibiting the study of Torah and the practice of the Jewish faith. The name of Judea is wiped from Roman maps and replaced with Syria Palaestina; Yerushalayim becomes Aelia Capitolina. So great is the devastation that some historians date the Jewish exile from the end of this revolt, and not from the earlier date of the Temple's destruction.

In retrospect, questions must be asked. Would it have been better to compromise with Roman rule, rather than risk our physical exile? Had we compromised, would we have lost our spiritual way? Would we still be here today, long after the Roman Empire has faded into dust? What constitutes defeat and what constitutes victory?

While the particulars may have changed, the basic physical and spiritual battles facing the Jewish people remain constant over the centuries. When do we resist and when do we compromise? What are our red lines? What principled stands must we take today to ensure our future survival?

Perhaps some of these very debates raged around that Pesach table of scholars, those many centuries ago, in Bnei Brak.

---

16 Talmud Bavli Gittin 56a; *Avot D'Rabi Natan* 4:5.
17 Talmud Yerushalmi Ta'anit 4:5.
18 Bamidbar 24:17.
19 Talmud Yerushalmi Ta'anit 4:5.

Aside #2: *Amar Rebbe Elazar ben Azarya*: Elazar ben Azarya's Observation

Rebbe Elazar ben Azarya, one of the scholarly discussants in the previous paragraph, is now quoted in a Mishnaic passage concerning the daily mitzva of remembering the Exodus. As noted before, this year-round obligation of Exodus remembrance differs from the Seder's mitzva of *sippur Yetziat Mitzrayim* in a number of substantive ways (see see pp. 16, 56).

אָמַר רַבִּי אֶלְעָזָר בֶּן עֲזַרְיָה: הֲרֵי אֲנִי כְּבֶן שִׁבְעִים שָׁנָה,
וְלֹא זָכִיתִי שֶׁתֵּאָמֵר יְצִיאַת מִצְרַיִם בַּלֵּילוֹת, עַד שֶׁדְּרָשָׁהּ בֶּן זוֹמָא,
שֶׁנֶּאֱמַר: לְמַעַן תִּזְכֹּר אֶת יוֹם צֵאתְךָ מֵאֶרֶץ מִצְרַיִם כֹּל יְמֵי חַיֶּיךָ.
יְמֵי חַיֶּיךָ - הַיָּמִים. כֹּל יְמֵי חַיֶּיךָ - הַלֵּילוֹת. וַחֲכָמִים אוֹמְרִים: יְמֵי חַיֶּיךָ -
הָעוֹלָם הַזֶּה, כֹּל יְמֵי חַיֶּיךָ - לְהָבִיא לִימוֹת הַמָּשִׁיחַ.

Rabbi Elazar ben Azarya said: "Behold, I am like a man of seventy years, yet I did not succeed in proving that the Exodus from Egypt must be mentioned at night–until Ben Zoma explained: The Torah states, 'In order that you may remember the day you left Egypt all the days of your life.'[20] The phrase 'the days of your life' would signify days only, but 'all the days of your life' includes the nights, as well."

The sages, however, maintain: "'The days of your life' would refer only to the present-day world; 'all the days of your life' indicates the inclusion of the messianic era."[21]

Food for Thought

A. The inclusion and placement of this paragraph in the Haggada poses an obvious challenge. We have suggested that, at this point in the Seder, the Haggada digresses from its primary narrative in order to analyze the mitzva of *sippur Yetziat Mitzrayim*. The passage before us, however, does not deal with this mitzva at all. It focuses instead on an entirely different obligation: the year-round mitzva to remember the Exodus.[22]

What place, then, does this passage have at this point in the Seder or, for that matter, in the Seder at all?

B. An intriguing technical explanation for the inclusion of this paragraph is suggested by an additional word in the Rambam's version of the Haggada. The Rambam's text reads: *"Amar **lahem** Rebbe Elazar ben Azarya"* (Rabbi Elazar ben Azarya said **to them**).[23] According to the Rambam, the paragraph

---

20 Devarim 16:3.
21 Mishna Pesachim 1:5.
22 For this reason, apparently, Rav Sa'adia Gaon omits this paragraph from his text of the Haggada. *Haseder Ha'aruch* 3:135.
23 Rambam, *Mishneh Torah*, Hilchot Chametz U'matza, Nusach Hahaggada.

before us is a natural extension of the immediately preceding passage describing the scholarly dialogue in Bnei Brak. Rabbi Elazar's declaration concerning daily remembrance of the Exodus arises out of that very conversation.

Even according to the Rambam's text, however, the philosophical question remains. Whether at Rabbi Akiva's Seder in Bnei Brak or at ours, what place is there for a discussion of the year-round mitzva of Exodus remembrance? The Seder's focus, one could argue, should remain on the central mitzva of the evening, the mitzva of *sippur Yetziat Mitzrayim*.

C. Two opposite approaches are suggested by the scholars in response to this question.

Some commentaries maintain that the paragraph before us teaches through *contrast*. The Haggada raises the topic of year-round observance, these scholars argue, in order to crystallize our understanding of the Seder night's uniqueness. While simple remembrance of the Exodus may suffice throughout the year, much more is required of us this evening. Tonight, each of us must travel along the historical path mandated by the Seder's central mitzva, the mitzva of *sippur Yetziat Mitzrayim*.[24]

Other authorities argue that this paragraph's message is of *continuity* rather than contrast. Our year-round obligation to remember the Exodus, these scholars explain, arises directly out of the Seder experience. Like so many other periodic mitzvot, the mitzva of *sippur Yetziat Mitzrayim* is meant to affect us well beyond the moments of its fulfillment. The Torah therefore mandates a continuing mitzva of Exodus remembrance, as an ongoing "reminder" to weave the lessons of the Seder into our daily lives.[25]

---

24 *Haggadat Ma'aseh Nissim*, quoted in *Haseder Ha'aruch* 3:384.
25 *Sefat Emet*, Pesach 5641.

Aside #3: *K'neged Arba'a Banim*: The Four Sons

The Haggada now turns its attention to the mechanics of the mitzva of *sippur Yetziat Mitzrayim*. Through a series of imagined conversations with four very different sons, we are reminded of the complex challenges inherent in the transmission of *mesora*, the eternal traditions of our people. "Train a child according to his way," King Solomon declares in Proverbs, "and even when he ages, he will not depart from it."[26] Success in teaching is ultimately dependent, Solomon emphasizes, upon reaching the heart and mind of each individual, very different child.

בָּרוּךְ הַמָּקוֹם, בָּרוּךְ הוּא. בָּרוּךְ שֶׁנָּתַן תּוֹרָה לְעַמּוֹ יִשְׂרָאֵל, בָּרוּךְ הוּא.
כְּנֶגֶד אַרְבָּעָה בָנִים דִּבְּרָה תוֹרָה. אֶחָד חָכָם, וְאֶחָד רָשָׁע, וְאֶחָד תָּם, וְאֶחָד
שֶׁאֵינוֹ יוֹדֵעַ לִשְׁאוֹל:

חָכָם מַה הוּא אוֹמֵר? מָה הָעֵדוֹת וְהַחֻקִּים וְהַמִּשְׁפָּטִים, אֲשֶׁר צִוָּה יי אֱלֹהֵינוּ
אֶתְכֶם? וְאַף אַתָּה אֱמָר לוֹ כְּהִלְכוֹת הַפֶּסַח: אֵין מַפְטִירִין אַחַר הַפֶּסַח
אֲפִיקוֹמָן.

רָשָׁע מַה הוּא אוֹמֵר? מָה הָעֲבֹדָה הַזֹּאת לָכֶם? לָכֶם – וְלֹא לוֹ. וּלְפִי שֶׁהוֹצִיא
אֶת עַצְמוֹ מִן הַכְּלָל, כָּפַר בָּעִקָּר. וְאַף אַתָּה הַקְהֵה אֶת שִׁנָּיו וֶאֱמָר לוֹ: בַּעֲבוּר
זֶה עָשָׂה יי לִי בְּצֵאתִי מִמִּצְרָיִם, לִי – וְלֹא לוֹ. אִלּוּ הָיָה שָׁם, לֹא הָיָה נִגְאָל.

תָּם מַה הוּא אוֹמֵר? מַה זֹּאת? וְאָמַרְתָּ אֵלָיו: בְּחֹזֶק יָד הוֹצִיאָנוּ יי מִמִּצְרַיִם
מִבֵּית עֲבָדִים.

וְשֶׁאֵינוֹ יוֹדֵעַ לִשְׁאוֹל, אַתְּ פְּתַח לוֹ, שֶׁנֶּאֱמַר: וְהִגַּדְתָּ לְבִנְךָ בַּיּוֹם הַהוּא
לֵאמֹר: בַּעֲבוּר זֶה עָשָׂה יי לִי בְּצֵאתִי מִמִּצְרָיִם.

Blessed is the Omnipresent One, blessed be He! Blessed is He who gave the Torah to His people Israel, blessed be He! The Torah speaks of four sons: one is wise, one is wicked, one is simple and one does not know how to ask.

The wise one, what does he say? "What are the testimonies, the statutes and the laws which the Lord, our God, has commanded you?"[27] You, in turn, shall instruct him in the laws of Passover, [up to] "one is not to eat any dessert after the Passover lamb."[28]

The wicked one, what does he say? "What is this service *to you*?!"[29] He says "to you," but not to him! By thus excluding himself from the community, he has denied that which is fundamental. You, therefore, blunt his teeth and say to him: "It is

---

26 Proverbs 22:6.
27 Devarim 6:20.
28 Mishna Pesachim 10:8.
29 Shmot 12:26.

because of this that the Lord did *for me* when I left Egypt";[30] "*for me*" – but not for him! If he had been there, he would not have been redeemed!

The simple one, what does he say? "What is this?"[31] Thus you shall say to him: "With a strong hand the Lord took us out of Egypt, from the house of slaves."[32]

As for the one who does not know how to ask, you must initiate him, as it is said: "You shall tell your child on that day, 'It is because of this that the Lord did for me when I left Egypt.'"[33]

Food for Thought

A. No section of the Haggada has become more popular over the years than the imagined conversation with the four sons. Consequently, a vast literature of commentary has developed surrounding this passage. We will limit our comments to a few salient observations concerning the origin of this paragraph and the significant lessons that it conveys.

B. The short blessing of *Baruch HaMakom*, introducing the passage of the "four sons," is a blessing of thanks. Recognizing the grandeur of the task before us, we pause to thank God for granting us the privilege of teaching our children the traditions of our fathers.

This blessing is not found in the Talmudic or Midrashic sources of the four sons narrative. It does appear, however, in later ancient Haggadot, including the ninth-century Haggada of Rav Amram Gaon.

C. Differing versions of the conversations with the four sons are found in the Talmud Yerushalmi and the Midrash. The depiction

in our Haggadot most closely matches the version found in the *Mechilta*.[34]

The rabbis base their portrayal of these conversations on four sources in the Torah in which the text specifically focuses on the transmission of information concerning the Exodus to a child.[35] The rabbinic text, however, departs from the original in a series of significant ways:

1. The Torah does not openly identify the children involved as respectively "wise, wicked, simple," and "unable to ask." That delineation is made by the rabbis, based on perceived hints in the biblical text (see below).

2. While some Torah verses are repeated verbatim in the rabbinic passage, other verses are replaced with alternative text. The questions of the wise and wicked sons, for example, are quoted directly from the Torah, while the answers given to those children are entirely different from the responses in the biblical text.

3. The biblical sources upon which the

---

30 Shmot 13:8.
31 Shmot 13:14.
32 Ibid.
33 Shmot 13:18.
34 *Mechilta D'bei Rebbi Yishmael*, Parashat Bo 18.
35 Shmot 12:26, 13:8, 13:14; Devarim 6:20.

rabbinic passage is based are not quoted in order of their appearance in the Torah. They are instead cited in the sequence that fits most logically into the narrative's flow.

D. The question asked by the first son, a direct quote from the biblical book of Devarim,[36] instantly identifies this child to the rabbis as "wise." Only a *chacham*, a wise individual, the scholars maintain, possesses the knowledge to categorize the mitzvot of Pesach into "testimonies, statutes and laws."[37] The answer provided by the rabbis to the *chacham*'s question, however, seems bewildering: "You, in turn, shall instruct him in the laws of Pesach; one is not to eat any afikomen (dessert) after the Passover offering." How does this response answer the *chacham*'s question concerning the overall significance of the Pesach laws? Why do the rabbis single out the specific edict prohibiting "a dessert" after the consumption of the Korban Pesach?

Many scholars interpret the response to the wise son as a charge toward comprehensive review of the entire body of law associated with the Seder. *To understand the significance of this evening, we tell the chacham, continue to study and review all relevant laws, up to and including the final Mishnaic edict concerning the Korban Pesach:* "One is not to eat any afikomen after the Passover offering."[38] The response to the wise son is clearly tailored to this specific child. The

chacham approaches the Seder from an intellectual vantage point, categorizing the mitzvot into groupings understandable to him. We therefore encourage this child to continue his intellectual striving, assuring him that, with further comprehension of the mitzvot, philosophical understanding will come, as well.[39]

Other, more abstract interpretations of the response to the *chacham* are offered by a variety of scholars across the ages. As an example, the Abravanel suggests that we are warning the wise son: *Do not assume, because you have attained a level of understanding of the Pesach rituals, that you have exhausted all that you can learn from them. Just as the Korban Pesach was meant to be the final taste of the evening, so too, the "taste" of the rituals is meant to remain with you. Continue to review and study even the material you think you have already mastered, for there is always new meaning to be discovered even in the "familiar."*[40]

E. Like the first son's question, the question raised by the second son is a direct quote from the Torah, this time from the book of Shmot.[41] Rabbinic use of this quote, however, to identify the second child as a *rasha*, a wicked individual, seems puzzling.

The rabbis argue that the second son excludes himself from the community when he asks, "What is this *avoda* (service) *to you*?" Strikingly, however, the first son employs similar language in his question: "What are the testimonies, statutes and laws that the

36 Devarim 6:20.
37 Ritva, Zevach Pesach (Abravanel).
38 Mishna Pesachim 10:8.
39 Ritva; Peirush Maharal al Hahaggada; *Haggada shel Pesach Baruch She'amar* (Baruch Halevi Epstein).
40 Abravanel, Zevach Pesach.
41 Shmot 12:26.

Lord, our God, *has commanded you?*" Given the clear parallel, why do the rabbis view these two children so differently?

A variety of answers are suggested by the commentaries:

1. Many scholars maintain that the distinction between the wise and wicked sons lies in the *chacham*'s inclusion of the phrase "the Lord, our God," in his question. By citing the divine name and by referring to God as "our God," the wise son effectively includes himself in the community of believers.[42]

2. Other authorities, citing a source in the Talmud Yerushalmi,[43] base the identification of the wicked son on his usage of the term *avoda* to describe Jewish practice. Dependent upon the context, this term can be translated either as "service" or as "work." When the *rasha* declares, "What is this *avoda* to you," he effectively reveals that he views the laws of Pesach as a burden, rather than as meaningful service to God.[44]

3. Yet other commentaries trace the distinction between the *chacham* and the *rasha* to the way in which the Torah introduces their respective queries.[45] The wise son's question is introduced in the Torah with the statement "If your child *asks* you in times to come, saying..."[46] In contrast, the Torah's introduction to the evil son's question is "And it shall come to pass if your children *say* to you..."[47] Unlike the *chacham*, the *rasha* does not "ask." He does not approach the Seder table in order to question or explore. The

rasha joins the proceedings solely to "say," to declare his previously determined positions. He is not open to discussion, nor is he interested in hearing other points of view. The Haggada therefore directs us to "blunt his teeth." We do not push the *rasha* away entirely; we do not banish him from the table; but we also do not engage him in futile conversation. *Stay with us*, we say, *and when you are ready to discuss, we will engage with you. We don't have to agree from the outset, but our conversation must begin from a point of mutual respect and openness.*

The exact nature of the *rasha*'s failing may be dependent upon nuanced variations in the Haggada text. Some editions of the Haggada separate the wicked son's sin into two, through the addition of the word *and*: "Because he has excluded himself from the community *and* he has denied that which is most fundamental." According to this version, the *rasha* is guilty of two separate sins: the sin of isolating himself from the community and the sin of apostasy.

In contrast, our Haggadot read, "Because he has excluded himself from the community, he has denied that which is most fundamental." By eschewing the division of the *rasha*'s sin into two, our texts underscore a powerful principle of Jewish thought: *Separation from the community is, by definition, a rejection of that which is most fundamental.* This principle is eloquently captured by the Rambam in his codification of Jewish law:

---

42 *Orchot Chaim*; Kol Bo.

43 Talmud Yerushalmi Pesachim 10:4.

44 *Shibbolei Haleket*; Rokeach.

45 These introductions are not quoted in the Haggada, but are found in the Torah text directly before each of the questions cited.

46 Devarim 6:20.

47 Shmot 12:26.

"One who separates himself from the ways of the community, even though he commits no [other] sin, but isolates himself from the community of Israel, and does not perform mitzvot together with them, and separates himself from their pain, such a person has no share in the world to come."[48]

By emphasizing the critical nature of communal connection in its reaction to the *rasha*, our text of the Haggada also subtly emphasizes the pivotal philosophical role played by the Exodus at the dawn of Jewish history.

The Jewish nation is born in a *two-stage process*, the first stage being the Exodus from Egypt and the second being the Revelation at Sinai. To be a Jew, you must first "belong." Before arriving at Sinai, each Israelite had to be willing to be part of the community, to throw his or her lot in with a nascent nation journeying into an unknown wilderness. Centuries later, this two-stage initiation into the Jewish faith is mirrored in the Talmud's insistence that a potential convert to Judaism must first be confronted with the challenge, *What did you perceive that prompted you to come? Do you not know that Israel (i.e., the Jewish people) is, in this day, afflicted, oppressed, downtrodden and harassed – and that hardships are frequently visited upon them?* Only once the potential convert essentially answers *I know, and I am not even worthy (to share in their hardships)* do we begin to teach him or her Jewish thought and law.[49] The convert's positive response to this challenge marks a personal Exodus, an experience of national affiliation that must precede his acceptance of mitzvot. Finally, the clear calendar connections drawn between the festival of Pesach and the festival of Shavuot (commemorating Revelation) yearly remind each Jew that before he can meet his God at Sinai, he must first rejoin his people leaving Egypt.

F. The third son merely asks, *"Ma zot?"* (What is this?) This minimalistic question, quoted again from the book of Shmot,[50] prompts the rabbis to identify this child as the *tam*, the simple son.

The exact character of the *tam*, however, is a matter of debate among the commentaries. Some scholars view this child as possessing a limited ability to learn.[51] Such a child, the Haggada maintains, must be appropriately included in the educational process. Every effort must be made to provide him with the tools that he needs to understand the significance of the Seder night.

Other scholars, however, base their understanding of this child on an alternate interpretation of the word *tam*, supported by several biblical verses.[52] In the eyes of these scholars, the third son is not learning disabled at all, but rather an individual of pure, wholehearted faith. The Vilna Gaon is among those who see the *tam* not as the antithesis of the *chacham* (the wise child), but as the antithesis of the *rasha* (the devious wicked child).[53] The *tam* is honest,

---

48 Rambam, *Mishneh Torah*, Hilchot Tshuva 3:12.
49 Talmud Bavli Yevamot 47a.
50 Shmot 13:14.
51 Rashi, Shmot 13:14.
52 Bereishit 6:9, 17:1; 25:27; Devarim 18:13, 32:4.
53 Haggadat Hagra (Jerusalem: Ha'am Hatorah Institute), p.58.

straightforward and guileless; his worship emerges more from his heart than from his head. Such "simple" belief, often derided by the more intellectually inclined, is not simple at all, but a courageous expression of spiritual will. The belief of the *tam* is to be appreciated and nurtured through educational interactions that touch the depth of this child's soul.

G. Finally, the fourth son emerges from a biblical source that features no question at all: "And you shall tell your child on that day: 'It is because of this that the Lord did for me when I left Egypt.'"[54]

This verse is familiar to us as the "response" already offered to the wicked child. Now, however, the rabbis consider this sentence as it appears in the Torah, without a prompting question from "the child." The absence of such a query leads the rabbis to conclude that here the Torah speaks of a fourth child, the *she'eino yode'a lishol*, the child who does not know how to ask.

With the inclusion of this fourth, final child, the Haggada reminds us that to be successful, parenting must be *proactive*, rather than *reactive*. Our children will not always be able to "ask." Their questions and their doubts will often lie unexpressed, not only for want of the right words, but because they will not always comprehend the nature of their own disquiet. The Haggada therefore instructs us that, upon confrontation with this fourth child, "*At psach lo*" (You must open for him). Our task, as parents, is to "open the door," to initiate, prompt and share, to actively encourage our children to express themselves. If we do so, then the "child who

does not know how to ask" will learn to ask – and to open doors of wonder, exploration and discovery – thereby enriching his or her life each day.

H. For continued discussion.

Hidden lessons course beneath the surface of the narrative of the four sons, bringing to life the complexity of human nature and the consequential challenges of parenting.

Among the easily missed issues that emerge are the following.

1. The difficulty the commentaries have in distinguishing the *chacham* from the *rasha* may mirror a fundamental truth: perhaps these children are not so different, after all. If the Haggada wanted to portray the antithesis of a *rasha*, it would have introduced a *tzaddik*, a righteous child, rather than a wise child. In and of itself, wisdom carries no moral imperative, and there is therefore no guarantee that every *chacham* will be a *tzaddik*.

The similar questions asked by the *chacham* and the *rasha*, in fact, indicate that the line separating these two children can potentially be thin, indeed. Channeling the intellect of the wise son can be as difficult as reaching the *rasha*.

2. The simple child reminds us that there are many ways to learn and many paths toward God. If the *tam* is understood as a "difficult learner," the Haggada declares that the "difficulty" may lie with us, rather than him. Contemporary educators are quick to point out that many children who, in the past, were labeled unable to learn can actually learn well, albeit differently.

---

54 Shmot 13:8.

Centuries ago, the rabbis already sense this truth. They thus charge us in the Haggada to "leave no child behind," to teach each *tam* in the individualized manner appropriate to that child.

If, on the other hand, the *tam* is understood as a child of "pure" faith, the Haggada's message is that we should appreciate those whose paths to God might be different from our own. Across the face of its historical journey, the Jewish nation has developed into a tapestry woven of many different cultural and philosophical threads: Chassidim and Mitnagdim, Ashkenazim and Sephardim, scientists and mystics, searchers and unquestioning believers. Judaism considers the many possible paths toward God as equally authentic and challenges each of us to find the personal path that works for us without denigrating the routes chosen by others.

Understood in this way, the Haggada's approach to the *tam* captures the essence of parenting at its core. Too often, when parents protest, *I want my child to be his or her own person*, what they really mean is, *I want my child to be his or her own person, as long as he or she turns out exactly like me*. Our task is not to raise our children into the people that we think they should become, but to raise them into the people that they each uniquely need to be. All this, while still modeling for them the essential values that we hold dear and that we hope they will hold dear, as well.

3. The final child, the one who does not know how to ask, may be the most important for consideration in our day. While generalities are always dangerous, in recent years I and many of my rabbinic colleagues have noticed a troubling phenomenon. A growing number of parents in our communities are unwilling to actively "parent." Whether the reason is lack of time and energy, or whether it's because many parents today want to be their children's friends, parental direction and discipline are often lacking. As a result, many of our children end up with an outsized sense of personal entitlement and without any real feeling for Jewish communal connection or personal behavioral boundaries.

If we don't educate our children, the world will – and most likely not in the way we would like. If we do not actively encourage our children to participate and explore within the safety of our homes, synagogues and schools, they will eventually explore over the internet, on the college campus or in the workplace.

As stated above, to be successful, parenting must be proactive rather than reactive. It takes energy and creativity, but parenting requires that we find ways to discuss issues with our children that we feel are critical to their moral and ethical development. Even more importantly, it requires that we clearly model and actively instruct toward the very behaviors that we would expect from them.

Every child is, at times, a child who does not know how to ask. In those moments we must ask and answer for them.

Aside #4: *Yachol Mei'rosh Chodesh*:
When Should the Story Be Told?

In this final aside, the Haggada focuses on the timing of the mitzva of *sippur Yetziat Mitzrayim* by quoting a midrashic passage[55] that offers two theoretical alternatives to the practice of retelling the Exodus narrative on the Seder night: either that the obligation should begin on Rosh Chodesh Nisan or that this mitzva should be performed during the day (on the fourteenth of Nisan, when the Korban Pesach was slaughtered, or on the fifteenth, when the Exodus actually occurred).

The Midrash responds to its own proposals by proving through textual sources that the fulfillment of this mitzva must specifically take place on the Seder night, "when the matza and *maror* lie before us."

יָכוֹל מֵראש חֹדֶשׁ, תַּלְמוּד לוֹמַר בַּיּוֹם הַהוּא.
אִי בַּיּוֹם הַהוּא, יָכוֹל מִבְּעוֹד יוֹם. תַּלְמוּד לוֹמַר, בַּעֲבוּר זֶה.
בַּעֲבוּר זֶה לֹא אָמַרְתִּי, אֶלָּא בְּשָׁעָה שֶׁיֵּשׁ מַצָּה וּמָרוֹר מֻנָּחִים לְפָנֶיךָ.

One might think that [the discussion of the Exodus] must begin from the first of the month. The Torah therefore states, "On that day."[56] "On that day," however, could mean while it is yet daytime; the Torah therefore states, "It is because of this."[57] The expression "because of this" can only be said when matza and *maror* are placed before you.

Food for Thought

A. Understanding the *hava amina* (original assumption) in any Talmudic discussion is critical to the course of Talmud study. The logic behind the rabbis' initial positions, even if those positions are ultimately disproven, provides valuable insights into the nature of rabbinic thought and methodology.

Later scholars, therefore, question the Midrashic suggestion that the mitzva of *sippur Yetziat Mitzrayim* should be launched yearly on the first day of Nisan. Why would we even assume, these authorities ask, that the mitzva of retelling the Exodus story would begin fifteen days before the date the Exodus actually occurred?

B. Numerous authorities explain that the *hava amina* of the Midrash is based on the conviction that the Israelites' path toward freedom begins in earnest not on the date of the actual Exodus, but earlier, on the first day of Nisan. We have previously reviewed the foundations of this belief (see p. 40), but will again summarize them here.

1. On Rosh Chodesh Nisan, the Israelites receive their first mitzvot as a nation:

---

55 *Mechilta*, Shmot 13:8.
56 Shmot 13:8.
57 Ibid.

the mitzva of Kiddush Hachodesh (sanctification of the new moon) and the commandments associated with the Korban Pesach. God's transmission of these edicts constitutes a critical first step in the redemptive process, marking the moment when the nation's allegiance to divine law begins. Freedom from servitude to man must be immediately accompanied by a new sense of service to the Divine, if the nascent Jewish nation is to succeed across time.

2. The content of these first mitzvot also shapes the nation's first real steps toward independence. By commanding the Israelites concerning the sanctification of time, God underscores the dividing line between slavery and freedom. A slave's time is controlled by others, while a free man is in control of his time. *By granting you dominion over your calendar,* God essentially declares to the Israelites, *I grant you control over time itself. Use your moments wisely; fill them with significance and meaning, and you will truly learn to be free.*

3. Many scholars maintain that the instructions concerning the Korban Pesach also constitute a declaration of freedom from Egyptian mastery. God directs the nation to publicly set aside a lamb, a god of Egypt, on the tenth day of Nisan, to slaughter that lamb as an offering on the fourteenth of the month, and to consume that lamb in its entirety on the eve of the fifteenth. The very awareness of these looming events, granted to the Israelites on Rosh Chodesh Nisan, increases their growing spiritual severance from the powerful culture around them.

4. Because these events occurred on the first day of Nisan, a case can be made that the mitzva of *sippur Yetziat Mitzrayim* should be yearly launched on that date.

C. In spite of these and other possible arguments, however, the Midrash rejects Rosh Chodesh Nisan as the starting point for the performance of the mitzva of *sippur Yetziat Mitzrayim*. Rejected, as well, is the possibility that this mitzva should be fulfilled during the daylight hours of the fourteenth or the fifteenth of the month. Based on the biblical phrase *"ba'avur zeh"* (because of this),[58] the rabbis conclude that the mitzva must be performed in the presence of the physical symbols of the Seder night, "when the matza and the *maror* are lying before us."[59]

The full significance of the role played by physical symbols in the mitzva of *sippur Yetziat Mitzrayim* has been discussed in our introductory essay "More Than a Mitzva: *Sippur Yetziat Mitzrayim*" and will be further clarified when we reach the final section of Maggid (pp. 133–38).

---

58 Shmot 13:8.
59 *Mechilta D'bei Rebbi Yishmael,* Parashat Bo.

Mi'tchila Ovdei Avoda Zara Hayu Avoteinu: The Second Answer to the *Ma Nishtana*

Having concluded the lengthy digression exploring the technical parameters of the mitzva of *sippur Yetziat Mitzrayim*, the Haggada returns to its primary narrative by offering a second answer to the *Ma nishtana*.

מִתְּחִלָה עוֹבְדֵי עֲבוֹדָה זָרָה הָיוּ אֲבוֹתֵינוּ. וְעַכְשָׁו קֵרְבָנוּ הַמָּקוֹם לַעֲבוֹדָתוֹ, שֶׁנֶּאֱמַר: וַיֹּאמֶר יְהוֹשֻׁעַ אֶל כָּל הָעָם: כֹּה אָמַר יי אֱלֹהֵי יִשְׂרָאֵל: בְּעֵבֶר הַנָּהָר יָשְׁבוּ אֲבוֹתֵיכֶם מֵעוֹלָם, תֶּרַח אֲבִי אַבְרָהָם וַאֲבִי נָחוֹר, וַיַּעַבְדוּ אֱלֹהִים אֲחֵרִים. וָאֶקַּח אֶת אֲבִיכֶם, אֶת אַבְרָהָם, מֵעֵבֶר הַנָּהָר, וָאוֹלֵךְ אוֹתוֹ בְּכָל אֶרֶץ כְּנָעַן. וָאַרְבֶּה אֶת זַרְעוֹ, וָאֶתֶּן לוֹ אֶת יִצְחָק. וָאֶתֵּן לְיִצְחָק אֶת יַעֲקֹב וְאֶת עֵשָׂו. וָאֶתֵּן לְעֵשָׂו אֶת הַר שֵׂעִיר לָרֶשֶׁת אוֹתוֹ. וְיַעֲקֹב וּבָנָיו יָרְדוּ מִצְרָיִם.

In the beginning our fathers served idols; but now the Omnipresent One has brought us close to His service, as it is said: "Joshua said to all the people: Thus said the Lord, the God of Israel, 'Your fathers used to live on the other side of the river – Terach, the father of Abraham and the father of Nachor, and they served other gods. And I took your father Abraham from beyond the river, and I led him throughout the whole land of Canaan. I increased his seed and gave him Isaac, and to Isaac I gave Jacob and Esau. And I gave to Esau Mount Seir, to possess it. And Jacob and his sons went down to Egypt.'"[60]

Food for Thought

A. We open our discussion of the Haggada's second answer to the *Ma nishtana* with a few basic points noted above (see p. 65).

1. The paragraph of *Mi'tchila* is incorporated into the Haggada at the suggestion of the Talmudic sage Rav, who interprets the midrashic directive "One opens with shame and closes with praise" broadly. In contrast to his colleague, Shmuel, Rav insists that the response to the *Ma nishtana* should not be limited to the story of the Exodus, but should begin centuries earlier with a statement reflecting the negative spiritual origins of the Jewish people.[61]

2. Following a tradition that may have developed as early as the Geonic period (seventh to eleventh centuries CE),[62] our Haggada incorporates the positions of both authorities. Shmuel's response to the *Ma nishtana*, *Avadim hayinu*, was offered immediately after the

---

60 Yehoshua 24:2–4.
61 Talmud Bavli Pesachim 116a.
62 Quoted in Rabbeinu Chananel, Talmud Bavli Pesachim 116a. Note that debate develops among the early scholars as to whether Rav and Shmuel are actually disagreeing with each other or whether their views were always meant to be seen as complementary. See Kasher, *Haggada Shleima*, introduction, chapters 3–4.

questions were asked. Now, as we return to the main flow of the Haggada text, Rav's broader response is presented.

3. The order in which these responses are recorded in the Haggada reflects sound pedagogical technique, as opposed to simple chronological rendering. Although the historical events cited by Rav occur well before those referenced by Shmuel, Shmuel's response is recorded first. The rabbis recognize that when a question is raised, that question should be addressed directly. Shmuel's response, which contains the immediate answers to the *Ma nishtana*, is therefore offered as soon as those questions end. Now, we turn to the questioner and say: *We have answered your questions directly. If you want to understand the Exodus story in its full context, however, we must follow Rav's directions and go back further in time, to the beginning...*

B. The Haggada buttresses Rav's position with a quote from the final speech delivered by Yehoshua, Moshe's successor, prior to his death.[63] Yehoshua opens his farewell charge to the nation with a review of their humble spiritual origins. With this dramatic gesture, Yehoshua mirrors the honesty with which Jews have always confronted their own history, an honesty that forms the basis of the Seder. Unlike other ancient nations that claim noble – even divine – origins, the Jewish nation "celebrates" its lowly beginnings. We also recognize that our accomplishments stem not only from our own efforts, but from God's great benevolence, for which we must be eternally grateful.

C. The last sentence of Yehoshua's declaration contrasts the early setbacks of Jewish history with the triumphant early accomplishments of the descendants of Esav, Yaakov's brother and the progenitor of numerous gentile peoples, including Amalek and Rome. Rabbi Joseph Soloveitchik sees this sobering comparison as projecting a fundamental truth: "The destinies of Yaakov and Esav are inversely proportional."[64]

Even before their birth, the fates of Yaakov and his twin brother, Esav, are negatively intertwined. Upon seeking an explanation for the strange struggles in her womb, Rivka, their mother, receives a prophetic prediction that states, in part: "Two nations are in your womb, and two regimes will separate themselves from your insides; *and the might will pass from one regime to the other...*"[65]

Centuries later, Talmudic authorities build upon this prophecy by declaring:

> If an individual tells you that Jerusalem and Caesarea are both standing, do not believe him. If an individual tells you that Jerusalem and Caesarea are both destroyed, do not believe him. If an individual tells you that Jerusalem stands and Caesarea is destroyed, or that [God forbid] Caesarea stands and Jerusalem is destroyed, believe him.[66]

The spiritual descendants of Yaakov and Esav cannot triumph in this world simultaneously. The victory of good is ultimately dependent upon the destruction of evil.

---

63 Yehoshua 24:1–4.
64 Genack, *The Seder Night: An Exalted Evening*, p. 54.
65 Bereishit 25:23.
66 Talmud Bavli Megilla 6a.

Baruch Shomer Havtachato:
Blessing, Perspective and Gratitude

As the first section of the Maggid draws toward its close, the Haggada offers a blessing of thanks to God for fulfilling the prophecy unveiled during the Brit bein Habetarim (Covenant between the Pieces). As part of this divine covenant, contracted with the first patriarch, Avraham, at the dawn of Jewish history, God predicts the eventual servitude of Avraham's descendants into a "land not their own" and their ultimate redemption from that servitude.[67] This prophecy marks the first biblical foreshadowing of the Exodus narrative.

בָּרוּךְ שׁוֹמֵר הַבְטָחָתוֹ לְיִשְׂרָאֵל. בָּרוּךְ הוּא. שֶׁהַקָּדוֹשׁ בָּרוּךְ הוּא חִשַּׁב
אֶת הַקֵּץ, לַעֲשׂוֹת כְּמָה שֶׁאָמַר לְאַבְרָהָם אָבִינוּ בִּבְרִית בֵּין הַבְּתָרִים, שֶׁנֶּאֱמַר:
וַיֹּאמֶר לְאַבְרָם: יָדֹעַ תֵּדַע, כִּי גֵר יִהְיֶה זַרְעֲךָ בְּאֶרֶץ לֹא לָהֶם, וַעֲבָדוּם וְעִנּוּ
אֹתָם אַרְבַּע מֵאוֹת שָׁנָה. וְגַם אֶת הַגּוֹי אֲשֶׁר יַעֲבֹדוּ דָּן אָנֹכִי. וְאַחֲרֵי כֵן יֵצְאוּ
בִּרְכֻשׁ גָּדוֹל.

Blessed is He Who keeps His promise to Israel, blessed be He! For the Holy One, Blessed Be He, calculated the end [of the bondage], in order to do as He had said to our father Abraham at the Covenant between the Pieces, as it is said: "And He said to Abraham, 'You shall know that your seed will be strangers in a land that is not theirs, and they will enslave them and make them suffer, for four hundred years. But I shall also judge the nation whom they shall serve, and after that they will come out with great wealth.'"[68]

Food for Thought

A. As we approach the close of the first stage of Maggid, two goals are accomplished through the recitation of this paragraph.

1. Having established in the previous paragraph that the Exodus story must be seen within the context of Jewish history as a whole, the Haggada now shows how profoundly intertwined the eras of our people's story actually are. The enslavement and redemption of the Israelites is divinely foretold to their progenitor, Avraham, centuries before the events actually occur. God's clear plan for the Jewish nation is then played out in the drama that subsequently unfolds.

The Brit bein Habetarim, perhaps more than any other biblical passage, thus demonstrates God's concrete involvement in the history of the Jewish nation from its very beginning. As we reach the end of the first section of Maggid, the section

---

67　Bereishit 15:9–21.
68　Bereishit 15:13–14.

designed to cultivate a sense of historical awareness, this passage underscores God's active role in moving the Jewish people along the path defined in the Mishna as the way from shame to praise.

2. The Haggada leads us through the critical step from narrative to thanks, a step essential to the mitzva of *sippur Yetziat Mitzrayim*. Simply retelling the story is not enough. Jewish thought views *hakarat hatov* (gratefulness) as an indispensable moral trait. The retelling and reexperiencing of the Exodus narrative must inexorably lead us to an appreciation of the monumental goodness bestowed upon us by God. Rabbi Joseph Soloveitchik goes so far as to argue that "The essence of the Seder, and hence that of *sippur Yetziat Mitzrayim*, is the expression of gratitude to the Almighty for the great liberation and miracles that He wrought for us in Egypt."[69]

This paragraph establishes a pattern that will be repeated with each of the three stages of Maggid. *Each stage will be complete only once we have moved from narrative to thanks.*

B. A perplexing historical discrepancy, however, is raised by the commentaries regarding God's prediction during the Covenant between the Pieces: "Know full well that your offspring will be strangers in a land not their own – and they will serve them; and they will oppress them *four hundred years.*" In reality, the period of Israelite enslavement in Egypt was much less than that, probably about *two hundred ten* years.

Compounding the problem further is the Torah's declaration at the actual time of the Exodus: "And the habitation of the children of Israel during which they dwelled in Egypt was *four hundred thirty years.*"[70]

C. A well-known solution to this discrepancy is proposed, with some variations, by the *Mechilta*, Targum Yonatan, Rashi, and other early commentaries. These scholars suggest that the four-hundred-year count of exile is to be numbered from the birth of the second patriarch, Yitzchak, and that the four-hundred-thirty-year count begins with the earlier Brit bein Habetarim itself.[71]

A rationale for the counting of the years of exile from the time of Yitzchak's birth can be found in the biblical account of this patriarch's relationship with his homeland. In describing Yitzchak's residence in Canaan, the Torah repeatedly uses the word *lagur* (to dwell) rather than the word *lashevet* (to settle). As we have noted in other settings[72] and as we will note further in our studies (see p. 95), there is a vast difference between these two Torah terms, generally used to describe an individual's tenancy on the land. *Lashevet* invariably indicates living on the land with a sense of permanence and comfort. In contrast, *lagur* connotes a degree of impermanence and discomfort. While Yitzchak is the only patriarch never to leave the Land of Canaan, he is, counterintuitively, the least settled in his surroundings. Yitzchak is literally a stranger in his own land. The period of exile can thus be said to begin with his birth.

---

69 Steven F. Cohen and Kenneth Brander, eds., *The Yeshiva University Haggada* (New York: Student Organization of Yeshiva, 1985), Articles, p. 7.
70 Shmot 12:40.
71 Rashi, Bereishit 15:13, Shmot 12:40; Targum Yonatan, Bereishit 15:13,14, Shmot 12:40.
72 See my *Unlocking the Torah Text: Bereishit*, pp. 85, 103.

D. Another traditional approach suggests that God substitutes quality for quantity in ultimately determining the tenure of the Israelites' exile in Egypt. The harshness of their suffering at the hands of the Egyptians causes the two-hundred-ten-year period of enslavement to become the equivalent of four hundred years.[73]

E. A fascinating alternative approach is offered by the contemporary scholar Rabbi Jacob Rabinowitz, who was for many years a renowned teacher and administrator at Yeshiva University. Building on the observations of secular biblical scholars, Rabinowitz notes that the numbers forty and four hundred are often used in the Torah to convey the sense of a "huge" entity, such as an extensive block of time. Rabinowitz goes on to note that in gematria, a system of biblical exegesis based on the numerical value of Hebrew letters, the last letter of the Hebrew alphabet, *taf*, has the numerical value of four hundred. "Just as moderns might say 'from A to Z' to denote completion," Rabinowitz explains, "ancient literature used the value of the letter *taf*, the apex of the letters, to suggest relative largesse."[74]

When God prophesies to Avraham that his descendants will be "strangers in a strange land for four hundred years," Rabinowitz suggests, it might well be that He is simply saying, *Your descendants will be strangers in a strange land for a very long time.*

F. Whatever the explanation for the phenomenon, the parameters of the exile's reduction may actually be captured in a striking linguistic nuance in the Haggada's introduction to the Brit bein Habetarim: "*Hakadosh Baruch Hu chishev et hakeitz*" (The Holy One, Blessed Be He, computed the end [of enslavement]). Returning to the Midrashic world of gematria, numerous scholars note that the numerical value of the Hebrew word *keitz* (end) is one hundred ninety. Subtract one hundred ninety from four hundred, these scholars explain, and the result is two hundred ten. Although God predicted to Avraham that his descendants would be enslaved for four hundred years, God, in his mercy, *chishev et hakeitz*. One hundred ninety years of servitude were divinely deducted from the predetermined four hundred – and the Israelites were slaves for only two hundred ten years.

F. The final phrase of the quote from the Brit bein Habetarim, "and afterwards they will leave with great wealth," introduces a puzzling theme that appears repeatedly in the unfolding Exodus story.[75]

God promises Avraham that his descendants will not only be redeemed from bondage, but that they will enter their newfound freedom "with great wealth." This idea is picked up again, centuries later, when God informs Moshe during their first encounter at the burning bush: "and it shall be that when you leave you shall not leave empty-handed. And each woman shall request of her neighbor and from the one who lives in her house silver vessels, and gold vessels, and garments; and you shall

---

73 Tiferet Yisrael, Mishna Pesachim 10:5; Avi Ezer, commentary on the Ibn Ezra, Shmot 2:34.
74 Cohen and Brander, *The Yeshiva University Haggada*, Articles, p. 5.
75 A more extensive review of the issues raised in this discussion can be found in my *Unlocking the Torah Text: Shmot*, Bo 2.

place them upon your sons and your daughters and you shall clear Egypt out."[76] Yet later, on the eve of the Exodus, God charges Moshe: "Please speak in the ears of the people and they shall request, each man from his fellow and each woman from her fellow, silver vessels and gold vessels."[77] Finally, as the Exodus actually transpires, the Torah testifies: "And the children of Israel fulfilled Moshe's words, and they requested from Egypt silver vessels, and gold vessels, and garments. And the Lord gave the people favor in the eyes of Egypt; and they granted their request, and they cleared Egypt out."[78]

G. The questions raised by this recurring theme are deeply troubling. Why does God specifically and repeatedly inform the Israelites that the first footfalls of their shared journey will be marked by the accumulation of material wealth? Is the acquisition of wealth really so critical to the Exodus and the birth of the Jewish nation? Are there not more lofty concerns upon which the Israelites should focus as they take their first steps toward freedom?

These issues are acknowledged by scholars across the ages, and a variety of approaches are offered.

H. Many authorities maintain that the wealth transferred from the Egyptians to the Israelites represents payment for the Israelites' centuries of servitude and/or reparation for the pain and torment experienced during those years. Central to this approach is the recognition of the moment of the Exodus as a powerful formative moment for the Jewish people. The Israelites' self-perception as they leave Egypt is of vital importance to the development of their national character. God therefore designs the details of the Exodus to ensure that the Israelites will leave Egypt as a proud nation, cognizant of their own self-worth. Payment received from their erstwhile masters is a critical component in this overall design.[79]

For this reason, God does not miraculously provide the Israelites with the gathered wealth, nor does he *command* them to acquire that wealth from the Egyptians. Remarkably, God instead couches the directive to Moshe in the form of a *request*: "Please speak in the ears of the people and they shall request..."[80] The people must see these received riches as earned from the Egyptians on their own, coming to them justly, as a result of their own sweat and tears.

I. From another vantage point, the wealth accumulated by the Israelites can also be seen as a critical component of their newfound freedom, as the medium through which they will be able to actualize their choices for good or for bad. Freedom is only meaningful if you have something to lose. Had the Israelites left Egypt with nothing precious, nothing they truly saw as their own, their liberation would have been incomplete. They would have had no way

---

76 Shmot 3:21–22.
77 Shmot 11:2.
78 Shmot 12:35–36.
79 Talmud Bavli Sanhedrin 91a; Kli Yakar, Shmot 11:12.
80 Shmot 11:2.

to turn thought into action, to concretize their independent decisions.

The gold and silver of Egypt is ultimately used by the Israelites for two vastly different purposes: the creation of the golden calf and the building of the Mishkan, the portable sanctuary in the desert. This wealth thus serves as a challenge to the newly freed slaves: *How will you use your own prosperity, which you have earned through the sweat of your brow? The choices you make, in answer to this challenge, will determine the very quality of your freedom.*

J. One final, telling point concerning these issues is noted by Rabbi Joseph Soloveitchik. The Israelites' Exodus from Egypt stands in stark contrast to other slave upheavals across time. History is replete with accounts of violently destructive slave insurrections, of newly freed slaves wreaking terrible vengeance upon their erstwhile masters. "Would we have blamed the Jews," asks the Rav, "if they had engaged in a few acts of vandalism and even murder on the night of the fifteenth of Nisan, killing a few taskmasters who had thrown their babies into the Nile?"

"Still the Jews," the Rav goes on to note, "at the command of God, said no. They defied themselves and refused to gratify a basic need of the human being, the need for revenge. But by defeating themselves, they also won the greatest of all victories: they became free."[81]

K. For continued discussion.

The mysterious equation between

predestination, prescience (God's foreknowledge of events), and man's free will becomes acutely relevant when we consider an event such as the prophetic Brit bein Habetarim.

Amidst great discussion and debate across the centuries, the vast majority of scholars conclude that God's awareness of future events does not affect man's choice when those events actually unfold. To suggest a simple theoretical model: were an individual to take a time machine into the future, witness his friend crossing the street at a particular place and time, return to the present and not tell his friend, that friend would still be acting as a free agent when he actually crosses the street. As long as the future is not revealed to the actor in a specific event, the actor's free will remains unencumbered by someone else's prior knowledge of his choice.

The equation changes dramatically, however, when the future is revealed to the actor. If, for example, the time traveler reveals the future to his friend upon his return to the present, his friend can no longer be said to be acting "freely." The knowledge he has attained of his future actions will, in some unquantifiable way, affect those actions as they unfold.

Here, then, is the problem: By revealing the future to Avraham, it would seem that God clouds the free agency of the patriarch's descendants. Once the future is openly predetermined, how much choice do Yosef and his brothers have in the events surrounding Yosef's sale, the catalyst for their family's descent into Egypt? How much freedom do

---

81 Genack, *The Seder Night: An Exalted Evening*, p. 57.

the members of Yaakov's family enjoy when they eventually resettle in Egypt in the face of famine, if God has already ordained the inevitability of their subsequent enslavement in that land?

And yet, the series of events launched by the Brit bein Habetarim can actually help us understand the paradigm that shapes Jewish history in its entirety.

While God broadly predicts the descent of Avraham's progeny into exile and hardship in a strange land, the details of those events as they occur are determined by the actions of the personalities at the time. If sibling hatred and jealousy, for example, had not been the catalysts for our Egyptian exile, perhaps that exile would have been less painful. If the Israelites had not tarried in Egypt longer than necessary after the famine, perhaps their years of servitude would have unfolded elsewhere, in a different way.

When it comes to the Exodus, God paints the broad brushstrokes of history. He allows man, however, to fill in the details. This equation, one could argue, holds true when we consider the overall destiny of the Jewish people, as well.

Jewish tradition maintains that our national history will culminate with the arrival of the Mashiach (Messiah). If the Mashiach's arrival is preordained, however, what purpose is there to the spiritual striving of each generation? Have we not been effectively promised that, even absent our effort, our national destiny will inexorably be realized?

The answer lies in recognizing that, while the realization of our destiny is a certainty, the details of that realization have yet to be determined. The Mashiach will certainly one day arrive. When he will arrive, however, how he will arrive, how much difficulty or ease will precede his arrival and who among us or our descendants will be there to greet him are all issues to be determined by our actions. The brushstrokes of our history have been divinely painted, but we fill in the all-important details.

V'hi She'amda: A Closing Declaration

The matzot are covered, the wine cup is raised
and the following declaration is recited aloud:

וְהִיא שֶׁעָמְדָה לַאֲבוֹתֵינוּ וְלָנוּ,
שֶׁלֹּא אֶחָד בִּלְבָד עָמַד עָלֵינוּ לְכַלּוֹתֵנוּ,
אֶלָּא שֶׁבְּכָל דּוֹר וָדוֹר עוֹמְדִים עָלֵינוּ לְכַלּוֹתֵנוּ,
וְהַקָּדוֹשׁ בָּרוּךְ הוּא מַצִּילֵנוּ מִיָּדָם.

And this [promise] is what has stood [remained constant]
for our fathers and for us!
For not just one [oppressor] alone has risen against us to destroy us,
but in every generation they rise against us to destroy us;
and the Holy One, Blessed Be He, saves us from their hand!

Food for Thought

A. The first section of the Maggid, the section of historical awareness, closes with this emphatic declaration: "*V'hi she'amda la'avoteinu v'lanu*" (And this is what has stood by our ancestors and us), we proclaim. Reflecting back on the previous paragraph, we declare that God's promise of redemption to Avraham, at the dawn of our history, has stood us in good stead across the centuries. In each generation, our enemies have struggled to halt our inexorable historical passage. And, in each generation, with God's help, we have triumphed.

B. We thus fulfill the Mishnaic mandate that shapes the first section of Maggid:

"*Matchil b'genut u'mesayeim b'shevach*" (One opens with shame and closes with praise).[82]

We announce that we have reached the stage of historical awareness as we proclaim: "*She'b'chol dor va'dor* (in each generation), they rise against us to destroy us, and the Holy One, Blessed Be He, saves us from their hand."

God continually redeems us from our enemies as we travel toward the ultimate realization of our national destiny. Just as the Exodus story describes a journey from servitude to redemption, so too, Jewish history in its entirety can be viewed as a continuing journey from darkness to light; an ultimate passage from shame to praise.

---

82 Mishna Pesachim 10:4.

Seder Section 5b • MAGGID's Second Goal
Historical Personalization/Participation

Having concluded the first major stage of Maggid, the stage of historical awareness, we are now about to embark upon the second major stage, the stage of historical personalization/participation.

This stage of Maggid is shaped by the Mishnaic directive *"V'doresh mei'Arami oved avi ad she'yigmor kol haparasha kula"* (And one studies the biblical passage beginning with the words "An Aramean tried to destroy my father..." until he finishes the entire passage).[1]

This section consists primarily of an experience in shared Torah study. The aforementioned biblical passage, selected from the beginning of Parashat Ki Tavo in the book of Devarim, is recited piece by piece and elaborated upon through the use of sources from the Oral Law.

As suggested in our introductory essay "More Than a Mitzva: *Sippur Yetziat Mitzrayim*" and in our ongoing commentary on the text (below), both the substance and the process of this section are designed to move the Seder participants toward a real sense of personal participation in the flow of Jewish history.

The second stage of Maggid closes with a declaration of gratitude to God, expressed through the well-known song "Dayenu" and a subsequent closing paragraph.

Tzei U'lemad: Shared Torah Study

The wine is put down, the matzot are uncovered and the Seder participants embark upon an experience in shared Torah study.

A biblical passage from the book of Devarim, beginning with the phrase "An Aramean tried to destroy my father" (or alternatively "My father was a wandering Aramean") is quoted, dissected and analyzed, verse by verse, through the prism of Written and Oral Law.[2] This lengthy section of shared Torah study continues through p. 128.

The material in these sections is not meant to be read, but to be "learned"; and the interpretations offered are designed to catalyze further exploration and discussion. To assist in this widening process of study, we will offer additional comments and observations concerning each verse, from among the many that can be offered on the unfolding text. (Note: For the sake of clarity, throughout this section of learning, the verses quoted from the central biblical passage are recorded in bold print, while the additional biblical and rabbinic sources are not bolded.)

---

1 Mishna Pesachim 10:4.
2 Midrashic sources used in this section include Sifrei, Parashat Ki Tavo; Midrash Lekach Tov, Parashat Ki Tavo; Yalkut Shimoni, Devarim 538.

Vidui Bikkurim, Verse 1

צֵא וּלְמַד, מַה בִּקֵּשׁ לָבָן הָאֲרַמִּי לַעֲשׂוֹת לְיַעֲקֹב אָבִינוּ. שֶׁפַּרְעֹה לֹא גָזַר אֶלָּא עַל הַזְּכָרִים, וְלָבָן בִּקֵּשׁ לַעֲקֹר אֶת הַכֹּל, שֶׁנֶּאֱמַר: אֲרַמִּי אֹבֵד אָבִי, וַיֵּרֶד מִצְרַיְמָה, וַיָּגָר שָׁם בִּמְתֵי מְעָט. וַיְהִי שָׁם לְגוֹי גָּדוֹל, עָצוּם וָרָב.

Go forth and learn what Laban the Aramaean intended to do to our father Jacob. For Pharaoh decreed [the destruction of] male children only, while Laban sought to uproot all, as it is said: **"An Aramaean sought to destroy my father,**[3] **and he [my father] went down to Egypt and sojourned there, few in number; and he became there a nation – great and mighty and numerous."**[4]

Food for Thought

A. As noted in our introductory essay on *sippur Yetziat Mitzrayim*, the rabbis seem to make a strange choice in their selection of Torah text for study at the Seder. The passage they choose emerges from Parashat Ki Tavo in the book of Devarim and constitutes the majority of the *vidui bikkurim*, the formula to be recited yearly by an Israelite farmer upon bringing his first fruits to the Temple. In the verses before us, the farmer briefly reviews the early history of his people, including the events surrounding the Exodus.

Given the host of available primary Torah sources concerning the Exodus, why do the rabbis deliberately select a secondary textual source referring to that episode solely in retrospect? The *vidui bikkurim* is designed, after all, to be recited by Israelite farmers only after the land of Canaan is conquered and settled, centuries after the events surrounding the Exodus have occurred.

To compound the problem, the *vidui bikkurim* is associated in the Torah with a festival other than Pesach. The first fruits are to be brought to the Temple each year on Shavuot. Why designate a passage associated with Shavuot as the Torah study centerpiece of the Pesach ritual?

B. Rabbi Joseph Soloveitchik maintains that the incorporation of the *vidui bikkurim* into the Haggada highlights the identical foundation lying at the core of both the first fruit and the Seder rituals.

Both rituals, the Rav argues, are fundamentally acts of *hakarat hatov*, the expressing of thanks to the Almighty; their retelling of the Exodus is calculated to awaken within the participant a heightened sense of gratitude for God's guiding hand in the course of human events.[5] Neither of these ceremonies is to be perceived as sterile storytelling. If we retell the historical tales

---

3 As indicated above, this phrase can also be translated as "My father was a wandering Aramaean." At this point in our translation, however, we only quote the alternative accepted by the Haggada (see Food for Thought below).

4 Devarim 26:5.

5 Rabbi Joseph B Soloveitchik, "The Nine Aspects of the Haggada," in *The Yeshiva University Haggada*, ed. Cohen and Brander.

but are not moved to thanks, we have not performed either of these mitzvot at all (see previous discussion on this point, p. 86).

C. Another, more basic explanation for the choice of the *vidui bikkurim* text was offered in our introductory essay on *sippur Yetziat Mitzrayim* (see pp. 19–21) and will be further explained below (see pp. 99–100).

D. The first three words of the *vidui bikkurim* also serve as the focus of significant rabbinic dispute. Who, the scholars ask, is the "Aramean" referred to in this verse, and who is the "father"? Two widely disparate interpretations are offered by the classical commentaries in their approach to this phrase. Some scholars view the terms "Aramean" and "father" as referring to the same person, specifically to one of the patriarchs. The phrase *"Arami oveid avi,"* these commentaries maintain, is to be translated as *"My father was a wandering Aramean."* The Rashbam, for example, argues that the text refers to the patriarch Avraham, who upon leaving his home at God's command, becomes "lost and in exile from the land of Aram [his homeland]."[6] The Ibn Ezra, in contrast, maintains that the subject of the verse is Avraham's grandson, Yaakov, who sojourns for decades in the land of Aram when he flees from Canaan to escape his brother Esav's wrath.[7]

E. The Haggada, however, reflects a totally different interpretation, proffered by Targum Onkelos and accepted by Rashi and others. These sages view the "Aramean" in the verse not as a protagonist but as an antagonist: specifically, Yaakov's father-in-law, Lavan. According to this second approach, the phrase reads: *"An Aramean (Lavan) sought to destroy my father (Yaakov)."*[8] Lavan's deceit and trickery are well chronicled. From substituting Leah for Rachel as Yaakov's betrothed to deceiving the patriarch over and over again in monetary matters, this biblical figure is portrayed in biblical and rabbinic thought as a charlatan who deliberately undermines the welfare of others while denying responsibility for any personal wrongdoing. Such an individual, the Haggada testifies, is willing to "uproot everything" in pursuit of his own gain.

The full extent of Lavan's evil is mirrored in his own words during his final confrontation with Yaakov: "It lies within the power of my hand *la'asot imachem ra* [to do evil to you]."[9] Rabbi Joseph Soloveitchik notes that the word *imachem* is in the plural form. Lavan threatens not only Yaakov's welfare, but the welfare of his family, including Lavan's own daughters and grandchildren. As attested to by the Haggada, Lavan thus emerges as a greater villain than Pharaoh. Pharaoh, for all his evil, did not threaten to wipe out the Israelites entirely, nor would he have been willing to harm the members of his own family.[10]

---

6   Rashbam, Devarim 25:5.
7   Ibn Ezra, Devarim 25:5.
8   Targum Onkelos and Rashi, Devarim 25:5.
9   Bereishit 31:29.
10   Genack, *The Seder Night: An Exalted Evening*, p. 59.

The Haggada Analyzes Verse 1

Having quoted the first sentence of the *vidui bikkurim*, the Haggada now proceeds to dissect and analyze each portion of that verse through the eyes of additional sources from the Written and Oral Law. (Reminder: The phrases quoted from the central biblical passage are recorded in bold blue text, while the additional biblical and rabbinic sources are not bolded.)

וַיֵּרֶד מִצְרַיְמָה, אָנוּס עַל פִּי הַדִּבּוּר.

And he went down to Egypt: forced, by divine decree.

וַיָּגָר שָׁם. מְלַמֵּד שֶׁלֹּא יָרַד יַעֲקֹב אָבִינוּ לְהִשְׁתַּקֵעַ בְּמִצְרַיִם, אֶלָּא לָגוּר שָׁם, שֶׁנֶּאֱמַר: וַיֹּאמְרוּ אֶל פַּרְעֹה, לָגוּר בָּאָרֶץ בָּאנוּ, כִּי אֵין מִרְעֶה לַצֹּאן אֲשֶׁר לַעֲבָדֶיךָ, כִּי כָבֵד הָרָעָב בְּאֶרֶץ כְּנָעַן, וְעַתָּה, יֵשְׁבוּ נָא עֲבָדֶיךָ בְּאֶרֶץ גֹּשֶׁן.

and he sojourned there: this teaches us that our forefather, Yaakov, did not go down to Egypt to settle, but only to live there temporarily. As it is said: "And they stated to Pharaoh, we have come to dwell in the land, for there is no pasture for the sheep that belong to your servants, for the famine is heavy in the Land of Canaan; and now, please allow your servants to settle in the Land of Goshen."[11]

Food for Thought

A. וַיָּגָר שָׁם. The Haggada's observation that the phrase *va'yagar sham* indicates temporary tenancy is based on the distinction between the two biblical terms *lagur* (to dwell) and *lashevet* (to settle). As we have previously noted (see p. 86), *lashevet* invariably indicates living on the land with a sense of permanence and comfort. In contrast, *lagur* connotes a degree of impermanence and discomfort. Through the use of the phrase *va'yagar sham*, the rabbis explain, the Israelite farmer offering his first fruits to the Kohen testifies, centuries after the fact, to Yaakov's view of his family's descent into Egypt. Yaakov, the Haggada underscores, initially has no intention of "settling" in the land of Egypt. The move is

to be temporary, until the need created by the famine in Canaan has passed.

A problem emerges, however, when the Haggada proceeds to prove its point from a primary source in the book of Shmot describing the first encounter between a delegation of Yaakov's sons and Pharaoh. The Israelites open the meeting with the statement *"Lagur ba'aretz banu"* (We have come to *dwell* in the land), consistent with the idea of transient tenancy in the land. They end their request, however, with the plea *"V'ata yeishvu na avadecha b'eretz Goshen"* (And now therefore, we pray thee, let your servants *settle* in the land of Goshen). This latter statement, employing the verb *lashevet* (to settle), seems to reflect a desire for

---

11 Bereishit 47:4.

permanence that contradicts the brothers' earlier words.

How are we to explain the apparent inconsistency in the brothers' presentation to the Egyptian king? Do Yaakov's sons realize midway through their royal audience that a request for temporary residence in Egypt would be an affront to Pharaoh? Do they, therefore, adjust their words accordingly? Or, does the inconsistency in their words reflect something darker – a Freudian slip, centuries before Freud, reflecting a subliminal desire on the part of the Israelites to remain permanently in the Land of Egypt, a land of obvious power, opulence and wealth?

B. Once the door is opened to this second possibility, the statements of Yaakov's sons may well foreshadow the Torah's own later testimony concerning the Israelites' eventual settlement in Egypt: "*Va'yeshev Yisrael b'eretz Mitzrayim, b'eretz Goshen, va'yei'achazu va va'yifru va'yirbu me'od*" (And Israel settled in the land of Egypt, in the land of Goshen, and they acquired possessions therein, and they were fruitful and multiplied exceedingly).[12] Any sense of transience on the part of the Israelites is apparently gone by this time, as they "settle and acquire possessions" in the land

of Egypt. Egypt has become their home, no longer a temporary way station on their journey back to Canaan.

Even the Torah's geographical description of the Israelite settlement underscores this tragic truth: "And Israel settled in the land of Egypt, in the land of Goshen." Written in the singular conjugation to illustrate the Israelites' unity of purpose, this phrase goes out of its way to specify "in the land of Egypt, in the land of Goshen." By this point in the Torah's narrative, we are fully aware that Goshen is in the "land of Egypt." Why does the Torah feel the need to stress this fact again? The Torah, it would seem, is conveying the mindset of the Israelites. From their perspective, the important fact is that Goshen is "in Egypt." The children of Yaakov no longer see themselves as a separate people living in Goshen – isolated from the Egyptians – as their brother Yosef had intended when he specifically instructed them to request the Land of Goshen for settlement.[13] They are instead, in their own minds, full Egyptian citizens, living "in the land of Egypt, in the land of Goshen." This transformation reflects a dangerous loss of perspective. Tragically, the Israelites' false sense of security as they assimilate into Egyptian culture will help set the stage for their eventual enslavement.

---

12 Bereishit 47:27.
13 Bereishit 46:31–34.

בִּמְתֵי מְעָט. כְּמָה שֶׁנֶּאֱמַר: "בְּשִׁבְעִים נֶפֶשׁ יָרְדוּ אֲבֹתֶיךָ מִצְרָיְמָה, וְעַתָּה שָׂמְךָ
יי אֱלֹהֶיךָ כְּכוֹכְבֵי הַשָּׁמַיִם לָרֹב."

Few in number: As it is said: "With seventy souls your fathers went down to Egypt
and now, the Lord, your God, has made you as numerous as the stars of heaven."[14]

וַיְהִי שָׁם לְגוֹי. מְלַמֵּד שֶׁהָיוּ יִשְׂרָאֵל מְצֻיָּנִים שָׁם.

And he became there a nation: This teaches that the Israelites maintained
themselves as a distinct people there.

גָּדוֹל עָצוּם. כְּמָה שֶׁנֶּאֱמַר: "וּבְנֵי יִשְׂרָאֵל פָּרוּ וַיִּשְׁרְצוּ וַיִּרְבּוּ וַיַּעַצְמוּ בִּמְאֹד
מְאֹד, וַתִּמָּלֵא הָאָרֶץ אֹתָם."

Great and mighty: As it is said: "And the children of Israel were fruitful and
increased abundantly, and multiplied and waxed exceedingly mighty; and the land
became filled with them."[15]

וָרָב. כְּמָה שֶׁנֶּאֱמַר: "רְבָבָה כְּצֶמַח הַשָּׂדֶה נְתַתִּיךְ, וַתִּרְבִּי, וַתִּגְדְּלִי, וַתָּבֹאִי בַּעֲדִי
עֲדָיִים, שָׁדַיִם נָכֹנוּ וּשְׂעָרֵךְ צִמֵּחַ וְאַתְּ עֵרֹם וְעֶרְיָה." "וָאֶעֱבֹר עָלַיִךְ וָאֶרְאֵךְ
מִתְבּוֹסֶסֶת בְּדָמָיִךְ, וָאֹמַר לָךְ בְּדָמַיִךְ חֲיִי, וָאֹמַר לָךְ בְּדָמַיִךְ חֲיִי."

And numerous: As it is said: "I caused you to thrive like the plants of the field, and
you increased and grew and became very beautiful, your bosom formed and your
hair grown long; but you were naked and bare."[16] "I passed over you and saw you
wallowing in your blood, and I said to you, 'by your blood shall you live,' and I said to
you, 'by your blood shall you live.'"[17]

C. וָרָב. In commenting on the term *va'rav*
(and numerous), our Haggadot quote
two verses from the prophetic book of
Yechezkel. The second of these verses is
absent from early Haggadot, first appearing at the Seder only in the sixteenth century – apparently at the suggestion of the
towering sage and mystic the Ari (Rabbi
Isaac Luria).[18] Perhaps to mark this two-
stage development of the text, these verses
are quoted in inverse order, with the more
recently added sentence listed second,
even though it appears first in the book of
Yechezkel.

D. The connection between these two
verses and the biblical narrative before
us, however, remains elusive. How does
Yechezkel's prophetic comparison of Israel
to a young woman who thrives "like the
plants of the field," yet remains "naked

---

14 Devarim 10:22.
15 Shmot 1:7.
16 Yechezkel 16:7.
17 Yechezkel 16:6.
18 Chida, *Haggadat Simchat Haregel.*

and bare" inform the Torah's description of the Israelite slaves as "numerous"? And what is the meaning of God's mysterious double proclamation in Yechezkel's vision: "By your blood shall you live; by your blood shall you live"?

E. Numerous interpretations are offered to explain the details of Yechezkel's vision and their possible relationship to the Exodus narrative.

The Ritva, for example, maintains that the prophet compares the Israelite slaves to thriving "plants of the field" because the more one prunes a plant, the healthier it grows. Miraculously, the more the Egyptians afflicted their Israelite victims, the more those victims miraculously "multiplied and flourished."[19]

Other commentaries point to the birth of plants from seeds buried deep within the ground. Just when these seeds appear to have disintegrated, a shoot sprouts forth and a thriving plant begins to grow. So too, after years of darkness and pain, when all seems lost, the Israelite nation springs forth from Egypt.[20]

Yechezkel's description of the nation as "naked and bare," the Midrash claims, mirrors the reality that, at this point, the Israelites are bereft of any "good deeds" through which to merit their own redemption. In response, God provides this people, "wallowing in the blood" of their own suffering, with two commandments that deal with blood: the Korban Pesach and the mitzva of circumcision. "By your blood shall you live; by your blood shall you live," God declares to His people. *Through the performance of these mitzvot, you shall live – you shall earn your own redemption.*[21]

Commenting on this midrashic tradition, Rabbi Joseph Soloveitchik declares:

> The most amazing thing about the Exodus, far greater than the signs and wonders, is the transformation of a nation of slaves.... Their life was a naked one, a beastly one, controlled by lusts and desires. And then there occurred the greatest of all miracles.... The slaves suddenly felt the duty of commandments, the power of a life devoted to higher ideals and goals. They understood what it means to possess spiritual ideals, and what it means to enter into a covenant with the Almighty. This transformation is a hidden miracle of great import.[22]

---

19 Shmot 1:12.
20 Cohen and Brander, *The Yeshiva University Haggada*, p. 13.
21 *Mechilta D'bei Rebbi Yishmael*, Bo 5.
22 Genack, *The Seder Night: An Exalted Evening*, pp. 68–69.

Vidui Bikkurim, Verse 2

וַיָּרֵעוּ אֹתָנוּ הַמִּצְרִים וַיְעַנּוּנוּ, וַיִּתְּנוּ עָלֵינוּ עֲבֹדָה קָשָׁה.

"The Egyptians dealt cruelly with us and they made us suffer, and they put hard work upon us."

Food for Thought

A. At this point in the biblical text, a fascinating transition in the *vidui bikkurim* begins to emerge. And, as we have mentioned earlier, this transition may well provide the most direct explanation for the rabbinic choice of this text for study at the Seder.

The farmer opened his proclamation in the third person: "…An Aramean tried to destroy my father, and *he descended* to Egypt and dwelt there, few in number, and *he became* there a nation, great, strong and numerous."

Now, however, as the farmer references the origins of the Jewish nation from the depths of Egyptian slavery, a startling change occurs. Though these historical events took place hundreds of years earlier, the farmer shifts to speaking of them *in the first person*: "And the Egyptians mistreated *us* and afflicted *us*, and they placed *upon us* hard work. And *we* cried out to the Lord, the God of *our* fathers, and the Lord heard *our* cries, and He saw *our* affliction and *our* travail and *our* oppression. And the Lord took *us* out of Egypt with a strong hand and an outstretched arm and with great awesomeness and with signs and with wonders."

Through the course of the *vidui*, the farmer switches from reporting what happened to others to describing these events as personal memories.

We can now answer the question we raised above: Why is this particular text chosen for study and analysis at the Seder?

The rabbis selected the passage of *vidui bikkurim* as the study text for *sippur Yetziat Mitzrayim* because no other biblical text can more clearly lead us towards the fulfillment of the second stage of our Maggid journey: the stage of *historical personalization/participation*. This is the point in the Seder when we recognize that it is not enough to become aware of the flow of Jewish history. We must *become part of that flow*, as well.

As we study the words of our farmer ancestor bringing his first fruits to the Temple, we recognize that with the birth of the Jewish nation, past, present and future blur together. Anything that happens to any Jew at any time happens to all Jews at all times.

We are unified with our forefathers in the land of Egypt, experiencing the Exodus as if it is currently happening to us, thereby fulfilling the halachic mandate to see ourselves as if we actually left Egypt.

B. This message is conveyed not only through the particular text that we study, but through *the very act of studying Torah* at the Seder, as well.

As noted in our introductory essay "More Than a Mitzva: *Sippur Yetziat Mitzrayim*," no single act in Jewish experience injects a participant more personally into the flow of Jewish history than the act of Torah study. When we enter the Seder's *beit midrash* (house of study), the constraints of time fall away. We find ourselves suddenly involved in an ongoing dialogue that spans the centuries. Present at our table are personalities from Mosaic times onward, discussing, debating, analyzing and arguing the details of Jewish thought and law. Moshe speaks to us through words recorded in the biblical text; Talmudic personalities from the periods of the Mishna and the Gemara interpret and elaborate upon those words; towering scholarly figures from across the generations and around the globe all add their voices to the mix; and we are invited to add our voices, as well, contributing yet another layer to a conversation that will stretch to the end of days.

By incorporating Torah study into the Seder proceedings, the rabbis ensure our active, personal participation in the unfolding story of our people.

The Haggada Analyzes Verse 2

Having quoted the second sentence of the *vidui bikkurim*, the Haggada now proceeds to dissect and analyze each portion of that verse through the prism of additional sources.

In this instance, the supplementary sources quoted by the Haggada consist of primary texts from the book of Shmot detailing the Egyptians' enslavement of the Israelites.

A frighteningly prescient reality emerges from these quoted texts. The birth pangs of the Jewish nation are shaped by a familiar step-by-step blueprint for persecution that, tragically, will be reused by our enemies, over and over again, during the ensuing centuries.

This blueprint is carefully designed to "prepare" both the perpetrators and the victims for the horrific events to come.

On the one hand, Pharaoh and his advisers must devise a plan of action that will make the decimation of the Israelites ultimately "acceptable" to their Egyptian neighbors. The king's program against the Israelites cannot begin abruptly. As the Ramban and other scholars note, the citizens of Egypt will not tolerate a sudden, unprovoked attack upon a people previously welcomed into their midst.[23]

On the other hand, the Israelite victims must be slowly robbed of their confidence and any vestige of their own self-worth so that, beaten down, they will become unwitting participants in their own demise.

The distinct steps in this cruel, double-edged process become painfully clear as the Haggada proceeds with its analysis of the text.

---

23 Ramban, Shmot 1:10.

וַיָּרֵעוּ אֹתָנוּ הַמִּצְרִים. כְּמָה שֶׁנֶּאֱמַר: "הָבָה נִתְחַכְּמָה לוֹ פֶּן יִרְבֶּה, וְהָיָה כִּי תִקְרֶאנָה מִלְחָמָה, וְנוֹסַף גַּם הוּא עַל שֹׂנְאֵינוּ, וְנִלְחַם בָּנוּ וְעָלָה מִן הָאָרֶץ."

And the Egyptians dealt cruelly with us: as it is said: *"Hava nitchakma lo…"* [And a new king rose up over Egypt who did not know Yosef. And he said to his nation: "Behold the nation, the children of Israel are more numerous and stronger than we.] Come let us be wise to them, lest they become numerous and it will be that if war occurs, they will join our enemies and wage war against us and go up from the land."[24]

וַיְעַנּוּנוּ. כְּמָה שֶׁנֶּאֱמַר: "וַיָּשִׂימוּ עָלָיו שָׂרֵי מִסִּים לְמַעַן עַנֹּתוֹ בְּסִבְלֹתָם, וַיִּבֶן עָרֵי מִסְכְּנוֹת לְפַרְעֹה, אֶת פִּתֹם וְאֶת רַעַמְסֵס."

and they afflicted us: as it is said: "And they appointed taskmasters over them in order to afflict them with their burdens, and they built storage cities for Pharaoh, Pitom and Raamses."[25]

וַיִּתְּנוּ עָלֵינוּ עֲבֹדָה קָשָׁה. כְּמָה שֶׁנֶּאֱמַר: "וַיַּעֲבִדוּ מִצְרַיִם אֶת בְּנֵי יִשְׂרָאֵל בְּפָרֶךְ."

and they placed hard work upon us: as it is said: "And the Egyptians made the children of Israel work with crushing harshness."[26]

Food for Thought

A. וַיָּרֵעוּ אֹתָנוּ. Stage one: propaganda.

Persecution invariably begins with propaganda, with the verbal isolation of a people from surrounding society. Pharaoh's words, as he sets the stage for the subjugation of the Israelites, are a clear case in point. The king's claim to his people, "Behold the nation, the children of Israel are more numerous and stronger than we," seems patently false, even ludicrous. Could the immigrant Israelites have possibly become "more numerous and stronger" than the native Egyptians? And yet the king knows that lies, boldly spoken, will be readily accepted by those who want to believe them.

Pharaoh's evil genius is also evident in his specific accusations against the Israelites. He consciously plays upon his own nation's envy, xenophobia and fear of a fifth column within their borders. *Why,* he asks, *should we tolerate a dangerous separate "nation" in our own land?*

B. וַיְעַנּוּנוּ. Stage two: physical isolation.

Pharaoh's edicts move to the next level with the designation of taskmasters and projects specific to the Israelites. *These people are different,* the Egyptian king proclaims through these actions, *and they require special attention and treatment.*

C. וַיִּתְּנוּ עָלֵינוּ. Stage three: degradation.

When the Israelites respond to Pharaoh's

---

24 Shmot 1:10.
25 Shmot 1:11.
26 Shmot 1:13.

initial decrees with resilience, the Egyptians ratchet the process up to the next level. Commentators note that the biblical term *b'pharech* conveys varied aspects of this new level of persecution.

Rashi leads a number of scholars who, choosing the path of *pshat* (straightforward explanation of the text), explain that the term refers to labor that crushes and breaks the body.[27] According to these commentaries, the term *b'pharech* is not descriptive but definitional. The toil thrust upon the Israelite slaves, like the toil thrust centuries later upon the victims of Nazi persecution, has no real purpose beyond physical torment and psychological degradation. Going a step further, the Talmudic sages suggest that, in order to mock and demean the slaves, men's work is given to the Israelite women and women's work to the men.[28] In a brilliant stroke, Rabbi Shimshon Raphael Hirsch connects the term *b'pharech* to the *parochet* – the dividing curtain which, centuries later, separated the Holy of Holies from the rest of the Temple. The purpose of the work placed upon the Israelites, suggests Hirsch, is to further *divide* the Israelites from their neighbors.[29] Finally, one particularly telling Talmudic source sees the word *pharech* as a consolidation of the two Hebrew words *peh* (mouth) and *rach* (soft). Like so many enemies rising against the Jews in centuries to come, the Egyptians beguile the Israelites with soft, enticing speech. Through lies and false promises of security, the taskmasters induce the slaves to cooperate in their own enslavement.[30]

D. Stage four: murder.

Having set the stage through the physical and psychological subjugation of the Israelites, Pharaoh now feels free to embark upon his true plan: the physical destruction of the fledgling Israelite nation. (Although the Haggada alludes to this fourth, final stage of Pharaoh's plan only in its analysis of the next verse of the *vidui bikkurim*, we mention it here to paint a complete picture of Pharaoh's carefully planned persecution of the Israelites.)

Murder carried out in the public arena, even after painstaking preparation, must be perpetrated slowly and cautiously. Pharaoh, therefore, opens the final devastating stage of his design against the Israelites in a manner that secretly attacks the weakest among them.

"And the king of Egypt said to the Hebrew midwives…, 'When you deliver the Hebrew women, you shall see on the birthing stool, if it is a son you are to kill him, and if it is a daughter, she is to live.'"[31]

Pharaoh, the rabbis explain, commands the Hebrew midwives to kill the male infants in such a way that "even the birthing mothers themselves will remain unaware."[32] The king's actions, however, may well be governed by even deeper, more devious motivations. To protect himself, the Egyptian king launches the extermination of the Israelites in territory that carries a degree,

---

27 Rashi, Shmot 1:13.
28 Talmud Bavli Sota 11b.
29 Rabbi Shimshon Raphael Hirsch, Shmot 1:13.
30 Talmud Bavli Sota 11b.
31 Shmot 1:16.
32 Ramban, Shmot 1:10.

however slight, of moral ambiguity. The Talmud postulates that Pharaoh conveys to the midwives a method of determining the gender of the Israelite children before their birth.[33] Rabbi Shimshon Raphael Hirsch explains that, in this view, Pharaoh is deliberately commanding abortion rather than infanticide.[34] *We are not really murdering the Israelite males. We are only preventing their birth.* Like Hitler and his henchmen centuries later, whose first step on the path of genocide will consist of "mercy killing" (the execution of the infirm and disabled), Pharaoh tests the waters by beginning his own murderous journey in the least morally objectionable arena available to him. When this subterfuge is thwarted by the righteous midwives, Pharaoh finally proclaims his true intentions and commands that all male infants be cast into the Nile.[35]

Even with this open step, however, Pharaoh ingeniously shields himself from blame. The Ramban notes that Pharaoh couches this horrific edict in language that distances the murder from the official seat of government. The king does not command his army or his officers to carry out this terrible act. Instead, he instructs "his entire people" to murder the Hebrew infants.[36] In retrospect, Pharaoh will be able to protest: *What do you want from me? This was not an official action. This was a spontaneous, popular pogrom.*

E. Pharaoh's ultimate success in manipulating both the Egyptian perpetrators and the Israelite victims may well be reflected in two telling biblical passages.

"And Pharaoh commanded his entire people, saying: 'Every son that is born – into the river you shall throw him! And every daughter – you shall keep alive!'"[37]

Rashi notes a startling omission in the Egyptian king's directive. The king does not say, "Every *Israelite son* that is born – into the river you shall throw him!" He says, "*Every son* that is born…"

Rashi explains the omission by citing a Midrashic tradition quoted in the Talmud. Pharaoh's astrologers, the Talmud explains, had predicted to the king that the savior of the Jewish nation would soon be born. The astrologers also foretold that this savior would ultimately meet his downfall through water. Uncertain as to whether this savior-to-be would be born to an Egyptian or to an Israelite family, Pharaoh decrees that, for a limited time, all male infants, *including Egyptian infants*, be cast into the Nile. Astoundingly, the Egyptians comply.[38]

In Rashi's view, the omission in the biblical text indicates how completely Pharaoh had influenced his own nation. By the time the king's plan reaches its climax, Egyptian hatred of the Israelites is so great that the Egyptians are even willing to sacrifice their own children to the cause.

Pharaoh's Machiavellian manipulation, however, not only molds the mindset of his own Egyptian subjects, but the mindset of the Israelite slaves, as well.

---

33 Talmud Bavli Sota 11b.
34 Rabbi Shimshon Raphael Hirsch, Shmot 1:16.
35 Shmot 1:22.
36 Ramban, Shmot 1:10.
37 Shmot 1:22.
38 Rashi, Shmot 1:22.

Later in Parashat Shmot, after Pharaoh has increased the burden upon the slaves in response to Moshe's initial demands for freedom, the Israelites turn on Moshe and exclaim: "May the Lord look upon you and judge, for you have made our very scent abhorrent in the eyes of Pharaoh and in the eyes of his servants, to place a sword in their hands to kill us!"[39]

How astonishing! Pharaoh has subjugated the Israelites, tormented them physically and psychologically, murdered their children, and yet, these very Israelites now turn to Moshe and, in effect, protest: *Because of you, Pharaoh and his servants won't like us!*

The genius of the Egyptian king is in full evidence. He has successfully robbed the Israelites of their freedom in a way that nonetheless maintains their psychological dependence upon him. Unwilling to believe in the total evil that confronts them, the Israelite slaves still harbor a hope that somehow, if they have just the right approach, Pharaoh may still relent.

One is reminded of the very sad joke in which two Jews stand before a Nazi firing squad. The German commander orders: "Ready, aim..." Suddenly one of the Jewish victims shouts out at the top of his lungs, "Down with the Nazis!" "Mordy!" exclaims the other Jew. "Don't make trouble!"

Pharaoh's influence over both the Egyptians and the Israelites is complete. As a result, the Jewish nation finds itself in mortal danger even before it is born.

F. For continued discussion: eternal lessons.

The uncanny ability of the Torah text to speak across the centuries is nowhere more clearly nor more frighteningly evident than in its description of the enslavement of the Israelites at the hands of the Egyptians. Here, openly rooted at the dawn of our history, are the very methods devastatingly used against us and other innocent victims, by enemies in every era, including our own. From calculating Nazi murderers to zealous Islamic fundamentalists, willing to kill their own children in the pursuit of the destruction of Israel and all of Western culture, the adversaries and tactics we face today are much too familiar. Propaganda, demonization, debasement, subterfuge and the teaching of hatred remain the preliminary tools of the murderers' trade as, over and over again, words inexorably lead to deeds. Terrorist regimes hide behind the cloak of popular sentiment as they fund, sponsor and direct murderous plots against innocent civilians.

Constant, as well, is the unwillingness of decent people to accept the reality of the evil that confronts us. We cling to a desperate, illusory hope that somehow, with the right gesture, with the right concession, we will convince our enemies to totally change their ways. After all, we feel, they can't really mean what they say...

Laid down at the beginning of time, the painstaking tactics of prejudice and persecution have remained remarkably constant. Evil will be defeated only if the initial steps are recognized when they first appear and are confronted head-on.

---

39 Shmot 5:21.

Vidui Bikkurim, Verse 3

וַנִּצְעַק אֶל יי אֱלֹהֵי אֲבֹתֵינוּ, וַיִּשְׁמַע יי אֶת קֹלֵנוּ, וַיַּרְא אֶת עָנְיֵנוּ וְאֶת עֲמָלֵנוּ
וְאֶת לַחֲצֵנוּ.

**And we cried out to the Lord, the God of our fathers, and the Lord heard our voice
and saw our affliction and our toil and our oppression.**

The tide begins to turn in the third verse of the *vidui bikkurim* as the farmer recounts
how the pleas of the Israelites reach God's ears.

The Haggada Analyzes Verse 3

Having quoted the third sentence of the *vidui bikkurim*, the Haggada now proceeds to
dissect and analyze each portion of that verse. Primary text from the biblical Exodus
narrative continues to be employed at this point in the Haggada's analysis of the
farmer's words.

וַנִּצְעַק אֶל יי אֱלֹהֵי אֲבֹתֵינוּ. כְּמָה שֶׁנֶּאֱמַר: "וַיְהִי בַיָּמִים הָרַבִּים הָהֵם, וַיָּמָת
מֶלֶךְ מִצְרַיִם, וַיֵּאָנְחוּ בְנֵי יִשְׂרָאֵל מִן הָעֲבֹדָה וַיִּזְעָקוּ. וַתַּעַל שַׁוְעָתָם אֶל
הָאֱלֹהִים מִן הָעֲבֹדָה."

And we cried out to the Lord, the God of our fathers: as it is said: "And it came to
pass during that long period of time that the king of Egypt died, and the children of
Israel groaned because of the servitude, and they cried out. And their cry for help
from their servitude rose to God."[40]

Food for Thought

A. וַיָּמָת מֶלֶךְ. The connection the Torah
draws between Pharaoh's death and the
increased anguish of the Israelites is extremely puzzling. Why would the demise
of the Egyptian king have a negative impact on the condition of the slaves? If anything, shouldn't the opposite be true?

Three alternative explanations offered
by the commentaries ring tragically true
when viewed through the prism of ensuing
Jewish history.

B. A midrashic tradition quoted by Rashi
explains that Pharaoh does not actually
die, but instead falls victim to the plague
of leprosy, a malady that, according to
Jewish tradition, renders its victims so in-
capacitated as to be considered "dead." To
ease his suffering, the midrash continues,
the Egyptian king "bathes in the blood of
slaughtered Israelite infants."[41] It is this
horrific continuing practice that causes
the Israelites to "groan." For the first time,

---

40 Shmot 2:23.
41 Targum Yonatan, Shmot 2:23; Midrash Rabba Shmot 1:34.

וַיִּשְׁמַע יי אֶת קֹלֵנוּ. כְּמָה שֶׁנֶּאֱמַר: "וַיִּשְׁמַע אֱלֹהִים אֶת נַאֲקָתָם, וַיִּזְכֹּר אֱלֹהִים אֶת בְּרִיתוֹ, אֶת אַבְרָהָם, אֶת יִצְחָק, וְאֶת יַעֲקֹב."

And the Lord heard our voice: as it is said: "And God heard their groaning, and God remembered His covenant with Avraham, Yitzchak and Yaakov."[42]

---

the Israelites experience a phenomenon that will be reproduced time and time again across the face of history. *Any misfortune befalling a nation or its leaders will be automatically and absurdly tied to "the Jews."*

C. Other commentaries, including the Ramban, the Ba'alei Tosafot and Rabbi Shimshon Raphael Hirsch, accept the straightforward testimony of the text concerning the king's death and offer an alternate approach. These scholars explain that, as long as the king who had originally enslaved the Israelites lived, the victims held out hope that his horrific decrees would be reversed with his passing. Upon the king's death, however, as their torment continues, the Israelites come face-to-face with the stark, unyielding truth. Their enslavement and persecution is no longer the product of the hatred and megalomania of one specific ruler. *Egyptian society as a whole has turned against them. No end to their suffering is in sight.*[43]

D. Finally, other scholars offer a creative, almost counterintuitive approach to the increased anguish of the Israelites upon Pharaoh's death. The king's passing, these commentaries explain, actually results in a temporary lessening of the physical torment of the slaves. A transitory suspension

of public works is decreed in Egypt in conjunction with a national period of mourning for the king. During this interlude the Israelites experience a brief respite. When their servitude resumes, however, their pain becomes even more acute. Having tasted freedom, the slaves now fully experience the tragedy of their current condition. *An individual's sense of loss is most keenly felt only when he truly recognizes the beauty of that which has been taken from him.*[44]

E. וַיִּשְׁמַע. The rabbis maintain that the Torah often "speaks in the language of man."[45] God, these scholars explain, does not actually "see," "hear," "remember," or experience "anger." Such language is incorporated into the text solely in order to help the reader understand God's actions on the reader's own terms. Nonetheless, the study of attributes assigned to God at specific points in the text can be instructive. In each case, we are challenged to ask: *What message is the Torah conveying through the specific language employed?*

As a case in point, consider the occasions when the phenomenon of remembering is associated with God in the text. Arguably, only a being capable of forgetting is capable of remembering. How then can an all-knowing

---

42 Shmot 2:23.

43 Ramban, *Da'at Zekeinim Mi'ba'alei Hatosafot*, and Rabbi Shimshon Raphael Hirsch, Shmot 2:23.

44 Chiddushei Harim, quoted in *Seder Ha'aruch*, vol. 3, p. 200.

45 Talmud Bavli Brachot 31b, Yevamot 71a and numerous other Talmudic sources.

וַיַּרְא אֶת עָנְיֵנוּ. זוֹ פְּרִישׁוּת דֶּרֶךְ אֶרֶץ, כְּמָה שֶׁנֶּאֱמַר: "וַיַּרְא אֱלֹהִים אֶת בְּנֵי יִשְׂרָאֵל. וַיֵּדַע אֱלֹהִים."

And He saw our suffering. This refers to the forced separation of husband and wife, as it is said: "And God saw the children of Israel, and God knew."[46]

וְאֶת עֲמָלֵנוּ. אֵלוּ הַבָּנִים, כְּמָה שֶׁנֶּאֱמַר: "כָּל הַבֵּן הַיִּלּוֹד הַיְאֹרָה תַּשְׁלִיכֻהוּ, וְכָל הַבַּת תְּחַיּוּן."

and our toil: This refers to [the destruction of] the sons, as it is said: "Every son that is born shall you cast into the river, and every daughter shall you keep alive."[47]

וְאֶת לַחֲצֵנוּ. זֶה הַדְּחַק, כְּמָה שֶׁנֶּאֱמַר: "וְגַם רָאִיתִי אֶת הַלַּחַץ אֲשֶׁר מִצְרַיִם לֹחֲצִים אֹתָם."

and our oppression: This refers to the strain, as it is said: "I have seen the oppression with which the Egyptians are oppressing them."[48]

God, from Whom nothing is hidden at any time, be said to suddenly "remember"?

F. Perhaps the Torah views remembering as an active – as opposed to a passive – phenomenon. *To remember in biblical terms means to act upon remembrance.* Each time God is said to "remember," the Torah speaks of a point in time when God is prepared to actively intervene in a specific situation. God "remembers" Noach in the Ark when He is ready to stop the rainwaters of the flood;[49] God "remembers" the patriarchal covenant when He is prepared to fulfill that covenant through the redemption of the Israelite slaves.

G. The full importance of this point,

however, only emerges when the lesson comes full circle and is applied to human behavior, as well. When God commands man to "remember," the same definition of "remembrance" holds true: *God mandates active, as opposed to passive, remembrance.* The biblical commandment to "Remember the Sabbath day to keep it holy,"[50] for example, is understood by the rabbis as obligating the recitation of the verbal formula of Kiddush (see p. 40).[51] The Torah's imperative to remember the malevolent actions of Amalek includes a continuing obligation to counteract the evil designs of Amalek's physical or philosophical descendants across the ages.[52]

The Torah teaches us that passive remembrance is not sufficient. It is only when

---

46 Shmot 2:25.
47 Shmot 1:22.
48 Shmot 3:9.
49 Bereishit 8:1.
50 Shmot 20:8.
51 Talmud Bavli Pesachim 106a.
52 Devarim 25:17–19.

thought *leads to concrete commitment* that an act of remembering – be it earthly or divine – can be said to truly matter.

H. וַיַּרְא. The previously quoted biblical verse from the book of Shmot spoke of God "hearing" and "remembering" in response to the pleas of the Israelites (see above). The verse now quoted, which follows the first verse directly in the text of Shmot, speaks of God "seeing" and "knowing" in connection with the same phenomenon. Isn't the second sentence redundant, simply a repetition of the first? What message does the Torah convey through these multiple verbs describing God's reaction to the cries of the Israelites?

I. A beautiful explanation is suggested by Rabbi Joseph Dov Soloveitchik. The Rav maintains that "The real tragedy of the slave consists in the fact that he himself does not understand how shameful and horrible the experience of slavery is."[53]

The Israelites fail to comprehend the extent of their own degradation and consequently offer only a limited appeal to God. They rage against the physical labor thrust upon them, but, beaten down by their years of enslavement, remain blind to the deeper assault on their very humanity. They neither mourn nor struggle against the forced disintegration of their family units.

God, however, not only "hears" the voices of the Israelites, but He "sees" and "knows" what they, themselves, neither see nor know. He responds not only to their pleas, but to the reality of their deeper degradation. The divine redemption will reach beyond the Israelites' own aspirations and prayers. God will respond to the real damage done to His people, the true extent of which only He recognizes.

J. Going one step further, the Rav applies the lessons emerging from these verses to our own experiences across the ages. "We would be a most unfortunate people," this scholar proclaims, "if God were guided entirely by our own prayers."[54] Unaware of that which is truly to our benefit, we sometimes pray for things that are damaging to us and often fail to pray for that which we really need. The rabbis address this reality by injecting an inherent tension into the flow of our daily prayers. They instruct us to plead, in the culminating blessing of a series of requests, "*Shma koleinu, Hashem Elokeinu*" (Hear our voices, Lord, our God), but then instruct us to immediately stipulate, "*V'kabel b'rachamim u'v'ratzon et tefillateinu*" (and accept our prayers with compassion and favor). *Dear God*, we plead, *hear our supplications. Then, however, in Your mercy, please choose which prayers to fulfill and which to reject. For our own sake, we must rely on Your judgment, not on ours.*[55]

53 Genack, *The Seder Night: An Exalted Evening*, pp. 74–75.
54 Ibid.
55 Ibid.

Vidui Bikkurim, Verse 4

וַיּוֹצִאֵנוּ יי מִמִּצְרַיִם, בְּיָד חֲזָקָה, וּבִזְרֹעַ נְטוּיָה, וּבְמֹרָא גָּדֹל, וּבְאֹתוֹת, וּבְמוֹפְתִים.

And the Lord took us out of Egypt with a mighty hand, and with an outstretched arm, and with great terror, and with signs, and with wonders.

Food for Thought

A. An obvious and troubling technical difficulty emerges as the Haggada ends its analysis of the *vidui bikkurim* with a study of that text's fourth verse.

As we have repeatedly noted, the mandate shaping this second major section of Maggid reads: *"V'doresh mei'Arami oved avi ad she'yigmor kol haparasha kula"* (And one studies the biblical passage beginning with the words *Arami oved avi* [An Aramean tried to destroy my father...] until he finishes the entire passage).[56]

Our Seder study ends, however, short of completing that goal. The fourth verse of the *vidui bikkurim*, referencing the Exodus from Egypt, is presented and analyzed in our text. The fifth, final verse, however, mentioning the nation's entry into the land of Canaan, is glaringly omitted. If the Talmud instructs us to complete the study of the *vidui* on the Seder night, why do we deliberately stop short of the finish line?

B. Once again, we turn to the observations of Rabbi Joseph Soloveitchik for a solution to our problem. The Rav, with the characteristic intellectual honesty for which he is known, considers two widely disparate approaches to this problem. On a technical level, the Rav proposes, we should recognize that we may be using an edited version of the Haggada: "It is possible to suggest that during the time the Temple still stood, the text of the Haggada did include the last verses relating to the entry into the Land of Israel. Upon the destruction of the Temple and the subsequent exile, Chaza"l [the rabbis of blessed memory] amended the text in order to conform to the new reality in which Am Yisrael [the nation of Israel] found itself."[57] With this suggestion, the Rav reminds us that the Haggada chronicles Jewish history, not only through its content, but through its structure as well. Additions and emendations to the Seder service were made across the ages, often as a result of the changing circumstances of the Jewish people. This textual phenomenon, of course, is not limited to the Haggada, but is characteristic of many other Jewish texts and rituals. Jewish experience is often reflected in the technical details of the nation's liturgy and observance.

The reading of the Haftara (a portion from the books of the Prophets, recited after the reading of the Torah on Shabbat and festival mornings and on fast days) serves as an obvious example of this phenomenon.

---

56 Mishna Pesachim 10:4.

57 Rabbi Joseph B. Soloveitchik, "The Nine Aspects of the Haggada," in Cohen and Brander, *The Yeshiva University Haggada*, Articles, p. 11.

According to many authorities, the recitation of these prophetic passages traces to a time when alien rulers prohibited the study of Torah text within the Jewish community. Responding to this tragic challenge, the rabbis instituted the recitation of a prophetic text related to the theme(s) of the prohibited designated Torah portion.[58] Once the practice of reading Haftarot was established, it remained in force even after the ban on Torah study was lifted.

C. Moving in an entirely different direction, the Rav also offers a striking alternative philosophical theory as to why the verse concerning entry into the Land of Israel is omitted from the Seder service: "Although the Jewish people did enter the Land of Israel subsequent to the Exodus from Egypt, this was not the primary goal of Yetziat Mitzrayim, the Exodus from Egypt. *It [the land] was their destination but not their destiny* [my italics]. The direct goal of Yetziat Mitzrayim was the Revelation at Sinai. The goal was the transformation of a subjugated people into 'a nation of priests and a holy nation.' It was not just to grant them political and economic freedom, but also to create a sacred people."[59]

Textual proof that the Sinaitic Revelation, and not entry into Canaan, was the primary goal of the Exodus can be found, according to the Rav, in God's first response to Moshe's objections at the burning bush. When Moshe questions his own worthiness for leadership, God responds: "And this shall be unto you the sign that I have sent you: when you have brought forth the people out of Egypt, they will serve God upon this mountain."[60] *I am not choosing you, Moshe, to be a politician or a diplomat, but to serve as a Rebbe, a spiritual mentor, to this people. Together we will fashion them into a holy nation. That is the purpose of your ascension to leadership, and that will be the ultimate goal of your mission.*

From the Rav's perspective, the Haggada deliberately omits the verse in the *vidui bikkurim* chronicling entry into the land, in order to remind the reader that the Land of Israel must be seen as one component of a much greater whole. The Jewish nation, born and forged at Sinai, is wholly defined by its relationship to God. That relationship is built upon the study, observance and living of the totality of divine law.

---

58 Avudraham, *Sefer Tefillot shel Shabbat* 63.

59 Soloveitchik, *The Nine Aspects of the Haggada*, quoted in Cohen and Brander, *The Yeshiva University Haggada*, Articles, p. 11.

60 Shmot 3:12.

The Haggada Analyzes Verse 4

Having quoted the fourth sentence of the *vidui bikkurim*, the Haggada now proceeds to dissect and analyze each portion of that verse through the eyes of additional sources from the Written and Oral Law.

וַיּוֹצִאֵנוּ יי מִמִּצְרַיִם. לֹא עַל יְדֵי מַלְאָךְ, וְלֹא עַל יְדֵי שָׂרָף, וְלֹא עַל יְדֵי שָׁלִיחַ.
אֶלָּא הַקָּדוֹשׁ בָּרוּךְ הוּא בִּכְבוֹדוֹ וּבְעַצְמוֹ. שֶׁנֶּאֱמַר: "וְעָבַרְתִּי בְאֶרֶץ מִצְרַיִם
בַּלַּיְלָה הַזֶּה, וְהִכֵּיתִי כָל בְּכוֹר בְּאֶרֶץ מִצְרַיִם, מֵאָדָם וְעַד בְּהֵמָה; וּבְכָל אֱלֹהֵי
מִצְרַיִם אֶעֱשֶׂה שְׁפָטִים אֲנִי יי."
"וְעָבַרְתִּי בְאֶרֶץ מִצְרַיִם בַּלַּיְלָה הַזֶּה," אֲנִי וְלֹא מַלְאָךְ.
"וְהִכֵּיתִי כָל בְּכוֹר בְּאֶרֶץ מִצְרַיִם." אֲנִי וְלֹא שָׂרָף.
"וּבְכָל אֱלֹהֵי מִצְרַיִם אֶעֱשֶׂה שְׁפָטִים," אֲנִי וְלֹא הַשָּׁלִיחַ.
"אֲנִי יי." אֲנִי הוּא וְלֹא אַחֵר.

And the Lord took us out of Egypt: Not through an angel, and not through a seraph, and not through a messenger. Instead, the Holy One, Blessed Be He, in His own glory and He alone. As it is said: "And I will pass through the Land of Egypt on that night, and I will smite every firstborn in the land of Egypt, from man to beast; and against all the gods of Egypt I will carry out judgments – I am the Lord."[61]
"And I will pass through the Land of Egypt on that night" – I and not an angel.
"And I will smite every firstborn in the land of Egypt" – I and not a seraph.
"And I will carry out judgments against all the gods of Egypt" – I and not a messenger.
"I am the Lord" – it is I, and no other.

Food for Thought

A. וַיּוֹצִאֵנוּ. Based on several allusions within the Torah text, the Haggada determines that the final stage of the redemption from Egypt is handled directly by God, without the aegis of other heavenly agents.

This assertion, however, seems puzzling. Angels, after all, appear throughout biblical and rabbinic literature as divine messengers, each angel designated to fulfill a single aspect of God's will. While widely disparate views are found among the rabbis as to the exact nature of these heavenly beings, general consensus does form around a series of basic points. Angels are entities without free will, serving as direct manifestations and extensions of God's resolve, meant to bridge the monumental chasm between an unfathomable Creator and limited man.[62]

If such entities serve an essential purpose on other occasions, why does God

---

61 Shmot 12:12.
62 Midrash Rabba Bereishit 48:11; Talmud Bavli Bava Metzia 86b; Midrash Tanchuma Vayeira 20.

reject their involvement during the climactic moments of the Exodus story?

B. A variety of answers are proposed by classical and contemporary scholars. Some authorities suggest that, due to its complex nature, the final plague of the death of the firstborn could only be administered by God directly. Unlike the preceding plagues, this affliction was directed against a specific subset of individuals, firstborn Egyptian sons. The difficult task of identifying the members of this subset – a population that includes not only all sons firstborn to their mothers, but all sons firstborn to their fathers, as well – requires knowledge that only God possesses.[63] As this plague marks the event that ultimately launches the Exodus, the final stages of the Israelites' redemption from Egypt must unfold under God's direct control.

C. Choosing an entirely different tack, other authorities point to the tarnished character of the Israelite slaves as the factor necessitating God's direct intervention in the final stages of the Exodus. By all rights, the Israelites do not deserve to be redeemed at this point in time. Broken in body and spirit, they have descended to the forty-ninth of fifty possible levels of defilement. God, Who alone can glimpse the majestic potential embedded in the soul of every man, has to personally "break His own rules" in order to bring about the slaves' immediate redemption.[64]

D. An additional explanation for God's direct involvement in the actual Exodus can be suggested if we consider the full impact of this event. The redemption from Egypt marks not only the first footfalls of Jewish national history but the beginning of an eternal relationship between God and His chosen people. For any relationship to be successful, the participants in that relationship must be "fully present." God, therefore, rejects the involvement of His oft-used heavenly messengers. *At the onset of our lasting bond*, He effectively says to the Israelites, *I myself will be here by your side.*

Soon after the Exodus, God seals His relationship with the nation at Sinai through the transmission of His Law. Not by accident, He launches that momentous process with the first of the Ten Declarations: "I am the Lord your God, Who took you out of the land of Egypt." *Our bond is built upon the foundation that I – and no one else – led you on your first steps as a nation out of Egypt.*

---

63 Rabbi David Cohen, *Haggada Simchat Ya'avetz* (Brooklyn: Mesorah, 1991), pp. 95–96.
64 Genack, *The Seder Night: An Exalted Evening*, p. 80.

בְּיָד חֲזָקָה. זוֹ הַדֶּבֶר, כְּמָה שֶׁנֶּאֱמַר: "הִנֵּה יַד יי הוֹיָה, בְּמִקְנְךָ אֲשֶׁר בַּשָּׂדֶה, בַּסּוּסִים, בַּחֲמֹרִים, בַּגְּמַלִּים, בַּבָּקָר, וּבַצֹּאן; דֶּבֶר כָּבֵד מְאֹד."

with a mighty hand: This refers to the [plague of] pestilence, as it is said: "Behold, the hand of the Lord is upon your livestock that are in the field, upon the horses, upon the donkeys, upon the camels, upon the oxen, and upon the sheep – a very severe pestilence."[65]

וּבִזְרֹעַ נְטוּיָה. זוֹ הַחֶרֶב, כְּמָה שֶׁנֶּאֱמַר: "וְחַרְבּוֹ שְׁלוּפָה בְּיָדוֹ, נְטוּיָה עַל יְרוּשָׁלָיִם."

and with an outstretched arm: This refers to the sword, as it is said: "And His sword is drawn in His hand, stretched out over Yerushalayim."[66]

וּבְמוֹרָא גָּדוֹל. זֶה גִּלּוּי שְׁכִינָה, כְּמָה שֶׁנֶּאֱמַר: "אוֹ הֲנִסָּה אֱלֹהִים, לָבוֹא לָקַחַת לוֹ גוֹי מִקֶּרֶב גּוֹי; בְּמַסֹּת, בְּאֹתֹת, וּבְמוֹפְתִים, וּבְמִלְחָמָה, וּבְיָד חֲזָקָה, וּבִזְרוֹעַ נְטוּיָה, וּבְמוֹרָאִים גְּדֹלִים; כְּכֹל אֲשֶׁר עָשָׂה לָכֶם יי אֱלֹהֵיכֶם בְּמִצְרַיִם, לְעֵינֶיךָ."

and with great awe: This refers to the Revelation of the Divine Presence, as it is said: "Has God ever tried to take unto Himself a nation from the midst of another nation – with trials, with signs, with wonders, with war, with a mighty hand and an outstretched arm, and with awesome revelations – like all that the Lord your God did for you in Egypt before your eyes?"[67]

E. וּבְמוֹרָא גָּדוֹל. In the eyes of the Israeli scholar Rabbi Yosef Zvi Rimon, this paragraph of the Haggada underscores the basic aim of the Exodus from Egypt, the Revelation of the Divine Presence to the world: "The Exodus from Egypt was not only an ex post facto rectification of the injustice of the enslavement of the nation of Israel. Its aim was not merely technical-to punish the Egyptians, and to take Israel out of Egypt. The aim was to reveal God's glory in the world, to reveal the Divine Presence."[68]

F. Rabbi Rimon's observation is supported by the two major themes reflected in our weekly observance of Shabbat. On Friday night, the Kiddush and Ma'ariv prayers focus on Shabbat Ma'aseh Bereishit (the Shabbat of Creation), reflecting God's act of "resting" on the seventh day of the world's creation. In contrast, the Kiddush and Shacharit prayers of Shabbat morning focus on Shabbat Yetziat Mitzrayim (the Shabbat of the Exodus), signaling God's giving of Shabbat as a mitzva to the newly forged Jewish nation. Each of these themes speaks to a different aspect of God's Revelation to man. The Shabbat of Creation attests to the fact of God's existence. The Shabbat of the Exodus attests to the fact of God's continued involvement in the affairs of man. As Rabbi Rimon suggests, God's introduction to the world is incomplete if it rests upon creation alone. The Exodus is a necessary, critical component in God's unfolding Revelation to mankind.

---

65 Shmot 9:3.
66 I Divrei Hayamim 21:16.
67 Devarim 4:34.
68 Haggada for Pesach Shirat Miriam, pp. 197–98.

וּבְאֹתוֹת. זֶה הַמַּטֶּה, כְּמָה שֶׁנֶּאֱמַר: "וְאֶת הַמַּטֶּה הַזֶּה תִּקַּח בְּיָדֶךָ, אֲשֶׁר תַּעֲשֶׂה בּוֹ אֶת הָאֹתֹת."

And with signs: this refers to the staff, as it is said: "And take into your hand this staff with which you shall perform the signs."[69]

At this point in the proceedings, as the Haggada begins to enumerate the specific plagues experienced by the Egyptians, we symbolize that our joy is diminished when we reflect upon the pain experienced by other human beings – even our enemies.

> Each Seder participant pours out a drop of wine with the recitation of each word of the enlarged red text:
> 1. each of the three terms *blood*, and *fire*, and *pillars of smoke*;
> 2. each of the ten plagues;
> 3. each word of the mnemonic *D'tzach Adash B'achav.*

וּבְמוֹפְתִים. זֶה הַדָּם, כְּמָה שֶׁנֶּאֱמַר: וְנָתַתִּי מוֹפְתִים, בַּשָּׁמַיִם וּבָאָרֶץ,

דָּם. וָאֵשׁ. וְתִימְרוֹת עָשָׁן.

And wonders: this refers to the plague of blood, as it is said: "And I shall show wonders in heaven and on earth: *blood*, and *fire*, and *pillars of smoke*."[70]

דָּבָר אַחֵר: בְּיָד חֲזָקָה שְׁתַּיִם, וּבִזְרֹעַ נְטוּיָה שְׁתַּיִם, וּבְמוֹרָא גָּדוֹל שְׁתַּיִם, וּבְאֹתוֹת שְׁתַּיִם, וּבְמוֹפְתִים שְׁתַּיִם:

אֵלּוּ עֶשֶׂר מַכּוֹת שֶׁהֵבִיא הַקָּדוֹשׁ בָּרוּךְ הוּא עַל הַמִּצְרִים בְּמִצְרַיִם, וְאֵלּוּ הֵן:

דָּם, צְפַרְדֵּעַ, כִּנִּים, עָרוֹב, דֶּבֶר, שְׁחִין, בָּרָד, אַרְבֶּה, חֹשֶׁךְ, מַכַּת בְּכוֹרוֹת.

רַבִּי יְהוּדָה הָיָה נוֹתֵן בָּהֶם סִמָּנִים:

דְּצַ"ךְ עַדַ"שׁ בְּאַחַ"ב.

Another explanation [can be offered for the verse]: **With a mighty hand,** denotes two [plagues]; **and with an outstretched arm,** denotes two; **and with great terror,** denotes two; **and with signs,** denotes two; **and with wonders,** denotes two.

[Referred to, thus,] are the ten plagues that the Holy One, Blessed be He, brought upon the Egyptians in Egypt:

Blood, Frogs, Lice, Wild Beasts, Pestilence, Boils, Hail, Locusts, Darkness, Slaying of the Firstborn.

Rabbi Yehuda would refer to them mnemonically (based upon their initials) as follows: *D'tzach Adash B'achav.*

---

69 Shmot 4:17.
70 Yoel 3:3.

G. עֶשֶׂר מַכּוֹת. Biblical tales such as the Exodus narrative become so familiar to us that we often fail to ask the obvious questions.

As a case in point, we could well ask: Why were the ten plagues necessary? God could have certainly orchestrated the Exodus in any way that He chose. Why not bring the Egyptians to their knees in one fell swoop with a single, overwhelming, enduring affliction? Or, conversely, why not simply redeem the Israelites miraculously without causing any plagues at all?

H. A cryptic answer to our question is perhaps offered by the Haggada itself. After listing the plagues, the text records Rabbi Yehuda's well-known mnemonic, *D'tzach Adash B'achav*, which divides the plagues into three groups. While Rabbi Yehuda himself offers no explanation for his proposed formula, scholars across the ages struggle to find deeper significance in this threefold division of the plagues. Their interpretations underscore a point made above. The Exodus is a formative teaching moment in the development of God's relationship with all of mankind, providing a vehicle through which He proclaims not only His existence, but His ongoing involvement in human affairs.

I. The Abravanel is one of the earliest scholars to interpret Rabbi Yehuda's division of the plagues. Based upon hints within Pharaoh's initial reaction to Moshe, the Abravanel identifies three basic principles

rejected by the Egyptian monarch: the existence of God, Divine Providence (the involvement of God in the life of man) and God's ability to control nature. The three sets of plagues are specifically designed to respond to Pharaoh's denials, as God's introduction to each set indicates. Before the first plague God proclaims, "With this you shall know that I am the Lord,"[71] indicating that the plagues of blood, frogs and lice are meant to counter Pharaoh's denial of God's existence. The fourth plague is preceded by the proclamation "that you may know that I am the Lord in the midst of the land."[72] This assertion specifies that the afflictions of beasts, pestilence and boils are designed to prove the reality of Divine Providence. Finally, before the seventh plague God announces, "And you may know that there is none like Me in all the land."[73] The plagues of hail, locusts and darkness demonstrate God's ability to control nature.

The tenth and final plague of the firstborn joins all three elements together in one devastating blow.[74]

The Maharal of Prague also discerns an educational dimension to the plagues. The first grouping of afflictions – blood, frogs and lice – represents an attack upon the Egyptians from below, as the land and sea turn against them. The second cluster – beasts, pestilence and boils – consists of an assault upon the Egyptians originating on their own level. Finally, the third set – hail, locusts, darkness and the plague of the firstborn – comprises an attack on

---

71 Shmot 7:16.
72 Shmot 8:18.
73 Shmot 9:14.
74 *Zevach Pesach* (Abravanel's commentary on the Haggada).

the Egyptians from above. Through the plagues, the Maharal maintains, God demonstrates His total mastery of the world by turning each level of existence against the Egyptians.[75]

Taking an entirely different tack, Rabbi Shimshon Raphael Hirsch sees in the structure of the plagues measure-for-measure punishment meted out against the Egyptians for their crimes. The persecution of the Israelites in Egypt, Hirsch explains, progressed through three phases: *gerut* (estrangement within their adopted land), *avdut* (enslavement) and *inui* (torment).

The first plague of each group, says Hirsch – blood, beasts and hail – is structured to make the Egyptians feel like strangers in their own land. The second affliction in each set – frogs, pestilence and locusts – conveys the emptiness of pride and masterfulness. The third plague in each cluster – lice, boils and darkness – is designed to torment the Egyptians as they tormented the Israelites. Finally, the last plague of the death of the firstborn brings the process to a climax and accomplishes the redemption.[76]

J. A careful reading of the text reveals another level of design embedded within the progression of the plagues. Rabbi Yehuda's groupings mirror a consistent internal structure. In each set, the first plague is preceded by a public warning to Pharaoh, the second plague by a private notice to the monarch, while the third plague carries no warning at all.

This internal pattern, the Abravanel maintains, reflects God's desire to forestall the tragedies confronting the Egyptians. First God warns Pharaoh in the presence of his court, affording the king's powerful retinue the opportunity to object. Recognizing, however, that the monarch might balk at a public warning, God then instructs Moshe to serve notice before the next plague to the king in private. When both of these cautions are ignored, God initiates the third plague of each set in full view of the Egyptian population without any warning at all. He hopes, by doing so, to educate the populace to the moral bankruptcy of their royal leadership and to prompt the masses to rise up in opposition to their nation's self-destructive course.[77]

K. A final approach to the overall purpose of the plagues emerges if we consider the events from the perspective of the Israelites.

Redemption is a process that requires both time and gradation. As the world has since learned through bitter experience, a servile population cannot make the transition to freedom and responsibility in one single step.

In light of the challenges confronting the generation of the Exodus, the plagues acquire new significance. To truly become free, the slaves must witness the total decimation of all that has previously held them in thrall. Only if Egypt, its citizens, its royalty, its sorcerers and its gods are laid low in full view can the participants in the Exodus even begin their journey toward autonomy. Step by step, the plagues destroy all that the Israelites have learned to fear. As the

---

75 Maharal, commentary on the Haggada.
76 Rabbi Shimshon Raphael Hirsch, Shmot 7:26.
77 Abravanel, Shmot 7:26.

shackles are broken, the promise of freedom begins to emerge.

As we have noted (see p. 42), the gradual character of redemption is mirrored at the Seder through the rabbinic mitzva of the four cups of wine. According to many authorities, these cups symbolize not only the four languages of redemption employed by God in his announcement of the Exodus to Moshe, but four distinct stages in the Israelites' journey toward the actual moment of the Exodus.

Ultimately, however, the transition toward national autonomy will prove to be too difficult for the departing Israelites. In spite of the plagues, the parting of the Reed Sea, the Revelation at Sinai and all the accompanying miracles, a full generation will have to pass before the promise of freedom is realized. The generation that leaves Egypt never fully leaves Egypt behind. Unable to recognize their own potential, they will die in the desert. Only their children, who never knew slavery, will enter their land.

L. For continued discussion.

A dramatic yet easily missed anomaly appears when we consider the disposition of the Israelites during the course of the plagues. The testimony of the text is strangely inconsistent. When discussing the plagues of beasts, pestilence, hail and darkness, the Torah goes out of its way to indicate that the Israelites were spared any suffering. During the plague of the firstborn, the Israelites who follow God's instructions are also saved. In conjunction with the other plagues, however, no distinction is made

in the Torah between the Egyptians and the Israelites.

This textual variance gives rise to a remarkable disagreement between the commentaries.

The Ramban maintains that the Israelites are not affected by any of the plagues. The Torah, however, only mentions their protected status in conjunction with the plagues that are by nature "spreading" afflictions. Since we would have assumed that these plagues affected the Israelites in Goshen as well, the Torah clearly tells us otherwise.[78]

The Ibn Ezra, in stark contrast, maintains that the majority of the plagues afflict the Israelites together with their Egyptian masters. Only those plagues clearly indicated in the text, the plagues that carry the greatest potential for enduring pain and mortal danger, actually leave them unscathed.[79]

At first glance, the Ibn Ezra's position seems deeply puzzling. Why should the Israelite victims of Egyptian slavery suffer even a measure of the punishment meted out against their taskmasters? The Avi Ezer, a commentator on the Ibn Ezra, is so troubled by this notion that he claims it was erroneously incorporated into the text of the Ibn Ezra by a "mistaken poor student."[80]

Two rationales, however, might be suggested in support of the Ibn Ezra's recorded position that the slaves are affected by a number of the plagues.

1. The Israelites bear a measure of

---

78 Ramban, Shmot 8:18–19.
79 Ibn Ezra, Shmot 7:24.
80 Avi Ezer, ibid.

culpability in their own enslavement.

As noted above (see pp. 95–96), the descent of Yaakov's family to Egypt was meant to result only in a temporary sojourn.

Eventually, however, the Israelites "settle and secure a permanent foothold" in the land of Egypt. Clearly the children of Yaakov become too comfortable with the exile from the land of their fathers. Another measure of blame can be leveled against the Israelites for their attempt to assimilate into Egyptian society. Upon his family's descent to Egypt, Yosef carefully manipulates their settlement in Goshen, thereby orchestrating a clear separation from the Egyptians. As we have previously noted, however (see pp. 95–96), the text later testifies: "And the children of Israel were fruitful, multiplied, increased, and became strong...and the land became filled with them."[81] The Netziv comments, building upon an earlier Midrashic tradition: "They filled not only the land of Goshen, which had been especially assigned to them, but the whole land of Egypt.... Wherever they could purchase a dwelling, there the Israelites went.... They wanted to be like the Egyptians."[82] For these failings, the Israelites deserve partial punishment along with the Egyptians.

2. God does not want the Jewish nation to become a people so callous that they are capable of ignoring the pain of others, even their sworn enemies. As the nation is about to be born, therefore, God conveys a necessary, painful lesson. The Israelites cannot remain untouched while surrounded by a sea of agony. They must endure a number of the plagues together with their taskmasters in order to feel a measure of their pain.

As noted earlier, this same sentiment gives rise to the practice of spilling out a drop of wine with the mention of each plague at the Seder. Our own happiness must be diminished upon our encounter with the pain of others, even our adversaries. Unlike our enemies, we will never rejoice in violence, even when it is necessary. We will always regret the pain we must inflict upon others, even in our own defense.

M. Another philosophical problem emerges as we consider the pain inflicted upon the Egyptians over the course of the plagues.

At the very outset of Moshe's mission to Egypt, God predicts, "And I will harden [Pharaoh's] heart and he will not let the people go."[83] On a number of occasions that follow, the Torah states that God makes good on this promise and actually "hardens the heart" of the Egyptian king.[84]

By "hardening Pharaoh's heart," doesn't God rob the Egyptian king of his rightful free will, thereby predetermining both Pharaoh's choices and his (and his nation's) resulting fate? Jewish tradition views *tshuva* (repentance or return) as an inalienable right granted by God to every individual. How can God deny that right to Pharaoh?

Compounding the problem is the fact that the textual record is inconsistent. After each of the first five plagues, the Torah states that Pharaoh "hardens" his own heart, apparently of his own free will. Only

---

81 Shmot 1:7.
82 *Ha'amek Davar*, Shmot 1:7.
83 Shmot 4:21.
84 Shmot 9:12; 9:12; 10:1; 20:27; 11:10.

in conjunction with the sixth through tenth plagues does God fulfill His prediction by "hardening the heart" of the Egyptian monarch.[85] How can we account for this inconsistency? What causes the apparent change in Pharaoh's mindset and in God's response?

The rabbis were well aware that the issues surrounding the apparent suspension of Pharaoh's free will strike to the very core of Jewish belief. Thus, Rabbi Yochanan ben Zakkai is quoted in the Midrash Rabba as stating, "[The textual testimony concerning Pharaoh] provides an opening for heretics to say: '[Pharaoh] was not allowed to repent.'"[86] And, centuries later, both the Ramban and the Ibn Ezra wonder aloud, "If God hardened Pharaoh's heart, then what was [Pharaoh's] sin?"[87]

Rising to the obvious challenges raised by these concerns, the authorities suggest a wide array of approaches.

N. At one end of the spectrum lie those, such as Shmuel David Luzzatto (Shadal), who find the problems so troubling that they feel compelled to claim that the questions are not questions at all: *"Know that all acts can be ascribed to God, for all are caused by Him* – some through absolute decree and others through man's free choice which has been granted by Him.... It can therefore be said that [God], as the author of all acts, hardened Pharaoh's heart."[88]

Pharaoh's choices are made totally of his own free will. These very choices, however, like all events in the world, ultimately trace back to God, Who grants Pharaoh and all mankind free will in the first place. The assertion that God "hardens Pharaoh's heart" is simply the text's way of indicating a fundamental connection between Pharaoh's independent choices and the divine source of his free will.

This circular reasoning, however, raises an obvious question: How, then, can the Torah ever speak of actions independently performed by individuals? Why doesn't the text attribute every decision made by each of its characters to its ultimate source – God – as it does in the case of Pharaoh? Luzzatto addresses this objection by maintaining that only actions that defy logic, such as Pharaoh's obstinacy in the face of the plagues, are actually ascribed in the text to God.[89]

O. Other scholars, unwilling to dismiss the overwhelming textual evidence that God actually "hardens Pharaoh's heart," attempt mightily to reconcile that fact with Judaism's fundamental view on free will and repentance.

Two intriguing alternatives, for example, are offered by the Abravanel:

1. Different sins warrant different paths toward absolution. Sincere contrition, prayer and remorse can effect full atonement for sins committed against God. Crimes against one's fellow man, however, will not be forgiven as long as the ledgers remain open in the human sphere. Atonement

---

85 Shmot 7:22; 8:11, 15, 28; 9:7.
86 Midrash Rabba Shmot 13:3.
87 Ibn Ezra, Shmot 7:3; Ramban, ibid.
88 Shmuel David Luzatto, Shmot 7:3.
89 Ibid.

cannot, for example, be attained for the crime of thievery until the theft is returned or replaced and appropriate fines are paid. An individual guilty of murder must be punished in an earthly court before he can be cleared in the heavenly realm. Pharaoh and the Egyptians are guilty of horrendous crimes against the Israelites – crimes which, by definition, give rise to requisite physical punishment. By hardening Pharaoh's heart, God ironically clears the way for the atonement of Pharaoh and his people. The punishment of the plagues is the first, necessary step along the Egyptians' path of repentance.

2. The "hardening of Pharaoh's heart" was directly caused by the methodology of the plagues. Had God afflicted the Egyptians with one unending plague, Pharaoh would have eventually relented. In order to demonstrate His own power to the world, however, God specifically visits a series of plagues upon Egypt. As each calamity ends, the Egyptian king rationalizes that the event had occurred of natural causes. Clearly, he reasons, had the plague been divinely ordained, it would not have been lifted until the Israelites were freed. The "hardening of Pharaoh's heart" is not an independent phenomenon but an inevitable outgrowth of the manner in which God orchestrates the plagues.[90]

P. A number of commentaries, including the Sforno, insist that God's actions vis-à-vis Pharaoh do not impede but actually enhance the king's free will. Absent the "hardening of his heart," Pharaoh would have chosen the right path for all the wrong reasons. He would have certainly released the Israelites – not, however, because of a sincere desire to repent and submit to divine will, but because he could no longer bear the suffering caused by the plagues. God, therefore, fortifies Pharaoh's ability to endure the plagues, so that the king will not release the Israelites simply because of fear of the impending calamities.

According to these commentaries, God certainly seeks the repentance of Pharaoh and the Egyptians, but only if that repentance is sincere. God launches the plagues, therefore, hoping that the Egyptians will be moved by His power and His merciful insistence upon freedom for all. Recognizing that true repentance, however, cannot take place under duress, God hardens Pharaoh against the physical and mental effects of the calamities. By doing so, He affords the king and his subjects the opportunity to repent of their own free will, not because of the pain of the plagues, but because of their message.[91]

Q. The most revolutionary approach to the issues before us, however, actually emerges from an early source. In contrast to the positions cited above, the Midrash cites an opinion that accepts the suspension of Pharaoh's free will and right to repentance. The Talmudic scholar Rabbi Shimon ben Lakish (Reish Lakish) maintains that if an individual fails to return to God after repeated warnings, God then closes that individual's heart to repentance in order to "exact punishment for his sin." God,

---

90 Abravanel, Shmot 7:3.
91 Sforno, ibid.

continues Reish Lakish, gives Pharaoh five chances to repent: the first five plagues. On each of these occasions, however, the Egyptian monarch hardens his own heart, refusing to bend to God's will. At that point God intervenes, suspends Pharaoh's free will and closes the door to his spiritual return.[92] This opinion acquires greater poignancy when we recognize that its author, Reish Lakish, was himself no stranger to the path of repentance. Living in the wilderness where he made his livelihood as a bandit, Reish Lakish was swayed to turn his life around through a chance encounter with the man destined to become his scholarly colleague and brother-in-law, Rabbi Yochanan.[93]

Perhaps Reish Lakish felt himself nearing the point of no return before fate intervened and pulled him back from the brink.

Numerous commentaries are unwilling to accept the Midrash at face value, refusing to believe that God would deny even Pharaoh the right to repentance. The Rambam, however, clearly codifies Reish Lakish's position in his laws of repentance:

> It is possible that a man may commit a sin so grave, or so many sins...that repentance is denied to him and he is not given the opportunity to turn away from his evil.... Therefore the Torah states, "and I [God] will harden the heart of Pharaoh." Because Pharaoh initially sinned of his own volition, divine judgment was rendered that he be denied the possibility of repentance so that he would pay for his crimes.[94]

The Rambam's assertion brings our discussion full circle. In contrast to the attempts to explain away the apparent suspension of Pharaoh's free will, Maimonides himself is willing to accept what at first seemed unthinkable. The ability to repent, itself a gift from God, is not an inalienable right under all circumstances. This gift will be denied to the perpetrators of the most heinous crimes, to ensure that they receive the justice they deserve.

R. For further discussion.

Even our most basic assumptions must sometimes be reexamined. Our discussion of the topic of Pharaoh's free will opened with the contention that the whole fabric of Jewish tradition begins to unravel if free will and repentance are denied to any individual. That assumption, for the most part, certainly remains correct. There are, however, according to some authorities, exceptions to the rule. Some crimes are so unforgivable that God will suspend the perpetrator's basic rights in order to ensure that justice prevails.

How, however, does this assertion fare in the moral realm? If God denies even the most evil their rights, can these individuals ever be held culpable for their crimes?

We can, perhaps, better address this question by moving the issue into more familiar territory.

If, God forbid, Adolf Hitler stood before us today and proclaimed true remorse for his crimes, would God grant him absolution? Should the opportunity for repair be available to all, or should certain individuals,

---

92 Midrash Rabba Shmot 13:3.
93 Talmud Bavli Bava Metzia 84a.
94 Rambam, *Mishneh Torah*, Hilchot Tshuva 6:3.

through the nature of their crimes, lose their eligibility for repentance?

Which of these possible approaches captures the moral high ground?

Here, it would seem – according to the Rambam – that Jewish and Catholic traditions part company. For while fundamental Christian theology preaches that repentance remains available to all under all circumstances, the Rambam maintains that repentance is a right that can be lost. Actions speak louder than words. No amount of remorse, contrition, confession or prayer can truly erase the crimes of a Pharaoh, a Hitler or a Stalin. The mobster who confesses to his priest after scores of murders cannot, according to the Rambam, wipe the slate clean.

There comes a point when even a merciful God is unwilling to forgive.

This realization causes the concept of *tshuva* to become substantially more fragile within our own lives. While, please God, none of us will even come close to the point where the right of repentance is totally denied to us, who knows whether such denial might be applied piecemeal? Perhaps a particular failure can become so habitual, so embedded in our lives, that the opportunity to turn away from that failure is lost. Who knows where the tipping point might be? The gifts of free will and *tshuva* should never be taken for granted; we never know the exact moment when those gifts might be taken away.

Expanded Torah Study:
Computing the Number of Plagues

Having introduced the subject of the ten plagues in its analysis of the fourth verse of the *vidui bikkurim*, the Haggada now quotes early midrashic authorities who claim substantial increases in the actual number of plagues affecting the Egyptians.

With the inclusion of these midrashic sources, the Haggada closes the section of Torah study that began with the opening declaration *"Tzei u'lemad"* (Go out and learn; see p. 92). Like most exercises in Torah study, our analysis has been far ranging, while still remaining based on a central textual source – in this case, the *vidui bikkurim*.

Many early editions of the Haggada, including the version recorded by the Rambam in his Code of Law, omit both this final midrashic discussion and the paragraphs of thanks that immediately follow (see p. 129). These Haggadot continue directly with the next major section of the Maggid, *Rabban Gamliel haya omer.*[95]

---

95 Rambam, Nusach Hahaggada. Strangely, however, the Rambam's son Avraham is quoted as testifying to the fact that his father did actually recite this Midrashic discussion at the Seder. Kasher, *Haggada Shleima*, p. 185, quoting the Ma'aseh Rokeach.

רַבִּי יוֹסֵי הַגְּלִילִי אוֹמֵר: מִנַּיִן אַתָּה אוֹמֵר שֶׁלָּקוּ הַמִּצְרִים בְּמִצְרַיִם עֶשֶׂר מַכּוֹת,
וְעַל הַיָּם לָקוּ חֲמִשִּׁים מַכּוֹת? בְּמִצְרַיִם מָה הוּא אוֹמֵר: "וַיֹּאמְרוּ הַחַרְטֻמִּם אֶל פַּרְעֹה,
אֶצְבַּע אֱלֹהִים הִוא." וְעַל הַיָּם מָה הוּא אוֹמֵר? "וַיַּרְא יִשְׂרָאֵל אֶת הַיָּד הַגְּדֹלָה אֲשֶׁר
עָשָׂה יי בְּמִצְרַיִם, וַיִּירְאוּ הָעָם אֶת יי, וַיַּאֲמִינוּ בַּיי, וּבְמֹשֶׁה עַבְדּוֹ." כַּמָּה לָקוּ בְּאֶצְבַּע?
עֶשֶׂר מַכּוֹת. אֱמוֹר מֵעַתָּה, בְּמִצְרַיִם לָקוּ עֶשֶׂר מַכּוֹת וְעַל הַיָּם לָקוּ חֲמִשִּׁים מַכּוֹת.

Rabbi Yossi the Gallilean said: From where can you infer that the Egyptians were afflicted by ten plagues in Egypt, and at the [Reed] Sea by fifty plagues?

Concerning [the events in] Egypt, it is said: "The magicians said to Pharaoh, 'This is *the finger of God.'*" Concerning [the events at] the Sea, it says: "Israel saw *the great hand* that the Lord laid against Egypt; and the people feared the Lord, and they believed in the Lord and in Moshe, His servant." Now, how many [plagues] did the Egyptians experience through "one finger"? Ten plagues. You must therefore conclude that in Egypt (in relation to which the word *finger* is used) they were struck by ten plagues, and at the Sea (in relation to which the word *hand* is used) they were struck by fifty plagues.

רַבִּי אֱלִיעֶזֶר אוֹמֵר: מִנַּיִן שֶׁכָּל מַכָּה וּמַכָּה, שֶׁהֵבִיא הַקָּדוֹשׁ בָּרוּךְ הוּא עַל הַמִּצְרִים
בְּמִצְרַיִם, הָיְתָה שֶׁל אַרְבַּע מַכּוֹת? שֶׁנֶּאֱמַר: "יְשַׁלַּח בָּם חֲרוֹן אַפּוֹ, עֶבְרָה וָזַעַם וְצָרָה."
מִשְׁלַחַת מַלְאֲכֵי רָעִים. עֶבְרָה אַחַת. וָזַעַם שְׁתַּיִם. וְצָרָה שָׁלֹשׁ. מִשְׁלַחַת מַלְאֲכֵי רָעִים
אַרְבַּע. אֱמוֹר מֵעַתָּה, בְּמִצְרַיִם לָקוּ אַרְבָּעִים מַכּוֹת, וְעַל הַיָּם לָקוּ מָאתַיִם מַכּוֹת.

Rabbi Eliezer said: From where can you infer that each individual plague that the Holy One, Blessed be He, visited upon the Egyptians in Egypt consisted of four plagues?

For it is said: "He sent upon them His fierce anger: fury, and wrath, and trouble, a team of messengers of evil: 'fury' denotes one [plague]; 'wrath' makes two; 'trouble' makes three; 'a team of messengers of evil' makes four. You must therefore conclude that in Egypt they were struck by forty plagues, and at the Sea they were struck by two hundred plagues."

רַבִּי עֲקִיבָא אוֹמֵר: מִנַּיִן שֶׁכָּל מַכָּה וּמַכָּה, שֶׁהֵבִיא הַקָּדוֹשׁ בָּרוּךְ הוּא עַל הַמִּצְרִים
בְּמִצְרַיִם, הָיְתָה שֶׁל חָמֵשׁ מַכּוֹת? שֶׁנֶּאֱמַר: "יְשַׁלַּח בָּם חֲרוֹן אַפּוֹ: עֶבְרָה, וָזַעַם,
וְצָרָה, מִשְׁלַחַת מַלְאֲכֵי רָעִים." חֲרוֹן אַפּוֹ אַחַת. עֶבְרָה שְׁתַּיִם. וָזַעַם שָׁלֹשׁ. וְצָרָה
אַרְבַּע. מִשְׁלַחַת מַלְאֲכֵי רָעִים חָמֵשׁ. אֱמוֹר מֵעַתָּה, בְּמִצְרַיִם לָקוּ חֲמִשִּׁים מַכּוֹת,
וְעַל הַיָּם לָקוּ חֲמִשִּׁים וּמָאתַיִם מַכּוֹת.

Rabbi Akiva said: From where can you infer that each individual plague that the Holy One, Blessed be He, brought upon the Egyptians in Egypt consisted of five plagues? For it is said: "He sent upon them His fierce anger, fury, and wrath, and trouble, a team of messengers of evil." "His fierce anger" denotes one; "fury" makes two; "wrath" makes three; "trouble" makes four; "a team of messengers of evil" makes five. Thus you must now say that in Egypt they were struck by fifty plagues, and at the Sea they were struck by two hundred fifty plagues.

Food for Thought

A. This segment of the Haggada has troubled me for years. Just a moment ago, we symbolized our sorrow over the suffering of the Egyptians by pouring a drop of wine from our cups with the mention of each of the ten plagues. Now, in contrast, the rabbis seem intent upon interpreting the events surrounding the Exodus in ways that magnify the pain experienced by the Egyptians. How are we to explain this sudden change in approach?

Given that midrashic literature is primarily used, according to many authorities, as a rabbinic vehicle for the transmission of spiritual, ethical and moral ideas, what messages are the rabbis conveying through the discussion before us?

B. Clearly bothered by this phenomenon, the scholars struggle to determine a positive message that might emerge from a multiplication of the afflictions affecting the Egyptians.

Rabbi Eliyahu of Vilna, the Vilna Gaon, for example, points to a divine promise delivered to the Israelites shortly after the parting of the Reed Sea: "If you hearken diligently to the voice of the Lord, your God, and do what is straight in his eyes, and pay attention to his commandments and observe all his decrees, then all of the diseases that I brought forth in Egypt, I will not bring upon you, for I am the Lord, your healer."[96]

The greater the number of afflictions that we can discern as having struck Egypt, the Gaon explains, the greater the number of afflictions from which God will protect the Jewish nation as a reward for their loyalty across time.[97]

A fascinating midrashic observation in this vein is made by the nineteenth-century Hasidic sage Rabbi Aryeh Leib Alter, popularly known by the title of his most famous work, the *Sefat Emet*. Rabbi Alter notes that *the sum total of all the plagues presented in the Haggada* – the ten biblical plagues; the three phrases of the mnemonic presented by Rabbi Yehuda (*D'tzach Adash B'achav*); the sixty, two hundred forty, and three hundred plagues computed respectively by Rabbi Yossi Haglili, Rabbi Eliezer and Rabbi Akiva – *equals 613*. Subliminally, the Haggada reminds us that God's protection of His people is ultimately contingent upon their obedience to His law. Across time, observance of the 613 biblical mitzvot will protect the Jewish nation from numerous "afflictions of Egypt."[98]

Finally, the various interpretations we offered earlier concerning the purpose of the plagues as a whole can lend positive significance to their magnification, as well. Whether as vehicles for the revelation of God's existence, as teaching tools concerning the extent of God's involvement in human affairs, or as deserved punishment clearing the way for spiritual repentance on the part of the Egyptians, the plagues had a positive purpose. As painful as these afflictions were, they were ultimately designed to be of potential benefit to the Egyptians, the Israelites, and a watching world.

---

96 Shmot 15:26.
97 *Haggadat Hagra* (Jerusalem, Noam Hatorah, 1983), p. 80.
98 *Sefat Emet*, vol. 3, Pesach 5647.

C. With the rabbinic debate concerning the sum total of plagues, the Haggada moves us, for the first time, beyond the events occurring in Egypt to the climactic parting of the Reed Sea.[99] Seen in retrospect, that momentous event seems almost inevitable from the outset. If the Israelites are to ever be truly free, an unrepentant Egypt cannot be left whole. The newly redeemed slaves would forever be haunted by the continued existence of their erstwhile masters. Thus, Torah testifies: "And Israel saw the mighty hand that the Lord inflicted upon Egypt; and the people feared the Lord; and they believed in the Lord and in Moshe, His servant." Only upon seeing the might of Egypt drowning in the swirling waters of the Reed Sea do the Israelites finally "believe in the Lord and in Moshe, His servant."

D. The seeming inevitability of Egyptian destruction in the waters of the sea, however, should give us pause when we consider a troubling thread woven into the Exodus narrative from its beginnings. Speaking from the burning bush, God appoints a reluctant Moshe to leadership, commanding him to return to Egypt and lead the Israelite slaves to freedom. God's instructions concerning Moshe's initial approach to the Egyptian king, however, are surprising and puzzling: "You and the elders of Israel shall come to the king of Egypt and say to him: 'The Lord, God of the Hebrews, happened upon us. And now, please let us go on a three-day journey in the wilderness, and we shall bring offerings to the Lord, our God.'"[100]

E. Why is the expected powerful demand for freedom, *Let my people go*, replaced with the seemingly tepid request, *Please let my people go on a three-day journey into the wilderness to worship our God*? What could be more central to the Exodus story than the demand for total freedom?

And...if Pharaoh had agreed to Moshe's request, would the Israelites have returned after three days? If so, what would have been accomplished by their brief departure? If they would never have returned, if a three-day journey was not a truly viable option, why would God instruct Moshe to lie to the Egyptian king? Is the Jewish nation to be born through deceit?

Finally, and most pertinent to our discussion, a frightening possibility emerges when we consider the events leading up to the parting of the Reed Sea. The Torah records that, exactly three days after the Israelites' release from bondage, "it was told to the king of Egypt that the [Israelite] nation had fled."[101]

F. How are we to understand this bewildering statement? Clearly Pharaoh knows that the Israelites have left Egypt. The king himself, broken by the last of the ten plagues, ordered the slaves out of his country! Why must he now be told that the Israelites have fled? *Can it be that Pharaoh, even after the devastation of the plagues, still believes he has released the Israelites only for a three-day religious holiday*? Is that why the Egyptian king leads his army in pursuit of

---

99 Some identify the inclusion of these events as the Rambam's motivation for omitting this section of the Haggada from his edition. The Rambam believes, these authorities maintain, that the Seder evening should focus only on those events leading up to and including the actual departure from Egypt (see pp. 122, 129).

100 Shmot 3:18.

101 Shmot 14:5.

the Israelites three days after the Exodus, when the king concludes that the slaves are not returning? Has the entire Exodus been divinely structured, through the three-day request, to deceive Pharaoh and inexorably lead his army to their deaths in the Reed Sea?

G. Strikingly, the Midrash embraces, without apology or excuse, God's deliberate deception of Pharaoh and the Egyptians. Rashi, quoting a *Mechilta*, relates that Pharaoh sends spies with the departing Israelite slaves. When the third day after the Exodus arrives, the day on which the Israelites had promised to return, the spies see that no such return is imminent. These agents therefore report to Pharaoh, "The Israelites have fled."[102] According to the Midrash, the idea of a three-day journey is never truly abandoned by Pharaoh. Even after the devastation wrought upon his land, the Egyptian king fully expects the Israelites to return. When he realizes that he has been deceived, he immediately takes off in pursuit of the "fleeing" slaves. Numerous other commentaries mirror this Midrashic approach.[103]

From this point of view, the Exodus is designed, from its earliest stages, to ultimately lead Pharaoh and his army to the banks of the Reed Sea. As stated above, God knows that the Israelites will never truly be free of their taskmasters unless they witness the total destruction of Egyptian power in the roiling waters of that sea.

Concerning the moral issues raised by this divinely ordained deceit, Shmuel David Luzzatto (Shadal) argues: "[The deception] was justified by the fact that Pharaoh would certainly have enslaved the Israelites upon their return to Egypt. We should not be surprised, therefore, that God commanded the Israelites to give Pharaoh a taste of his own medicine."[104]

As Rabbi Yehuda Nachshoni essentially argues in his discussion of an earlier moral quandary raised by the Torah narrative, "All is fair in love and war." If we are obligated to kill on the battlefield in order to defeat evil, it stands to reason that we are obligated to use subterfuge, when necessary, to accomplish the same goal.[105]

H. Many other commentaries, however, are less than sanguine with the Midrashic acceptance of divinely ordained deceit. Refusing to accept the possibility that God – and upon his orders, Moshe, as well – could possibly be deceitful, these commentaries offer a number of alternative approaches.

Some scholars, including Abravanel[106] and the Akeidat Yitzchak,[107] explain the three-day request as an exercise meant to test and expose the limits of Pharaoh's obstinacy. As the Abravanel puts it, "The Almighty proffered this request in order to demonstrate to the world the extent of Pharaoh's stubbornness and to justify the divine judgment and punishment about to be brought upon Pharaoh and Egypt."[108]

---

102 Rashi, Shmot 14:5.
103 Ibn Ezra (Hakatzar), Shmot 11:4, 14:5; Chizkuni, Shmot 14:5.
104 Shmuel David Luzzatto, Shmot 3:18.
105 Yehuda Nachshoni, *Hagut B'parashiot HaTorah* (Tel Aviv: Zohar Publishing, 1979), p. 209.
106 Abravanel, Shmot 3:18.
107 Akeidat Yitzchak, Shmot, sha'ar 35.
108 Abravanel, Shmot 3:18.

This position could imply that the request for a three-day journey was offered as a serious option. Had the Egyptian king shown flexibility by agreeing to this first request presented to him, the Israelites would indeed have returned, and the Exodus might well have unfolded in a different, less painful fashion. Once Pharaoh refuses to accede even to this reasonable appeal, however, the three-day option is removed from the table and replaced with the demand for total freedom.

I. Other scholars maintain that the limited journey was never really presented as a viable option at all. God certainly had no intention of allowing His people to return to Egypt after three days of freedom. How, then, can the request be explained without bringing into play the possibility of divine deceit?

On this point, two contrasting schools of thought emerge.

The Abravanel and Rabbi Yaakov Mecklenberg are among those who maintain that, notwithstanding the implied commitment to return to Egypt, Moshe never clearly verbalizes a pledge to come back. He is therefore not guilty of an outright falsehood.[109]

The Chizkuni goes one step further and claims that the request for a three-day journey was factually truthful. He points to the fact that on the second day after the Exodus, the Israelites encamp at Eitam in the "edge of the wilderness," effectively halting their flight from Egypt.[110]

J. One final approach to the three-day request is offered by Rabbeinu Bachya, who views God's instructions from the perspective of the Israelite slaves, as opposed to the perspective of the Egyptians.

Abrupt, total change in the human condition is impossible. Consequently, the Israelites would have been unable to even conceive of an immediate transition from slavery to freedom. God, therefore, proceeds slowly. By introducing the concept of a limited excursion from Egypt, He presents the Israelites with a proposal that they can accept.

As the plagues progress, however, and as the Israelites witness the step-by-step decimation of their enslavers, the possibility of full freedom begins to become real.

God, Rabbeinu Bachya maintains, orchestrates the entry of the Israelites into a new world of responsibility through measured steps.[111]

K. For continued discussion...
What if...?

What if, as some of the sources quoted above maintain, the three-day request of Pharaoh was not a ruse at all, but a serious offer? And, what if Pharaoh had agreed to the request? Upon the return of the Israelites, how might the path of the Exodus have been altered? While it is impossible to answer this question with any degree of certainty, we can suggest the one variable that would have changed: the Israelites themselves.

Granted a taste of freedom after decades of carefully orchestrated slavery

---

109 Haktav V'hakabala, Shmot 3:18.
110 Chizkuni, Shmot 3:18.
111 Rabbeinu Bachya, Shmot 3:1.

and degradation, the Israelites would have returned to Egypt, in some measure, a changed people. Pharaoh knew this. He knew that he could not allow even a glimmer of hope to illuminate the lives of his slaves. Only through unremitting subjugation could he maintain their physical and spiritual servitude. A holiday from slavery, no matter how brief, could simply not have been countenanced.

As the Exodus unfolds, a fundamental truth is mirrored in the depth of a demagogue's fear – a truth that will be proven over and over again across the span of Jewish history. Even the most powerful subjugation and degradation cannot totally destroy the spark of human spirit burning deep in the hearts of the oppressed. Let the smallest glimmer of hope enter, and that spark will be quickly fanned into a rising flame.

Perspective and Gratitude

Having concluded the extensive section of Torah study upon which the second major section of Maggid is built, the Haggada now takes the critical step from narrative to thanks, a step taken at the close of each of the three major sections of Maggid (see p. 86).

As noted above, the well-known song "Dayenu" (It would have been enough for us), chronicling various acts of kindness performed by God toward His people; the paragraph following, along with the previous section discussing the sum total of plagues, are omitted in early editions of the Haggada. These sections do appear, however, in the ninth-century Haggada of Rabbi Amram Gaon.[112]

The song "Dayenu" is sung by the Seder participants.

כַּמָּה מַעֲלוֹת טוֹבוֹת לַמָּקוֹם עָלֵינוּ:

וְלֹא עָשָׂה בָהֶם שְׁפָטִים, דַּיֵּנוּ:	אִלּוּ הוֹצִיאָנוּ מִמִּצְרַיִם,
וְלֹא עָשָׂה בֵאלֹהֵיהֶם, דַּיֵּנוּ:	אִלּוּ עָשָׂה בָהֶם שְׁפָטִים,
וְלֹא הָרַג אֶת בְּכוֹרֵיהֶם, דַּיֵּנוּ:	אִלּוּ עָשָׂה בֵאלֹהֵיהֶם,
וְלֹא נָתַן לָנוּ אֶת מָמוֹנָם, דַּיֵּנוּ:	אִלּוּ הָרַג אֶת בְּכוֹרֵיהֶם,
וְלֹא קָרַע לָנוּ אֶת הַיָּם, דַּיֵּנוּ:	אִלּוּ נָתַן לָנוּ אֶת מָמוֹנָם,
וְלֹא הֶעֱבִירָנוּ בְּתוֹכוֹ בֶּחָרָבָה, דַּיֵּנוּ:	אִלּוּ קָרַע לָנוּ אֶת הַיָּם,
וְלֹא שִׁקַּע צָרֵינוּ בְּתוֹכוֹ, דַּיֵּנוּ:	אִלּוּ הֶעֱבִירָנוּ בְּתוֹכוֹ בֶּחָרָבָה,
וְלֹא סִפֵּק צָרְכֵּנוּ בַּמִּדְבָּר אַרְבָּעִים שָׁנָה, דַּיֵּנוּ:	אִלּוּ שִׁקַּע צָרֵינוּ בְּתוֹכוֹ,
וְלֹא הֶאֱכִילָנוּ אֶת הַמָּן, דַּיֵּנוּ:	אִלּוּ סִפֵּק צָרְכֵּנוּ בַּמִּדְבָּר אַרְבָּעִים שָׁנָה,
וְלֹא נָתַן לָנוּ אֶת הַשַּׁבָּת, דַּיֵּנוּ:	אִלּוּ הֶאֱכִילָנוּ אֶת הַמָּן,
וְלֹא קֵרְבָנוּ לִפְנֵי הַר סִינַי, דַּיֵּנוּ:	אִלּוּ נָתַן לָנוּ אֶת הַשַּׁבָּת,
וְלֹא נָתַן לָנוּ אֶת הַתּוֹרָה, דַּיֵּנוּ:	אִלּוּ קֵרְבָנוּ לִפְנֵי הַר סִינַי,
וְלֹא הִכְנִיסָנוּ לְאֶרֶץ יִשְׂרָאֵל, דַּיֵּנוּ:	אִלּוּ נָתַן לָנוּ אֶת הַתּוֹרָה,
וְלֹא בָנָה לָנוּ אֶת בֵּית הַבְּחִירָה, דַּיֵּנוּ:	אִלּוּ הִכְנִיסָנוּ לְאֶרֶץ יִשְׂרָאֵל,

How many levels of favors has the Omnipresent One bestowed upon us!
Had He brought us out from Egypt, and not executed judgments
against them [the Egyptians],
it would have sufficed us!
Had He carried out judgments against them, and not against their gods,
it would have sufficed us!
Had He executed judgment against their gods, and not slain their firstborn,
it would have sufficed us!
Had He slain their firstborn, and not given us their wealth,

---

112 Kasher, *Haggada Shleima*, pp. 46–47.

it would have sufficed us!

Had He given us their wealth, and not split the sea for us,
 it would have sufficed us!

Had He split the sea for us, and not taken us through it on dry land,
it would have sufficed us!

Had He taken us through it [the sea] on dry land, and not drowned our tormentors in it, it would have sufficed us!

Had He drowned our tormentors in it [the sea], and not supplied our needs in the wilderness for forty years,
it would have sufficed us!

Had He supplied our needs in the desert for forty years, and not fed us the manna,
it would have sufficed us!

Had He fed us the manna, and not given us the Sabbath,
it would have sufficed us!

Had He given us the Sabbath, and not brought us before Mount Sinai,
it would have sufficed us!

Had He brought us before Mount Sinai, and not given us the Torah,
it would have sufficed us!

Had He given us the Torah, and not brought us into the Land of Israel,
it would have sufficed us!

Had He brought us into the Land of Israel,
and not built for us the Chosen House [Holy Temple],
it would have sufficed us!

Food for Thought

A. Many commentaries question the fundamental postulate lying at the core of "Dayenu" that partial steps in the Israelites' redemptive path would have been satisfactory.

How would our ancestors have benefited, these scholars ask, *had God parted the Reed Sea but failed to lead the nation through on dry land? How would it have been "enough for us" had God brought the nation before Mount Sinai but failed to give us the Torah?*

B. Some scholars address this issue by responding, piecemeal, to problems raised by specific verses of "Dayenu." The Sefat Emet, for example, explains how an approach to Mount Sinai, without the actual giving of the Torah, might have benefited our forefathers. Upon nearing the site of Revelation, this scholar maintains, the nation immediately acquires a new level of spiritual perfection as a result of their proximity to the Divine Presence. Thus, we can recite, "If He had only brought us before Mount Sinai and had not given us the Torah, *dayenu!*"[113]

C. The key to "Dayenu" as a whole, however, may be hinted at in the Haggada itself. The text introduces the song with the proclamation "How many levels of favors has the Omnipresent One bestowed upon us!" Following the song, a closing declaration

is further introduced with the statement "Thus, how much more so should we be grateful to the Omnipresent One for the doubled and redoubled goodness that He has bestowed upon us!"

"Dayenu," it would seem, is *an exercise in appreciation.* As we express our gratitude to God at the close of the second major stage of Maggid, the section of historical personalization, we are reminded by the Haggada that a full appreciation of bestowed goodness requires recognition of each step and element involved in the process.

A son or daughter thanking his or her parents at a milestone moment becomes more fully grateful upon considering the many days of care, support, love and sustenance that have led to this day of achievement. An individual thanking friends for a particularly thoughtful gesture can only be fully grateful when truly considering each detail – the time, effort and planning behind the gift.

D. The steps leading to the redemption of the Israelites from Egypt and to their subsequent achievements were many, every one of them worthy of note. As we, their descendants, reexperience these steps, one by one, in song, we declare to our Creator: *Each of these kindnesses alone would have been sufficient to earn our gratitude. We therefore thank You for every step along the way. Dayenu!*

---

113 Sefat Emet, *Panim B'panim,* 5637.

Al Achat Kamma V'kamma: A Closing Declaration

The following declaration, reiterating the points of "Dayenu"
in narrative form, is recited:

עַל אַחַת כַּמָּה וְכַמָּה טוֹבָה כְפוּלָה וּמְכֻפֶּלֶת לַמָּקוֹם עָלֵינוּ: שֶׁהוֹצִיאָנוּ
מִמִּצְרַיִם, וְעָשָׂה בָהֶם שְׁפָטִים, וְעָשָׂה בֵאלֹהֵיהֶם, וְהָרַג אֶת בְּכוֹרֵיהֶם, וְנָתַן לָנוּ
אֶת מָמוֹנָם, וְקָרַע לָנוּ אֶת הַיָּם, וְהֶעֱבִירָנוּ בְתוֹכוֹ בֶּחָרָבָה, וְשִׁקַּע צָרֵינוּ בְּתוֹכוֹ,
וְסִפֵּק צָרְכֵּנוּ בַּמִּדְבָּר אַרְבָּעִים שָׁנָה, וְהֶאֱכִילָנוּ אֶת הַמָּן, וְנָתַן לָנוּ אֶת הַשַּׁבָּת,
וְקֵרְבָנוּ לִפְנֵי הַר סִינַי, וְנָתַן לָנוּ אֶת הַתּוֹרָה, וְהִכְנִיסָנוּ לְאֶרֶץ יִשְׂרָאֵל, וּבָנָה
לָנוּ אֶת בֵּית הַבְּחִירָה לְכַפֵּר עַל כָּל עֲוֹנוֹתֵינוּ.

Thus, how much more so should we be grateful to the Omnipresent One for the
doubled and redoubled goodness that He has bestowed upon us; for He brought
us out of Egypt, and executed judgments against them [the Egyptians] and against
their idols, and slayed their firstborn, and gave us their wealth, and split the sea
for us, and took us through it on dry land, and drowned our tormentors in it, and
supplied our needs in the wilderness for forty years, and fed us the manna, and
gave us the Sabbath, and brought us before Mount Sinai, and gave us the Torah,
and brought us into the Land of Israel, and built for us the Chosen House [Holy
Temple] to atone for all our sins.

Food for Thought

A. The second stage of Maggid, the stage
of historical personalization/participation,
closes with this emphatic declaration of
gratitude. Having engaged in the shared
experience of Torah study that comprised
the centerpiece of this Seder section, we
are acutely attuned to our roles as active
participants in the unfolding story of the
Jewish nation. Thrust into the flow of our
people's story, we recognize that what happens to one Jew at any time happens to all
Jews at all times.

B. We can now, therefore, fully express our
gratitude to God for events that occurred

thousands of years ago. These events, we
proclaim, are not shrouded in the mists
of history, but are a real part of our lives
today.

C. As we thank God for the gifts of the
past, however, we also recognize the subliminal message conveyed by this section
of the Haggada. *Just as the past lives on in
our lives, the present (defined by our contribution to the Jewish story) will directly shape
the lives of generations to come.* This recognition leads us directly into the third and
last stage of Maggid, the stage of historical
perpetuation.

Seder Section 5c • MAGGID's Third Goal
Historical Perpetuation

Having concluded the second major stage of Maggid, the stage of historical personalization/participation, we now turn our attention to the third and final stage, the stage of historical perpetuation.

This stage, the shortest of the three major stages of Maggid, consists almost entirely of a declaration recorded in the Mishna in the name of the towering first-century sage Rabban Gamliel: *Kol she'lo amar shelosha devarim eilu b'Pesach lo yatza yedei chovato, v'eilu hein – Pesach, matza, u'maror..."* (Anyone who has not said [spoken of] these three words on Pesach has not fulfilled his obligation – Pesach [the Korban Pesach], matza [unleavened bread], and *maror* [bitter herbs]...).[1]

The Haggada quotes Rabban Gamliel, elaborates briefly on each of the symbols he mentions, and continues with another paragraph quoted from the Mishna: *"B'chol dor va'dor chayav adam lirot et atzmo k'ilu hu yatza mi'Mitzrayim..."* (In every generation a person is obligated to look upon himself as if he personally came out from Egypt...).

Finally, this stage of Maggid closes with an extended section of gratitude; consisting of the first passages of Hallel Hamitzri and a concluding blessing.

As suggested in our introductory essay on *sippur Yetziat Mitzrayim* and in our ongoing commentary on the text below, this section of the Haggada is designed to move the Seder participants toward one final realization: our personal responsibility for the perpetuation of Jewish history.

Rabban Gamliel Haya Omer...

The three symbols of Pesach, matza and *maror* are discussed, in fulfillment of Rabban Gamliel's instructions. The matza and *maror* are each raised as they are referenced. The shank bone representing the Korban Pesach, however, is not raised. This variation serves to remind us that, while the Korban Pesach is recalled at the Seder, it is not observed as a mitzva in our day, in the absence of the Temple.

רַבָּן גַּמְלִיאֵל הָיָה אוֹמֵר: כָּל שֶׁלֹּא אָמַר שְׁלשָׁה דְבָרִים אֵלּוּ בַּפֶּסַח, לֹא יָצָא יְדֵי חוֹבָתוֹ, וְאֵלּוּ הֵן: פֶּסַח, מַצָּה, וּמָרוֹר.

Rabban Gamliel was wont to say: Anyone who has not said [spoken of] these three words on Pesach has not fulfilled his obligation, namely: **Pesach (the Korban Pesach)**, *matza* **(unleavened bread)**, and *maror* **(bitter herbs)**.

---

1   Mishna Pesachim 10:5.

פֶּסַח שֶׁהָיוּ אֲבוֹתֵינוּ אוֹכְלִים בִּזְמַן שֶׁבֵּית הַמִּקְדָּשׁ הָיָה קַיָּם, עַל שׁוּם מָה?
עַל שׁוּם שֶׁפָּסַח הַקָּדוֹשׁ בָּרוּךְ הוּא עַל בָּתֵּי אֲבוֹתֵינוּ בְּמִצְרַיִם, שֶׁנֶּאֱמַר:
"וַאֲמַרְתֶּם זֶבַח פֶּסַח הוּא לַיי, אֲשֶׁר פָּסַח עַל בָּתֵּי בְנֵי יִשְׂרָאֵל בְּמִצְרַיִם בְּנָגְפּוֹ
אֶת מִצְרַיִם, וְאֶת בָּתֵּינוּ הִצִּיל, וַיִּקֹּד הָעָם וַיִּשְׁתַּחֲווּ."

The Korban Pesach that our forefathers ate during the period of the Holy Temple –
for what reason [did they do so]?

Because the Holy One, Blessed Be He, passed over our forefathers' houses in
Egypt, as it is said: "You shall say, 'It is a Passover offering to the Lord, Who passed
over the houses of the children of Israel in Egypt when He smote Egypt and spared
our housholds.' And the people bowed and prostrated themselves."[2]

The broken middle matza is raised, and the following paragraph is recited:

מַצָּה זוֹ שֶׁאָנוּ אוֹכְלִים, עַל שׁוּם מָה? עַל שׁוּם שֶׁלֹּא הִסְפִּיק בְּצֵקָם שֶׁל
אֲבוֹתֵינוּ לְהַחֲמִיץ עַד שֶׁנִּגְלָה עֲלֵיהֶם מֶלֶךְ מַלְכֵי הַמְּלָכִים, הַקָּדוֹשׁ בָּרוּךְ הוּא,
וּגְאָלָם, שֶׁנֶּאֱמַר: "וַיֹּאפוּ אֶת הַבָּצֵק אֲשֶׁר הוֹצִיאוּ מִמִּצְרַיִם עֻגֹת מַצּוֹת, כִּי לֹא
חָמֵץ, כִּי גֹרְשׁוּ מִמִּצְרַיִם וְלֹא יָכְלוּ לְהִתְמַהְמֵהַּ, וְגַם צֵדָה לֹא עָשׂוּ לָהֶם."

This matza that we eat – for what reason [do we do so]?

Because the dough of our forefathers did not have time to ferment before the
Supreme King of kings, the Holy One, Blessed Be He, revealed Himself to them and
redeemed them. As it is said: "They baked the dough that they had brought out
of Egypt into unleavened cakes, for it had not fermented, because they had been
driven out of Egypt and could not delay, nor had they prepared any provisions for
themselves."[3]

The maror is raised and the following paragraph is recited:

מָרוֹר זֶה שֶׁאָנוּ אוֹכְלִים, עַל שׁוּם מָה? עַל שׁוּם שֶׁמֵּרְרוּ הַמִּצְרִים אֶת
חַיֵּי אֲבוֹתֵינוּ בְּמִצְרַיִם, שֶׁנֶּאֱמַר: "וַיְמָרְרוּ אֶת חַיֵּיהֶם בַּעֲבֹדָה קָשָׁה, בְּחֹמֶר
וּבִלְבֵנִים, וּבְכָל עֲבֹדָה בַּשָּׂדֶה, אֵת כָּל עֲבֹדָתָם אֲשֶׁר עָבְדוּ בָהֶם בְּפָרֶךְ."

This maror that we eat – for what reason [do we do so]?

Because the Egyptians embittered the lives of our forefathers in Egypt, as it is said:
"They embittered their lives with hard labor, with mortar and with bricks, and with all
manner of labor in the field; all their labor was imposed upon them with rigor."[4]

---

2 Shmot 12:27.
3 Shmot 12:39.
4 Shmot 1:14.

Food for Thought

A. In underscoring the need to speak about the symbols of Pesach, matza and *maror* at the Seder, Rabban Gamliel employs a Talmudic catchphrase. He maintains that one who fails to mention these symbols *"lo yatza yedei chovato"* (has not fulfilled his obligation). When applied in the Talmud, this phrase invariably refers to an individual who has attempted to perform a discrete halachic requirement, but has failed to do so properly.

In this case, however, a question can be raised. Which exact halachic obligation does Rabban Gamliel consider unfinished if we do not mention Pesach, matza and *maror*? What requirement of the Seder remains incomplete without the verbal mention of these symbols?

Some authorities maintain that Rabban Gamliel refers to the obligations embedded in the symbols themselves.[5] According to this approach, Rabban Gamliel argues, for example, that an individual who consumes matza during the Seder but fails to discuss the significance of this act has not properly fulfilled the mitzva of *achilat matza* (consuming matza on the Seder night). Many other sages, however, disagree and maintain that Rabban Gamliel refers to the mitzva of *sippur Yetziat Mitzrayim*.[6] According to this view, Rabban Gamliel argues that an individual cannot properly fulfill the obligation to retell the Exodus story on the Seder night without verbally mentioning the Korban Pesach, the matza and the *maror* in the process.

B. This second position seems baffling. Isn't Rabban Gamliel turning the medium into the message? Logically, the symbols of the Seder night are tools designed to aid in the reexperiencing of the Exodus story. Why would Rabban Gamliel transform them into essential features of the narrative itself? Surely, the story of the Exodus can be told without a verbal mention of these three symbols?

C. Rabban Gamliel's position becomes clear when we recognize that the most elusive and important step of Maggid yet remains before us: the step of *historical perpetuation*. Within this context, Rabban Gamliel reminds us that *concrete mitzvot* are essential to the perpetuation of Jewish tradition. Ideas, concepts and values, as important as they may be to any faith tradition, are individual and varied. An individual's understanding of Jewish thought is bound to be different from that of his ancestors – and different, as well, from that of his children and grandchildren. Religious perspective is greatly shaped, after all, by a person's personality, environment and experience.

In contrast, physical symbols and ritual worship possess the power of constancy. The tefillin that an individual puts on each morning are fundamentally the same as those that were worn by his great-great-grandfather and the same as those that will be worn, with God's help, one day by his great-great-grandsons. Concrete, physical, symbolic mitzvot

---

5   Commentary of Abudarham and Maharsha, as explained in Rabbi Shlomo Wahrman, *Sefer Orot Hapesach* (North Bergen, NJ: independently published, 1992), chapter 54.

6   Rambam, *Mishneh Torah*, Hilchot Chametz U'matza 7:5.

are critical to the uniform transmission of Jewish tradition, thought and law. Without such mitzvot, the Jewish nation would have long ago faded into oblivion.

D. Rabban Gamliel confronts a formidable challenge as he reaches this point of the Seder. This sage maintains that, although the previous stages of Maggid have enabled us to gain an awareness of the structured flow of Jewish history and a sense of personal participation in that history, our task is far from complete. Not by accident, the very formulation of the mitzva of *sippur Yetziat Mitzrayim* emerges, in part, from the biblical statement *"V'higgadeta l'vincha"* (and you shall relate to your child).[7]

To become full participants in history, on this night of history, we must ensure the future participation of our progeny. Rabban Gamliel therefore insists that we have not accomplished the mitzva of *sippur Yetziat Mitzrayim* unless the narrative includes a discussion of the concrete mitzvot of the Seder evening. While these are independent mitzvot, they are also critical components of the narrative itself. These mitzvot, and mitzvot like them, will guarantee the perpetuation of Jewish tradition. They must therefore be spoken of as we journey toward a full understanding of our personal place in history.

Thus, under Rabban Gamliel's guidance, we successfully fulfill the requirements of the third and final stage of the Maggid: the stage of historical perpetuation. We recognize that to become full participants in our nation's journey, we must actively

enable that journey to continue. Once we reach that realization and make that commitment, we fully rise to the philosophical challenge of the Seder night.

E. We now return to the mystery of matza...

As previously noted (see p. 60), the symbol of matza is discussed twice during the retelling of the Exodus narrative. The two references to this symbol, however, could not be more different.

In the opening paragraph of Maggid, matza is referred to as *lachma anya*, the "bread of affliction" or "a poor man's bread" – clearly a symbol of bondage and suffering. At this point in the Seder, however, as Maggid draws to a close, matza becomes synonymous with redemption: "This matza that we eat – for what reason [do we do so]? It is because the dough of our forefathers did not have time to become leavened before the King of kings, the Holy One, Blessed Be He, revealed Himself to them and redeemed them..."

Which is it? Is matza a symbol of slavery or a symbol of freedom?

F. While highlighted in the Haggada, the contradictory nature of matza is actually first evidenced much earlier, in the Torah text itself.

On the one hand, the Torah twice testifies to the popularly accepted notion that matza dramatically originates due to the speed of the Israelites' departure from Egypt: "And the people took up their dough before it became leavened";[8] "And they baked the dough that they had brought out of Egypt into unleavened cakes, for it had not fermented,

---

7 Shmot 13:8.
8 Shmot 12:34.

because they had been driven out of Egypt and could not delay, nor had they prepared any provisions for themselves."[9]

On the other hand, almost unnoticed, the Torah also testifies to the existence of matza as a symbol prior to the moment of the Exodus. God's commandments concerning the Korban Pesach in Egypt include the following: "And they shall eat that flesh on that night, roasted over the fire, *and matzot*; with bitter herbs shall they eat it."[10]

If the symbol of matza is born only at the moment of the Exodus, as a result of the haste characterizing the Israelites' departure, how can matza already be in existence as a symbol before that moment of redemption arrives?

G. It would seem that, unlike other static Seder rituals, matza is dynamic. While other symbols at the Seder represent either slavery or freedom, *somehow matza represents both*. Perhaps this is one reason why, of the three central Seder symbols mentioned by Rabban Gamliel, only matza remains a biblical obligation to this day (see p. 151). The Korban Pesach waits to be reinstated with the Temple's rebuilding. *Maror*, associated in the text with the Korban Pesach, is transformed into a rabbinic mitzva over the course of time, observed today in remembrance of the Temple. Only matza, the one dynamic symbol that best represents the volatile nature of Jewish history and the ever-changing lot of the Jew, remains in full force consistently over time.

But how can one substance simultaneously represent such vastly different states as slavery and freedom? What is the secret of the matza?

H. Perhaps the answer is hinted at in another curious aspect of matza…

The festival of Pesach is largely shaped by the antithetical relationship between matza and its opposite, *chametz* (leavened bread). Hours and hours of preparation are spent to ensure that, by the time the festival begins, our personal worlds are *chametz*-free. Eating, benefiting from, even owning *chametz* on Pesach is biblically prohibited. In order to enter the realm of matza, we must completely leave the realm of *chametz*. Matza and *chametz* simply cannot coexist.

And yet, *these two "opposites" are remarkably alike*. Their ingredients are, in fact, identical. The Talmud goes so far as to say that the only flour acceptable for the production of matza is flour that has the potential to become *chametz*.[11]

Other authorities suggest that even the Hebrew terms *chametz* and *matza* themselves reflect the fundamental similarity of the items they represent. *Matza* is spelled *mem, tzadik, heh*, while *chametz* is spelled *chet, mem, tzadik*. These terms are thus distinguished from each other by the variable of one letter alone. Furthermore, the differentiating letters *heh* and *chet* are themselves only separated by a tiny line which, when attached to the leg of a *heh*, turns that letter into a *chet*. This seemingly insignificant line, these scholars maintain, represents

---

9 Shmot 12:39.
10 Shmot 12:8.
11 *Shulchan Aruch*, Orach Chaim 459:2; *Mishna Berura* 459: 15.

the small yet critical factor that separates the realms of *chametz* and matza.[12]

That single factor? *A split second of time.*

A mixture of flour and water that remains untended for over eighteen minutes automatically becomes *chametz*. If we catch and bake that mixture within eighteen minutes or less, we have created matza.[13]

I. Here then, is a possible global approach to the mystery of matza. Just as matza is defined physically by a split second of time, matza philosophically represents a split second of time. *Matza captures the moment when everything changes.* It is the moment of transition from slavery to freedom. By freezing this moment in time, this symbol alone is able to reflect elements of both slavery and freedom.

Once a year, we enter the realm of matza, a realm wholly defined by a moment of time. We do so not only to capture the transitional instant that launched our national history, but to remind ourselves that life is never static. The line separating "opposites" in our lives is often razor thin. Every moment of our lives can be a transitional moment – moving forward or slipping back.

J. For further discussion.

The centrality of time as a theme within the Exodus narrative demands our attention. Over and over again, time emerges center stage in the unfolding drama.

The first mitzva transmitted to the Israelites as a nation is the sanctification of the new moon, a mitzva dealing with the sanctification of time (see p. 40); numerous aspects of the Korban Pesach in Egypt are designed to ritualize an atmosphere of haste, openly referenced in God's instruction "and you shall eat it in haste, it is a Pesach to the Lord";[14] the distinction between *chametz* and matza is a split second of time. In fact, the urgency meant to accompany the performance of all mitzvot is formalized in the overarching Midrashic dictum "One should not allow the mitzvot to become *chametz*."[15]

The festival of Pesach and its symbols remind us that our own lives are replete with fleeting opportunities taken or lost in an instant, often recognized only in retrospect. As we mark our nation's birth, paying tribute to those Israelites who seized the opportunity presented by the Exodus, we pray for the wisdom to recognize and seize the opportunities presented to us each day.

---

12 Quoted by many classical and modern commentators.
13 *Shulchan Aruch*, Orach Chaim 459:2; *Mishna Berura* 459: 15.
14 Shmot 12:11.
15 *Mechilta D'bei Rebbi Yishmael*, Parashat Bo, Mesechta D'pischa 9.

B'chol Dor Va'dor: A Closing Declaration

As the last section of Maggid begins to draw to a close, the Haggada departs from its previously established norm. For the first time, the closing declaration of this stage precedes the expression of gratitude.

This variation can be explained by the fact that, in this case, we close not only the last section of Maggid, but Maggid as a whole. A more expansive section of gratitude, consisting of the first portions of Hallel and reflecting back on the entire Maggid, is therefore recited after the closing declaration for this section.

The following declaration quoted from the Mishna is now recited:

בְּכָל דּוֹר וָדוֹר חַיָּב אָדָם לִרְאוֹת אֶת עַצְמוֹ כְּאִלּוּ הוּא יָצָא מִמִּצְרָיִם,
שֶׁנֶּאֱמַר: וְהִגַּדְתָּ לְבִנְךָ בַּיּוֹם הַהוּא לֵאמֹר: בַּעֲבוּר זֶה עָשָׂה יי לִי, בְּצֵאתִי
מִמִּצְרָיִם. לֹא אֶת אֲבוֹתֵינוּ בִּלְבָד גָּאַל הַקָּדוֹשׁ בָּרוּךְ הוּא, אֶלָּא אַף אוֹתָנוּ גָּאַל
עִמָּהֶם, שֶׁנֶּאֱמַר: וְאוֹתָנוּ הוֹצִיא מִשָּׁם, לְמַעַן הָבִיא אֹתָנוּ, לָתֶת לָנוּ אֶת הָאָרֶץ
אֲשֶׁר נִשְׁבַּע לַאֲבֹתֵינוּ.

In every generation a person is obligated to look upon himself as if he personally came out from Egypt, as it is said: "You shall tell your child on that day, saying: 'It is because of this that the Lord did [all these wonders] for *me* when I left Egypt.'"[16]

Not our forefathers alone did the the Holy One, Blessed Be He, redeem from Egypt, but He redeemed us also with them; as it is said: "and He brought *us* out from there, that He might bring us to, and give us, the land that He promised to our forefathers."[17]

Food for Thought

A. This familiar declaration, quoted directly from the Mishna, serves as a closing statement, not only for the third major section of Maggid, but for Maggid as a whole. Having reached this point in the Seder, we more clearly understand why our tradition demands that we must each see ourselves as if we left the Land of Egypt – why we are obligated to relive this historical event as we do no other. Our journey through Maggid has taught us that the departure from Egypt, the event that launches Jewish national history, is not meant to be reexperienced in isolation. *The Exodus is instead meant to be the portal through which we, every year on the Seder night, reenter the flow of Jewish history.*

Having concluded the three stages of Maggid, we proclaim that we are no longer spectators looking out on events that are distant from our lives. We were present as the Exodus framed the first footfalls of our

---

16 Ibid., 13:8.
17 Devarim 6:23.

nation's journey; and we will be present, if only through our progeny, at that journey's culmination.

B. Tellingly, the Rambam emphasizes the participatory nature of this obligation through a one-letter variation in his formulation of the laws concerning the Seder night. As he quotes this paragraph in the *Mishneh Torah* and as he formulates his version of the Haggada text, the Rambam adds the letter *heh* to the word *lir'ot* (to see), transforming it into the word *l'har'ot* (to show). The mandate thus reads: "In every generation a person must *show himself* as if he personally came out from Egypt."[18]

The Rambam converts the personal obligation of experiencing the Exodus from the passive to the active. On the Seder night, this Sage maintains, each individual *must act* as if he or she is participating in the Exodus at this very moment. The sense of freedom must be immediate, real and palpable. Even further, our internal experience must be shared with those around us.

While our versions of the the Haggada text do not reflect the Rambam's rendering of this passage, the lesson this great scholar conveys certainly rings true. By "showing ourselves" as if we personally came out from Egypt, we model for all those present, particularly for our children, the sense

of historical involvement so critical to the Seder.

C. For further discussion: joining the circle.

My rabbinic colleagues and I often hear complaints about the dearth of spirituality in Jewish observance today. *I'm waiting to be moved, to be inspired*, the litany often goes, *but nothing grabs me.*

While this important issue can and should be addressed on many levels, the Rambam may be hinting at a fundamental truth concerning the search for spirituality.

Much of Judaism is experiential in nature and can only be understood through involvement. An individual witnessing the dancing at a Simchat Torah celebration, for example, will never be "moved" until he joins the circle. There are times when you have to lead with your heart, when you have to jump in and trust that meaning will follow. If you wait to "feel" before entering the circle, you may forever be standing outside.

On the Seder night, the Rambam maintains, those present should not wait to "feel like" joining the proceedings. Each participant should instead thrust him- or herself into the experience, act as if he or she left the land of Egypt, and trust that the feelings will follow. The meaning we seek may well be waiting to be found, if only we are willing to join the circle.[19]

---

18 Rambam, *Mishneh Torah*, Hilchot Chametz U'matza 7:6, Nusach Hahaggada.
19 It is worth noting that an oft-quoted declaration in the Sefer Hachinuch mirrors this point – for good and for bad. "After actions are the hearts drawn," the author of the Chinuch proclaims. An individual who involves him- or herself in productive, spiritually uplifting activities will be drawn to their positive message, while an individual who falls prey to negative pursuits will find those activities corrupting to his soul (*Sefer Hachinuch*, mitzva 16).

Expressions of Gratitude: The First Sections of Hallel

The matzot are covered, the wine cups are raised
and the first sections of Hallel are recited.

לְפִיכָךְ אֲנַחְנוּ חַיָּבִים לְהוֹדוֹת, לְהַלֵּל, לְשַׁבֵּחַ, לְפָאֵר, לְרוֹמֵם, לְהַדֵּר, לְבָרֵךְ, לְעַלֵּה וּלְקַלֵּס לְמִי שֶׁעָשָׂה לַאֲבוֹתֵינוּ וְלָנוּ אֶת כָּל הַנִּסִּים הָאֵלּוּ: הוֹצִיאָנוּ מֵעַבְדוּת לְחֵרוּת, מִיָּגוֹן לְשִׂמְחָה, וּמֵאֵבֶל לְיוֹם טוֹב, וּמֵאֲפֵלָה לְאוֹר גָּדוֹל, וּמִשִּׁעְבּוּד לִגְאֻלָּה. וְנֹאמַר לְפָנָיו שִׁירָה חֲדָשָׁה, הַלְלוּיָהּ.

Therefore, it is our duty to praise, to laud, to praise, to glorify, to exalt, to acclaim, to bless, to esteem and to honor the One Who wrought all these miracles for our forefathers and for us. He brought us out from slavery to freedom, from sorrow to joy, and from mourning to festivity, and from deep darkness to great light and from bondage to redemption. Let us recite before Him a new song. Praise the Lord!

הַלְלוּיָהּ. הַלְלוּ עַבְדֵי יי. הַלְלוּ אֶת שֵׁם יי. יְהִי שֵׁם יי מְבֹרָךְ מֵעַתָּה וְעַד עוֹלָם: מִמִּזְרַח שֶׁמֶשׁ עַד מְבוֹאוֹ, מְהֻלָּל שֵׁם יי. רָם עַל כָּל גּוֹיִם יי, עַל הַשָּׁמַיִם כְּבוֹדוֹ. מִי כַּיי אֱלֹהֵינוּ, הַמַּגְבִּיהִי לָשָׁבֶת, הַמַּשְׁפִּילִי לִרְאוֹת בַּשָּׁמַיִם וּבָאָרֶץ. מְקִימִי מֵעָפָר דָּל, מֵאַשְׁפֹּת יָרִים אֶבְיוֹן, לְהוֹשִׁיבִי עִם נְדִיבִים, עִם נְדִיבֵי עַמּוֹ. מוֹשִׁיבִי עֲקֶרֶת הַבַּיִת, אֵם הַבָּנִים שְׂמֵחָה. הַלְלוּיָהּ.

Praise the Lord! Offer praise, you servants of the Lord; praise the name of the Lord. May the name of the Lord be blessed from this time forth and forever. From the rising of the sun to its setting, praised is the name of the Lord. The Lord is high above all nations; His glory is above the heavens. Who is like the Lord, our God, Who dwells on high, Who looks down low upon heaven and upon earth! He raises the poor from the dust, He lifts forth the needy from the dunghill, that He may seat them with princes, even with the princes of His people. He seats the barren woman in her home, as the joyful mother of children. Praise the Lord!

בְּצֵאת יִשְׂרָאֵל מִמִּצְרַיִם, בֵּית יַעֲקֹב מֵעַם לֹעֵז, הָיְתָה יְהוּדָה לְקָדְשׁוֹ, יִשְׂרָאֵל מַמְשְׁלוֹתָיו. הַיָּם רָאָה וַיָּנֹס, הַיַּרְדֵּן יִסֹּב לְאָחוֹר. הֶהָרִים רָקְדוּ כְאֵילִים, גְּבָעוֹת כִּבְנֵי צֹאן. מַה לְּךָ הַיָּם כִּי תָנוּס, הַיַּרְדֵּן תִּסֹּב לְאָחוֹר? הֶהָרִים תִּרְקְדוּ כְאֵילִים, גְּבָעוֹת כִּבְנֵי צֹאן? מִלִּפְנֵי אָדוֹן חוּלִי אָרֶץ, מִלִּפְנֵי אֱלוֹהַּ יַעֲקֹב. הַהֹפְכִי הַצּוּר אֲגַם מָיִם, חַלָּמִישׁ לְמַעְיְנוֹ מָיִם.

When Israel went out of Egypt, the House of Jacob from a people of foreign tongue, Judah became His sanctuary, Israel His dominion. The sea saw and fled; the Jordan turned backward. The mountains skipped like rams, the hills like young sheep. What ails you, O sea, that you flee; O Jordan, that you turn backward? You mountains, that you skip like rams; you hills, like young sheep? Tremble, O Earth, at the presence of the Master, at the presence of the God of Jacob, Who turned the rock into a pool of water, the flint into a flowing spring.

Food for Thought

A. As noted in our introductory essay and in our sidebar concerning the mitzva of Hallel (pp. 2–3, 183–84), many scholars view the recitation of Hallel on the Seder night as unique, distinct from its recitation at other times of the year. A number of these authorities maintain that the section of Hallel recited at this point in the Seder is an integral part of Maggid, an essential component in the fulfillment of the mitzva of *sippur Yetziat Mitzrayim*. Our reexperience of the Exodus remains incomplete, these authorities argue, until we express our gratitude to God for our miraculous redemption.[20]

Just as each of the two previous stages of Maggid led us through the critical step from narrative to thanks, the third stage of Maggid does the same. In this case, however, the expression of gratitude, consisting of the first paragraphs of Hallel Hamitzri, the year-round Hallel, reflects back upon the Maggid as a whole. For this reason, these passages follow, rather than precede, the closing statement for the third stage of Maggid.

The Mishna's introduction to these passages of Hallel, quoted in the Haggada, seems to support the contention that they are part of Maggid: "Therefore, we are obligated to thank, to laud, to praise, to glorify..."[21]

According to the Mishnaic scholars, this section of Hallel rises seamlessly out of our Seder experience. Having noted, in the previous paragraph, our obligation to feel as if we personally left the Land of Egypt, we now take the next mandatory step by thanking God for our redemption.

B. With an incisive eye for detail, Rabbi Joseph Soloveitchik sees the essential role played by this section of Hallel as the solution to an apparent inconsistency in the Haggada text. In the introduction to this section of Hallel, we note our obligation to praise the God "Who did all these miracles *for our ancestors and for us.*" In the closing blessing following these paragraphs, however, we reverse the order, and bless the God "Who has *redeemed us and redeemed our ancestors.*" The Rav explains that when we thank God for a historical event, we first mention our forefathers, to whom the event occurred, and then we mention ourselves. When, however, we speak of an event that we have experienced ourselves, we speak first of our own redemption and then we reference the redemption of others.

Before reciting the first passages of Hallel, we cannot fully claim success in the task of seeing ourselves as if we personally left Egypt. Our Maggid obligation has not yet been fulfilled. At that point of the Seder, we can only speak of the Exodus as a historical event. Once, however, we lift our voices in grateful song, praising God for the goodness that He has bestowed upon us, we have fully integrated the Exodus

---

20 *Mishnat Ya'abetz* 18, 19. Rabbi Joseph Soloveitchik maintains that, although the Rambam views the year-round recitation of Hallel as a rabbinical mandate, he considers the obligation on the Seder night to be of biblical origin – an essential component in the mitzva of *sippur Yetziat Mitzrayim*. Genack, *The Seder Night: An Exalted Evening*, p. 104.

21 Mishna Pesachim 10:5.

experience. We can now speak of our own redemption before mentioning that of our ancestors.[22]

C. A critical question, however, remains. Why is Hallel "split" at the Seder? Why is one section of praise recited before the meal while the second section is reserved for after the meal?

D. Some authorities trace the splitting of Hallel to Temple times when an obligation existed to recite Hallel in conjunction with the Korban Pesach.[23] In order to demonstrate the connection between the *korban* and the prayers, Hallel was divided to surround the offering.[24]

The two sections of Hallel can also be seen as playing two different halachic roles at the Seder. As noted above, the passages recited before the meals are, according to many authorities, part and parcel of the biblical obligation of *sippur Yetziat Mitzrayim*. Without their recitation, our performance of that mitzva would be incomplete. In contrast, the passages after the meal may well rise out of the general obligation – categorized by many authorities as rabbinically derived – to praise God for the goodness that He provides throughout our lives. Rabbi Joseph Soloveitchik suggests this distinction in his studies on the Haggada and offers a series of supporting proofs.[25]

Finally, as noted in our introductory essay (see pp. 12–14), the splitting of Hallel can also be seen as motivated by the structure of the Seder as a whole. To facilitate the evening's task of entering the flow of Jewish history, the Seder is structurally designed to mirror that flow. After a series of preliminary rituals, all of the passages in the Haggada that are recited before the meal focus primarily *on the past*. All of the passages recited after the meal focus *on the future*. And the meal itself reflects *the present* – a meal like no other, surrounded by the flow of the Jewish national journey.

Hallel is thus divided into two sections to comply with the Seder's overall construction. The portions of Hallel recited before the meal deal with thanks and praise for *past events*, while the portions recited after the meal focus on praise and prayer for the *ultimate redemption that is yet to come.*

---

22 Genack, *The Seder Night: An Exalted Evening*, pp. 101–2.
23 Mishna Pesachim 9:3.
24 Maharal, *Gevurot Hashem* 62.
25 Genack, *The Seder Night: An Exalted Evening*, p. 105.

Concluding Blessing and the Second Cup of Wine

With wineglasses still raised, the Maggid closes with a culminating
blessing, followed by the blessing over the wine.
(On Saturday night, substitute the portion in parentheses.)

בָּרוּךְ אַתָּה יי אֱלֹהֵינוּ מֶלֶךְ הָעוֹלָם, אֲשֶׁר גְּאָלָנוּ וְגָאַל אֶת אֲבוֹתֵינוּ מִמִּצְרַיִם,
וְהִגִּיעָנוּ לַלַּיְלָה הַזֶּה לֶאֱכָל בּוֹ מַצָּה וּמָרוֹר. כֵּן יי אֱלֹהֵינוּ וֵאלֹהֵי אֲבוֹתֵינוּ,
יַגִּיעֵנוּ לְמוֹעֲדִים וְלִרְגָלִים אֲחֵרִים, הַבָּאִים לִקְרָאתֵנוּ לְשָׁלוֹם, שְׂמֵחִים בְּבִנְיַן
עִירֶךָ, וְשָׂשִׂים בַּעֲבוֹדָתֶךָ, וְנֹאכַל שָׁם מִן הַזְּבָחִים וּמִן הַפְּסָחִים (במוצאי שבת
אומרים: מִן הַפְּסָחִים וּמִן הַזְּבָחִים), אֲשֶׁר יַגִּיעַ דָּמָם עַל קִיר מִזְבַּחֲךָ לְרָצוֹן,
וְנוֹדֶה לְךָ שִׁיר חָדָשׁ עַל גְּאֻלָּתֵנוּ וְעַל פְּדוּת נַפְשֵׁנוּ. בָּרוּךְ אַתָּה יי גָּאַל יִשְׂרָאֵל.
בָּרוּךְ אַתָּה יי אֱלֹהֵינוּ מֶלֶךְ הָעוֹלָם, בּוֹרֵא פְּרִי הַגָּפֶן.

Blessed are You, Lord, our God, King of the universe, Who has redeemed us and
redeemed our fathers from Egypt, and enabled us to attain this night to eat
matzah and *maror*. So too, Lord, our God and God of our fathers, enable us to
attain other holidays and festivals that will come to us in peace, gladdened in the
rebuilding of Your city, and rejoicing in Your [Temple] service. Then we shall eat of
the sacrifices and of the Korban Pesach (*on Motzaei Shabbat say*: of the Korban
Pesach and of the sacrifices), whose blood shall be sprinkled on the wall of Your
altar for acceptance. And we shall thank You with a new song for our redemption
and for the deliverance of our souls. Blessed are You, God, Who redeemed Israel.

Blessed are You, Lord, our God, King of the universe,
Who creates the fruit of the vine

The second cup of wine is consumed, while leaning to the left.

Food for Thought

A. The concluding blessing of Maggid reflects our accomplishments over the course of this lengthy central section of the Seder.

Fully immersed in our nation's historical flow, we can now experience past, present and future simultaneously.

We are thus able to bless our God:

1. "Who has redeemed us and redeemed our ancestors from Egypt." The Exodus has become for us immediate and real. We have personally experienced our nation's past.

2. "Who has enabled us to reach this night to eat matza and *maror*." The significance of present responsibilities is recognized and noted. Our current roles, as participants in the perpetuation of Jewish tradition and as contributors to the fabric of Jewish life, are real and clear to us.

3. Who will, we pray, enable us "to reach other holidays and festivals...gladdened in the building of Your city and rejoicing in Your service..." Future redemption is not a vague dream, but rather, with God's help and our efforts, a certainty. We are a destiny-driven people traveling toward a clear goal. We recognize our own responsibilities as participants in that directed journey.

רָחְצָה

מוֹצִיא מַצָּה

מָרוֹר

כּוֹרֵךְ

שֻׁלְחָן עוֹרֵךְ

צָפוּן

בָּרֵךְ

Seder Unit III
The Present

Seder Sections: Rachtza, Motzi Matza, Maror, Korech, Shulchan Orech, Tzafun, Barech

Having completed Maggid's step-by-step journey toward the fulfillment of the mitzva of *sippur Yetziat Mitzraim*, we are now ready to enter the third unit of the Seder evening with its focus on current challenge and responsibility.

The past interweaves with the present as we consume the matza and maror, in fulfillment of biblical and rabbinic obligations respectively; we join together in a festive Seder meal culminating with the eating of the afikomen (the portion of matza hidden away since the Seder's beginning); and we raise our voices in Birkat Hamazon, the Grace after Meals, as we thank God for the bounty divinely bestowed upon us.

A brief but extremely significant transitional ritual follows Birkat Hamazon.

Seder Section 6 • RACHTZA
The Second Washing of Hands

In preparation for the eating of the matza, the Seder participants wash their hands. Rabbinic law requires *netilat yadayim*, the washing of hands, before the consumption of bread year-round. As we prepare to eat matza – the Pesach bread – we therefore perform this familiar ritual.

> The washing cup is taken in the right hand, passed to the left hand, and water is poured twice over the right hand. The cup is then passed to the right hand and water is poured twice over the left hand. In contrast to the first handwashing at the Seder's beginning (Urchatz), during which no blessing was recited, the following *bracha* is now recited before the hands are fully dried:

בָּרוּךְ אַתָּה יי אֱלֹהֵינוּ מֶלֶךְ הָעוֹלָם, אֲשֶׁר קִדְּשָׁנוּ בְּמִצְוֹתָיו וְצִוָּנוּ עַל נְטִילַת יָדָיִם.

Blessed are You, Lord, our God, King of the universe, Who has sanctified us with His commandments and commanded us concerning the washing of the hands.

Food for Thought

A. As noted previously (see pp. 46–47), the obligation of handwashing before the consumption of bread is based upon two distinct foundations in rabbinic thought.

The first of these foundations traces to the Temple period, when a state of ritual purity was required for the handling and consumption of *teruma* – foodstuffs designated for the Kohanim, the priestly caste. In order to ensure that the populace would grow accustomed to maintaining the laws of purity when necessary, the rabbis decreed handwashing for bread, as well.[1]

The second foundation focuses on the dignified comportment that God generally requires from His people. By requiring handwashing before the consumption of bread, man's most basic nourishment, the rabbis seek to remind each Jew of his or her fundamental requirement to act at all times in a dignified, even sanctified, manner.[2]

B. The ritual of *netilat yadayim* provides us with an opportunity to focus on a basic general rule concerning *birchot hamitzva*, blessings recited over the performance of a mitzva.

The Talmudic authorities maintain that such blessings should always be recited *immediately prior* to the fulfillment of the commandments involved.[3]

As the mitzva of *netilat yadayim* is completed upon the drying of one's hands

---

1 Talmud Bavli Chullin 106a.
2 *Aruch Hashulchan*, Orach Chaim 158:3.
3 Talmud Bavli Pesachim 7b.

after their ritual washing, the blessing is recited immediately before, or as, the hands are dried.[4] Similarly, the blessings over tefillin are recited after the tefillin boxes have been placed on the arm and head but before they are adjusted,[5] and the blessing over the Shabbat (and, according to some customs, festival) candles is recited after they are lit, but before benefitting from their light (after kindling the candles, a woman closes her eyes, recites the blessing, then opens her eyes to benefit from the light [see p. 29]).[6]

---

4   *Mishna Berura* 158:42.
5   *Shulchan Aruch*, Orach Chaim 25:8; Rema, ibid.
6   Rema, *Shulchan Aruch*, Orach Chaim 263:5.

Seder Section 7 • MOTZI MATZA
The Consumption of Matza

After all the Seder participants have washed their hands and returned to the table, the leader of the Seder lifts the three matzot (the two whole matzot with the broken piece created at Yachatz between them) and recites the following blessing:

בָּרוּךְ אַתָּה יי אֱלֹהֵינוּ מֶלֶךְ הָעוֹלָם, הַמּוֹצִיא לֶחֶם מִן הָאָרֶץ.

Blessed are You, Lord, our God, King of the universe, Who brings forth bread from the earth.

The bottom matza is then put down and, with the top matza and the broken piece still in his hands, the leader of the Seder recites the following blessing:

בָּרוּךְ אַתָּה יי אֱלֹהֵינוּ מֶלֶךְ הָעוֹלָם, אֲשֶׁר קִדְּשָׁנוּ בְּמִצְוֹתָיו וְצִוָּנוּ עַל אֲכִילַת מַצָּה.

Blessed are You, Lord, our God, King of the universe, Who has sanctified us with His commandments and commanded us concerning the eating of matza.

Each of the Seder participants consumes a *kezayit*, minimum "olive-sized" portion, of the top matza and a *kezayit* of the broken matza while leaning to the left (see pp. 152–53, the sidebar concerning the mitzva of matza, for the exact amount that should be eaten). If necessary, additional matzot are used to ensure that all participants are able to consume the required amount.

Food for Thought

A. Some authorities require the use of only two matzot for Motzi Matza: a whole matza and the broken piece created at Yachatz (Seder section 4, above).[1] The prevailing practice, however, is to use three matzot – the broken piece between two whole matzot – in order to fulfill the year-round requirement for *lechem mishneh*, two whole loaves of bread (in this case, matzot), at Shabbat and festival meals.[2]

During the recitation of the *bracha* of *hamotzi*, the blessing recited on bread throughout the year, all three matzot are raised. In this way, the blessing references the *lechem mishneh*.

When *al achilat matza*, the specific blessing for matza, is recited, however, only those matzot associated with the unique obligation of the Seder night should be held. During the recitation of this *bracha*,

---

1 Rambam, *Mishneh Torah*, Hilchot Chametz U'matza 8:6; *Biur Hagra* (Vilna Gaon), *Shulchan Aruch*, Orach Chaim 472: 4.
2 *Shulchan Aruch*, Orach Chaim 473:4.

therefore, the bottom matza is put down, while the top whole matza and the broken piece remain in the leader's hands.

B. For continued discussion: the surviving mitzva.

In the course of a heartfelt plea to the Jewish community of the Italian city of Trieste, the renowned eighteenth–nineteenth-century halachic authority the Chatam Sofer offers a powerful observation concerning the mitzva of *achilat matza* (the consumption of matza).

This great scholar admonishes the leaders of Trieste for having allowed lax standards to develop in the supervision of the baking and preparation of matzot for Pesach. Urging the adoption of the supervisory standards practiced in his own community, the Chatam Sofer notes that of the numerous biblical mandates requiring the consumption of specific foods, only the consumption of matza remains in full force across time. Until the rebuilding of the Temple, the obligation to consume such foods as the Korban Pesach, *teruma* (the

priestly portions), *ma'aser* (the portions given to the Levites), sacrificial meats, etc., do not apply. "Only one mitzva of this type remains from year to year," the Chatam Sofer implores, "and if that mitzva will not be properly observed...will that find favor in God's eyes?"[3]

The observation of the Chatam Sofer could well serve as a starting point for continued consideration of the unique significance of matza. Why, indeed, of all mitzvot of its type has only matza survived?

Might the answer be found in some of the extraordinary characteristics of matza previously discussed, including this symbol's dynamic ability to capture the transitional moment from slavery to freedom, its message that each moment is a moment of potential transition, its reflection of the ever-changing nature of Jewish history, and its representation of humility and purity? These and other possibilities are worthy of ongoing discussion, as we consider the unique nature of the "surviving" mitzva of matza.

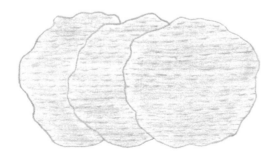

---

3   *She'eilot U'tshuvot Chatam Sofer* 196, in Hashmatot.

The Primary Mitzvot of the Seder
ACHILAT MATZA: The Consumption of Matza

A. The biblical obligation to consume matza on the Seder night emerges from the passage "In the first [month], on the fourteenth day of the month in the evening, you shall eat matzot..."[4]

B. Although women are generally exempt from biblical time-bound mitzvot, they are required to participate in the mitzva of *achilat matza*. Based on a connection drawn in the Torah between the eating of matza and the prohibition of *chametz*,[5] the rabbis conclude: "All those who are included in the prohibition of consuming *chametz* are included in the requirement to consume matza."[6]

C. Although the Torah states, "Seven days shall you eat matzot...,"[7] the rabbis determine from a combination of texts that the obligation to consume matza is limited to the first night(s) of Pesach. The biblical admonition concerning matza after that point is designed to underscore the prohibition of *chametz*.[8] Some authorities do maintain, however, that while one is not obligated to eat matza on the remaining days of Pesach, such consumption is still considered a mitzva.[9]

D. Various opinions are found among the authorities concerning the exact measure of matza that must be consumed at various points in the Seder. At issue is the measurement of a *kezayit* (the "olive-sized" portion required as a minimum for the basic mitzva) and whether or not that minimum measure must be doubled in the fulfillment of certain rituals. Accepted practice requires portions minimally equivalent to one-half of a hand-baked matza or two-thirds of a machine-baked matza for Motzi Matza; one-fourth of a hand-baked matza or one-third of a machine-baked matza for Korech; one-half of a hand-baked matza or two-thirds of a machine-baked matza for the afikomen. In cases of difficulty, portions equivalent to one-quarter of a hand-baked matza or one-third of a machine-baked matza can be used to fulfill all requirements.[10]

E. The authorities differ as to which consumption of matza at the Seder marks the actual fulfillment of the mitzva. While many scholars maintain that the mitzva is discharged with the eating of matzot during Motzi Matza as the meal begins,[11] others argue that the principal mitzva is the consumption of the afikomen at the meal's end.[12]

---

4   Shmot 12:18.
5   Devarim 16:3.
6   Talmud Bavli Pesachim 43b.
7   Shmot 12:15.
8   Rashi, Shmot 12:15.
9   Chizkuni, Shmot 12:18; *She'eilot U'tshuvot Chatam Sofer*, Yoreh Deah 191; *Aruch Hashulchan*, Ohr Hachaim 476:18.
10 Rabbi Shimon Eider, *Halachos of Pesach* (Jerusalem: Feldheim, 1985).
11 Rosh, Pesachim 10:34; *Sefer Hachinuch*, mitzva 21; Me'iri, Pesachim 119b.
12 Rashi and Rashbam, Pesachim 119b.

F. As noted earlier (see pp. 69–70), the Talmudic tractate of Pesachim records a debate between Rabbi Elazar ben Azarya and Rabbi Akiva concerning the time by which the Korban Pesach was to be consumed on the Seder night. Rabbi Elazar ben Azarya maintains that the ritual had to be completed by midnight,[13] while Rabbi Akiva argues that participants were allowed to consume the Korban Pesach until dawn.[14]

Based upon a textual connection drawn in the Torah,[15] the later Talmudic scholar Rava concludes that the consumption of matza on the Seder night is subject to the same time constraints as the Korban Pesach.[16]

Because many early authorities codify the law according to Rabbi Elazar ben Azarya and because others argue that even Rabbi Akiva agrees to the earlier time limit as preferable, the majority of halachic decisors decree that the mitzva of *achilat matza* should be performed before midnight. If one delayed past that time, the matza should still be eaten, but the *bracha* of *al achilat matza* should be omitted.[17]

---

13 In halachic matters dependent upon times of day, points such as midnight and midday will fluctuate based upon the solar calendar. The night is divided into twelve equal parts, each part constituting a halachic hour. Midnight on any particular night falls after the passage of six halachic hours.

14 Talmud Bavli Pesachim 120b.

15 Shmot 12:8.

16 Talmud Bavli Pesachim 120b.

17 See *Biur Halacha*, Orach Chaim 477, s.v. "V'yehei zahir," for a full discussion of the issue.

Seder Section 8 • MAROR
The Consumption of Bitter Herbs

Each Seder participant selects a *kezayit* of *maror* (see pp. 156–57, the halachic sidebar on *achilat maror*, for the exact amount), dips the *maror* into the *charoset*, shakes off some of the *charoset* and recites the following blessing:

בָּרוּךְ אַתָּה יְיָ אֱלֹהֵינוּ מֶלֶךְ הָעוֹלָם, אֲשֶׁר קִדְּשָׁנוּ בְּמִצְוֹתָיו וְצִוָּנוּ עַל אֲכִילַת מָרוֹר.

Blessed are You, Lord, our God, King of the universe, Who has sanctified us with His commandments and commanded us concerning the eating of *maror*.

The *maror* is consumed without leaning to the left.

Food for Thought

A. For continued discussion: a critical distinction...

A fundamental halachic distinction between the consumption of matza and *maror* underscores their respective roles at the Seder and conveys an important life lesson in the process.

The rabbis maintain that if an individual swallows matza without tasting it, he has performed the mitzva, albeit not in a preferred manner. In contrast, however, an individual who swallows the *maror* without allowing it to be tasted has not performed the mitzva at all.[1]

Matza's impact emerges from its intrinsic character and its inherent symbolism. Matza stands alone and does not derive its significance from its physical affect upon us.

Maror, on the other hand, possesses no independent symbolism. A means to an end, this substance gains its value solely from the way in which it affects each of us.

As always, the symbolic world serves as a paradigm for life.

There are phenomena in our environment that exist independently of us, and we ignore their autonomous value at our own peril.

What price are we paying – and will future generations pay – for centuries of insensitivity to the natural world around us? How many interpersonal human relationships are fundamentally flawed because the individuals involved see each other only in terms of their own potential benefit and fail to recognize the independent value of the "other"?

At the same time, however, there are phenomena in our surrounding world that acquire their meaning only via their practical impact upon our lives.

A bush burning in the wilderness is only significant if Moshe sees it and reacts. Presented opportunities have no

---

1   Talmud Bavli Pesachim 115b.

independent value. Their significance is realized only when we note them, understand them and bring them to fruition.

B. For continued discussion: adapting versus accepting.

As we have noted (see introductory essay and sidebar), the biblical obligation of *achilat maror*, the consumption of *maror*, does not apply in the absence of the Korban Pesach. Today, the mitzva is a rabbinic requirement, performed in remembrance of the Temple. The *maror* provides us with an opportunity to consider the crucial difference between adapting to reality and accepting reality.

The survival of the Jewish nation has clearly depended upon its ability to adapt to vastly changing circumstances. History has required us to transform ourselves from a people on our land to a "wandering nation," pushed from country to country, forced to find ways to exist in ever-shifting circumstances and surroundings. While we have tragically lost many of our number along the way, we are still here, against all odds, to tell the tale.

Counterintuitively, however, the key to our success does not lie in adaptability alone, but in its balance with an opposing force. We have survived because, while we have *adapted to* reality, we have not *accepted* reality.

From the time of his exile, the Jew has always looked upon his surroundings with a jaundiced eye, believing that he lives in a flawed reality. Until the return to his land, until the glorious culmination of his historical journey, the world in which he lives is simply unacceptable.

No set of edicts within Jewish tradition mirrors this truth more clearly than those rabbinic rules, such as the consumption of *maror* in our time, mandated *zecher l'Mikdash* (as a remembrance of the Temple) and *zecher l'Churban* (as a remembrance of the Temple's destruction).

Established as "pinpricks of discomfort" woven into the very fabric of Jewish life, these laws serve as an ever-present reminder that all is not as it should be and that it is the Jews' responsibility to make it better.

A number of years ago, during a visit to Jerusalem, my wife and I were relaxing at an outdoor café in the crowded pedestrian mall at Ben Yehuda Street when an alarm was raised announcing a suspicious object in the middle of the mall. Immediately, an area was cleared for the police to examine the object, and if necessary, deal with the danger. Astoundingly, however, on the periphery of the cleared area, everyone just sat down again and calmly resumed their conversations over coffee.

The citizens of Israel have heroically adapted to their often difficult reality, recognizing that victory lies in the continuity of normal life and in the triumph of steadfastness over fear.

At the same time, however, loudly and vociferously, the citizens of Israel have refused to accept that reality. No voice has been stronger than theirs in defense of principled morality across the globe; no one has been firmer in the quest for peace; no one has sacrificed more to establish an island of democracy in a sea of instability and violence.

To adapt but not accept remains one of the secrets of Jewish survival to this day.

The Primary Mitzvot of the Seder
ACHILAT MAROR: The Consumption of Maror

A. With the commandment *"U'matzot al merorim yochluhu"* (And matzot, with bitter herbs shall they eat it [the Korban Pesach]),[2] the Torah mandates the consumption of both matza and *maror* in conjunction with the Korban Pesach. Unlike matza, however, *maror* is not commanded again independently in the text.[3] Based on this distinction, the scholars conclude that while a biblical obligation to eat matza on the first night of Pesach remains in force even in the absence of the Korban Pesach, the biblical obligation to eat *maror* does not.[4] Nonetheless, the rabbis mandate that *maror* should remain at the Seder to this day, as a remembrance of the rituals performed during Temple times.[5] The consumption of *maror* at our Seder, therefore, is no longer performed in fulfillment of a biblical commandment, but in fulfillment of a rabbinic edict, *zecher l'Mikdash* (in remembrance of the Temple).

B. The blessing of *Borei pri ha'adama* (He Who creates the fruit of the ground), usually recited before the consumption of vegetables, is notably absent in conjunction with the eating of the *maror*. This omission is explained by the rabbis in a number of ways:

1. Some scholars maintain that the blessing recited earlier over the *karpas* (see p. 48) fulfilled the requirement for the blessing over *maror*, as well.[6]

2. Other authorities point to the general law that a blessing over bread establishes a meal and fulfills the obligation for all blessings pertaining to foodstuffs that are part of that meal. As *maror* is a component of the meal covered by the *bracha* over the matza, these scholars therefore maintain, the *maror* requires no additional blessing.[7]

3. Finally, other scholars argue that the general blessing over vegetables simply does not apply to *maror*. This blessing falls into the category of *birchot hanehenin*, blessings recited before gaining benefit from objects and phenomena in our environment. The consumption of *maror*, these scholars argue, conveys no personal benefit, as it is eaten solely as a reminder of the bitterness of slavery.[8]

C. The Mishna lists a series of vegetables through which one may fulfill the mitzva of *achilat maror*. The exact identification of these vegetables remains the subject of discussion from Talmudic times onward.

The first vegetable listed in the Mishna, *chazeret*, is identified by most authorities as romaine lettuce and is considered the preferred choice for *maror* because of its prioritized place in the Mishna.

---

2 Shmot 12:8.
3 Shmot 12:18.
4 Talmud Bavli Pesachim 120a.
5 *Shulchan Aruch Harav*, Orach Chaim 475:12.
6 Rashi, Rashbam, Rosh, Pesachim 114b.
7 Tosafot, Brachot 41b, s.v. "L'hachi"; Pesachim 119, s.v. "V'hadar."
8 *Shulchan Aruch*, Ohr Hachaim, Chok Yaakov, quoting the *Sefer Mitzvot Gedolot* 473:29; Magen Avraham 475:10.

While romaine lettuce is certainly not the most "bitter" of the possibilities offered, the Talmud Yerushalmi sees this substance as most clearly mirroring the experience of our ancestors in Egypt: "Just as *chazeret* is initially sweet and ultimately bitter, so did the Egyptians deal with our forefathers in Egypt." [9]

The initial descent of our forefathers to Egypt at the close of the patriarchal era was marked by an apparent welcome from Pharaoh and his subjects. This welcome, however, soon disintegrated into persecution, enslavement and murder, as the Egyptians turned against the Israelites, their erstwhile "guests."

D. The amount of *maror* required for fulfillment of the mitzva is once again a *kezayit* of the substance used. In the case of romaine lettuce, this entails consumption of a piece that covers roughly 8 x 10 inches.

E. Special care should be taken to ensure that, if lettuce is used, it is free of insects.

---

9   Talmud Yerushalmi Pesachim 2:5.

Seder Section 9 • KORECH
The Consumption of a Sandwich of Matza and Maror

Each Seder participant takes a *kezayit* of the bottom matza and a *kezayit* of *maror* (see the halachic sidebars, pp. 152–53 and 156–57, for the appropriate amounts) and combines them into a sandwich. If necessary, additional matzot are used to enable each participant to consume the required amount.

Many authorities maintain that the *maror* should be dipped into *charoset* before being placed in the sandwich. In the absence of a family custom to the contrary, one should do so.

The following formula is recited:

זֵכֶר לְמִקְדָּשׁ כְּהִלֵּל: כֵּן עָשָׂה הִלֵּל בִּזְמַן שֶׁבֵּית הַמִּקְדָּשׁ הָיָה קַיָּם. הָיָה כּוֹרֵךְ [פֶּסַח] מַצָּה וּמָרוֹר וְאוֹכֵל בְּיַחַד, לְקַיֵּם מַה שֶׁנֶּאֱמַר: "עַל מַצּוֹת וּמְרוֹרִים יֹאכְלֻהוּ."

As a remembrance of the Temple according to [the practice of] Hillel: Thus did Hillel do during the period of the Temple's existence. He would combine [the Korban Pesach], matza and *maror* and eat them together, to comply with the verse that says, "with matzot and bitter herbs shall they eat it [the Korban Pesach]."[1]

The sandwich is consumed while leaning to the left.

Food for Thought

A. The Talmud records a dispute between Hillel and his rabbinic colleagues concerning the meaning of the verse "with matzot and bitter herbs shall they eat it [the Korban Pesach]."[2]

Interpreting the verse literally, Hillel maintains that the matza and *maror* should be eaten together. His rabbinic colleagues argue that the two should be eaten separately.[3]

B. Later scholars debate the extent of each of these positions, arguing whether Hillel and/ or his colleagues are staking out the preferable or the required modes of observance.[4]

The Talmud concludes that since the law has not been decided conclusively in favor of either Hillel or his colleagues, proper procedure is to eat the matza separately, then eat the *maror* separately and finally to eat them together.[5]

---

1 Bamidbar 9:11.
2 Bamidbar 9:11.
3 Talmud Bavli Pesachim 115a.
4 See Rashbam, Ramban, Tosafot, Me'iri, Maharsha and other commentaries on Pesachim 115a for a discussion of the issues.
5 Talmud Bavli, ibid.

C. Most authorities maintain that the Talmud's concern for Hillel's position is limited to the Temple period. After the Temple's destruction, the suspension of the Korban Pesach, and the transition of *maror* from a biblical to a rabbinic requirement, these scholars argue, even Hillel would agree that the mitzvot of matza and *maror* should be performed separately.

The ritual of Korech is thus observed today, as our Haggadot instruct us to state: *"Zecher l'Mikdash k'Hillel,"* as a remembrance of the Temple period practice according to the opinion of Hillel.

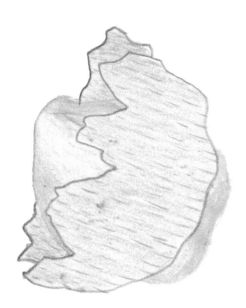

Seder Section 10 • SHULCHAN ORECH
The Seder Meal

A festive Seder meal is shared by all present.

Food for Thought

A. Important advisory: the Seder meal is not a break, a recess or an intermission in the Seder.

As indicated in our introductory essay "Making Sense of the Seder III" (see pp. 12–14), the Seder could well have been constructed differently, with all of the rituals and liturgy preceding or following the meal. What logic is there in the placement of the meal not only in the middle of the Seder proceedings, but in the middle of the recitation of Hallel?

The answer, as we have suggested above, lies in the Seder's tripartite structure. After a series of preliminary rituals, all of the passages in the Haggada that are recited before the meal focus primarily on the past. All of the passage recited following the meal, until the Seder's end, focus on the future. And the meal itself? The meal is meant to reflect the present. The Seder feast is truly a repast like no other in our experience – a meal literally surrounded by the past and future of Jewish history. This is a meal during which we are truly meant to explore the present, to examine our own place in the unfolding story of the Jewish nation.

B. Rabbi Joseph Soloveitchik identifies three dimensions of time awareness (see pp. 13–14): (1) retrospection, the reexperiencing of the past; (2) anticipation, the projecting of our vision and aspirations into the future; and (3) appreciation, the valuing of the present. Of these, the most difficult to attain is appreciation.

Within this dimension, we are challenged to view our lives through the lens of history. One hundred, two hundred, five hundred years from now, how will our time and our contribution to Jewish life be judged? No other moment on the calendar year is more appropriate for this assessment than the Seder meal.

C. For continued discussion: an exploration of the present.

Many difficult questions can and should be raised as we engage those at our Seder table in an exploration of the present. These questions might include: What is the quality of our religious commitment and observance – are we committed to halacha or to compromise? How accurate is the often-heard assessment that Jewish observance today lacks passion and spirituality? If this assessment is correct, what can be done about it? Are we successfully transmitting a sense of Jewish commitment to our children and grandchildren? How can we improve? Could today's committed American Jewish community do more to stem the rising tide of assimilation beyond its walls?

How will the diaspora community be judged years from now for continuing to live in a "diaspora of choice"? At a time when the possibility of return to Israel is personally available to us all, are we failing to meet the challenge of Jewish history by remaining where we are? Are we sensitive enough to the signs of a world changing around us? How should we respond to those signs?

What are our responsibilities as Jews to defend the rights of others?

On this night of history, these and other questions should be raised and debated.

Seder Section 11 • TZAFUN
The Eating of the Afikomen

At the conclusion of the meal, the afikomen (the broken piece of matza remaining from Yachatz) is retrieved (often from the children, who have "stolen" it and now barter for its return).

Each Seder participant consumes a portion of the afikomen equivalent to a *kezayit* while leaning to the left. Many authorities maintain that two such portions should be consumed (see halachic sidebar on *achilat matza*, pp. 152–53, for the recommended amounts). If necessary, additional matzot are used to ensure that all participants are able to consume the required amount. Every effort should be made to consume the matza before halachic midnight.[1]

Food for Thought

A. What exactly is the afikomen? What is the significance of this last remaining piece of matza, consumed as the "dessert" of the Seder meal?

B. The term *afikomen* first appears in halachic literature in the Mishnaic statement *"Ein maftirin achar haPesach afikomen"* (One may not, after the consumption of the Passover offering, conclude the meal with an afikomen).[2] While debate ensues in the Talmud concerning the interpretation of this mandate, the majority of scholars consider the term *afikomen* to be a word of Greek origin, referring to the wine, fruits and sweets that were commonly brought to the table at the end of a meal. The Mishna, referencing the time when the full Pesach ritual was yet observed, prohibits the eating of any *"afikomen"* or dessert after the consumption of the Korban Pesach.[3] In our day, the term is applied to indicate that the matza consumed at this point in the Seder must be the final course of the meal. No other food should be consumed on the Seder evening after we eat the matza afikomen.

C. Although all agree that the afikomen should be the last course of the Seder meal, dispute rages among the classical commentaries as to the exact significance and meaning of this "matza dessert." Strikingly, a number of authorities, including Rashi and the Rashbam, maintain that the afikomen is actually the *matzat mitzva*, the portion of matza consumed in fulfillment of the biblical mandate to eat matza on the Seder night. According to these scholars, the *bracha* of *achilat matza*, the blessing

---

1 As explained earlier, halachic midnight is determined by dividing the night into twelve equal "halachic hours." Midnight falls at the end of the sixth halachic hour.
2 Mishna Pesachim 10:8.
3 Talmud Bavli Pesachim 119b.

referencing the mitzva of matza, should have been recited at this point, rather than over the matzot at the beginning of the meal. On a technical level, however, reciting the blessing after the evening's first consumption of matza would have been inappropriate. These scholars therefore maintain that the blessing should be recited over the matza at the beginning of the meal, with the intent to include the afikomen under the blessing's rubric.[4]

Other scholars insist that the obligatory consumption of matza is fulfilled with the portions consumed at the meal's beginning. The afikomen, these authorities argue, is a rabbinic innovation, consumed at the meal's end in remembrance of the Korban Pesach, which was originally required to be the meal's last course.[5]

Finally, a third group of commentaries, agreeing that the primary mitzva of matza took place of the beginning of the meal, simply view the afikomen as a rabbinically ordained means of ensuring that the taste of the matza will linger in our mouths long after the meal has ended.[6]

---

4   Rashi, Rashbam, Pesachim 119b.
5   Rosh, Pesachim 34; *Sefer Hachinuch*, mitzva 21.
6   Tosafot, Pesachim 120a.

Seder Section 12 • BARECH
The Grace after Meals

The third cup of wine is poured, and the familiar Birkat Hamazon (Grace after Meals) is recited. Care should be taken to include the special additions for Pesach (as well as those for Shabbat, when appropriate).

If three or more males over the age of thirteen are present, a communal introduction is recited (see below). In that case, the leader raises his wine glass during the recitation of the grace. Some have a custom in which all present at the Seder raise their glasses.

The following psalm is recited as an introduction to the Birkat Hamazon. Some add the text in small print.

שִׁיר הַמַּעֲלוֹת בְּשׁוּב יי אֶת שִׁיבַת צִיּוֹן הָיִינוּ כְּחֹלְמִים. אָז יִמָּלֵא שְׂחוֹק פִּינוּ
וּלְשׁוֹנֵנוּ רִנָּה. אָז יֹאמְרוּ בַגּוֹיִם הִגְדִּיל יי לַעֲשׂוֹת עִם אֵלֶּה. הִגְדִּיל יי לַעֲשׂוֹת
עִמָּנוּ הָיִינוּ שְׂמֵחִים. שׁוּבָה יי אֶת שְׁבִיתֵנוּ כַּאֲפִיקִים בַּנֶּגֶב. הַזֹּרְעִים בְּדִמְעָה
בְּרִנָּה יִקְצֹרוּ. הָלוֹךְ יֵלֵךְ וּבָכֹה נֹשֵׂא מֶשֶׁךְ הַזָּרַע, בֹּא יָבֹא בְרִנָּה נֹשֵׂא אֲלֻמֹּתָיו.
תְּהִלַּת יי יְדַבֶּר פִּי וִיבָרֵךְ שֵׁם קָדְשׁוֹ לְעוֹלָם וָעֶד. וַאֲנַחְנוּ נְבָרֵךְ יָהּ מֵעַתָּה וְעַד עוֹלָם, הַלְלוּיָהּ.
הוֹדוּ לַיי כִּי טוֹב, כִּי לְעוֹלָם חַסְדּוֹ. מִי יְמַלֵּל גְּבוּרוֹת יי יַשְׁמִיעַ כָּל תְּהִלָּתוֹ.

A song of ascents: When the Lord returns the exiles of Zion, we will have been as dreamers. Then our mouths will be filled with laughter, and our tongues with joyous song. Then will they say among the nations, "The Lord has done great things with them." The Lord has done great things with us, we are rejoiced. Lord, return our exiles as streams in the Negev. Those who sow in tears, with joyous song will reap. Though he goes weeping on his way, he who bears the measure of seed; he shall return in joyful song, he who bears his sheaves.[1]

My mouth will utter the praise of the Lord, and all flesh shall bless His holy name forever and ever.[2] And we will bless the Lord from now and forever, praise the Lord![3] Give thanks to the Lord, for He is good; for His loving-kindness endures forever.[4] Who can describe the mighty deeds of the Lord, or make known all of His praises?[5]

---

1   Tehillim 126.
2   Tehillim 145:21.
3   Tehillim 115:18.
4   Tehillim 118:1.
5   Tehillim 106:2.

If three or more adult men are present at the Seder, one is chosen to lead the Grace after Meals and begins with the following introduction.

When ten or more adult men are present, the words in parentheses ("our God") are substituted for the word "He."

Leader:

Gentlemen, let us say grace!

רַבּוֹתַי נְבָרֵךְ!

The others respond:

May the name of the Lord be blessed from now and forever.

יְהִי שֵׁם יי מְבֹרָךְ מֵעַתָּה וְעַד עוֹלָם.

Leader:

May the name of the Lord be blessed from now and forever. With the permission of the masters, teachers and gentlemen, let us bless He (our God) of Whose bounty we have eaten.

יְהִי שֵׁם יי מְבֹרָךְ מֵעַתָּה וְעַד עוֹלָם.
בִּרְשׁוּת מָרָנָן וְרַבָּנָן וְרַבּוֹתַי,
נְבָרֵךְ (אֱלֹהֵינוּ) שֶׁאָכַלְנוּ מִשֶּׁלוֹ.

The others respond:

Blessed be He (our God) of Whose bounty we have eaten and through Whose kindness we live.

בָּרוּךְ (אֱלֹהֵינוּ) שֶׁאָכַלְנוּ מִשֶּׁלוֹ
וּבְטוּבוֹ חָיִינוּ.

Leader:

Blessed be He (our God) of Whose bounty we have eaten and through Whose kindness we live. Blessed be He and blessed be His name.

בָּרוּךְ (אֱלֹהֵינוּ) שֶׁאָכַלְנוּ מִשֶּׁלוֹ
וּבְטוּבוֹ חָיִינוּ. בָּרוּךְ הוּא וּבָרוּךְ שְׁמוֹ.

בָּרוּךְ אַתָּה יי אֱלֹהֵינוּ מֶלֶךְ הָעוֹלָם, הַזָּן אֶת הָעוֹלָם כֻּלּוֹ בְּטוּבוֹ בְּחֵן בְּחֶסֶד וּבְרַחֲמִים. הוּא נוֹתֵן לֶחֶם לְכָל בָּשָׂר כִּי לְעוֹלָם חַסְדּוֹ. וּבְטוּבוֹ הַגָּדוֹל תָּמִיד לֹא חָסַר לָנוּ, וְאַל יֶחְסַר לָנוּ מָזוֹן לְעוֹלָם וָעֶד בַּעֲבוּר שְׁמוֹ הַגָּדוֹל. כִּי הוּא אֵל זָן, וּמְפַרְנֵס לַכֹּל, וּמֵטִיב לַכֹּל, וּמֵכִין מָזוֹן לְכֹל בְּרִיּוֹתָיו אֲשֶׁר בָּרָא. בָּרוּךְ אַתָּה יי הַזָּן אֶת הַכֹּל.

Blessed are You, Lord, our God, King of the universe, Who, in His goodness, nourishes the whole world with grace, with kindness and with mercy. He gives food to all flesh, for His kindness is everlasting. And through His great goodness to us we have never lacked, nor may we ever lack, food forever; for the sake of His great name. For He is a God Who nourishes and provides for all, and does good to all, and prepares food for all His creatures whom He has created. Blessed are You, Lord, Who nourishes all.

נוֹדֶה לְךָ יי אֱלֹהֵינוּ עַל שֶׁהִנְחַלְתָּ לַאֲבוֹתֵינוּ אֶרֶץ חֶמְדָּה טוֹבָה וּרְחָבָה, וְעַל שֶׁהוֹצֵאתָנוּ יי אֱלֹהֵינוּ מֵאֶרֶץ מִצְרַיִם, וּפְדִיתָנוּ מִבֵּית עֲבָדִים, וְעַל בְּרִיתְךָ שֶׁחָתַמְתָּ בִּבְשָׂרֵנוּ, וְעַל תּוֹרָתְךָ שֶׁלִּמַּדְתָּנוּ, וְעַל חֻקֶּיךָ שֶׁהוֹדַעְתָּנוּ, וְעַל חַיִּים חֵן וָחֶסֶד שֶׁחוֹנַנְתָּנוּ, וְעַל אֲכִילַת מָזוֹן שָׁאַתָּה זָן וּמְפַרְנֵס אוֹתָנוּ תָּמִיד, בְּכָל יוֹם, וּבְכָל עֵת, וּבְכָל שָׁעָה.

We thank You, Lord, our God, for having given as a heritage to our forefathers a precious, good and spacious land; and for having brought us out, Lord, our God, from the land of Egypt and redeemed us from the house of servitude; and for Your covenant that You have sealed in our flesh; and for Your Torah that You have taught us; and for Your statutes that You have made known to us; and for the life, favor and kindness that You have graciously bestowed upon us; and for the food we eat with which You constantly nourish and provide for us every day, and at all times and at every hour.

וְעַל הַכֹּל, יי אֱלֹהֵינוּ, אֲנַחְנוּ מוֹדִים לָךְ, וּמְבָרְכִים אוֹתָךְ, יִתְבָּרַךְ שִׁמְךָ בְּפִי כָל חַי תָּמִיד לְעוֹלָם וָעֶד. כַּכָּתוּב: וְאָכַלְתָּ, וְשָׂבָעְתָּ, וּבֵרַכְתָּ אֶת יי אֱלֹהֶיךָ עַל הָאָרֶץ הַטּוֹבָה אֲשֶׁר נָתַן לָךְ. בָּרוּךְ אַתָּה יי, עַל הָאָרֶץ וְעַל הַמָּזוֹן.

And for all this, Lord, our God, we thank You and bless You. Blessed be Your name in the mouth of every living creature, continually and forever. As it is written: "And you will eat, and you will be satisfied, and you will bless the Lord your God, for the good land that He has given you."[6] Blessed are You, Lord, for the land and for the food.

רַחֵם נָא יי אֱלֹהֵינוּ, עַל יִשְׂרָאֵל עַמֶּךָ, וְעַל יְרוּשָׁלַיִם עִירֶךָ, וְעַל צִיּוֹן מִשְׁכַּן כְּבוֹדֶךָ, וְעַל מַלְכוּת בֵּית דָּוִד מְשִׁיחֶךָ, וְעַל הַבַּיִת הַגָּדוֹל וְהַקָּדוֹשׁ שֶׁנִּקְרָא שִׁמְךָ עָלָיו. אֱלֹהֵינוּ, אָבִינוּ, רְעֵנוּ, זוּנֵנוּ, פַּרְנְסֵנוּ, וְכַלְכְּלֵנוּ, וְהַרְוִיחֵנוּ, וְהַרְוַח לָנוּ, יי אֱלֹהֵינוּ, מְהֵרָה מִכָּל צָרוֹתֵינוּ. וְנָא אַל תַּצְרִיכֵנוּ, יי אֱלֹהֵינוּ, לֹא לִידֵי מַתְּנַת בָּשָׂר וָדָם, וְלֹא לִידֵי הַלְוָאָתָם, כִּי אִם לְיָדְךָ הַמְּלֵאָה, הַפְּתוּחָה, הַקְּדוֹשָׁה, וְהָרְחָבָה, שֶׁלֹּא נֵבוֹשׁ וְלֹא נִכָּלֵם לְעוֹלָם וָעֶד.

Please have mercy, Lord, our God, upon Israel Your people; and upon Jerusalem Your city; and upon Zion the abode of Your glory; and upon the kingship of the House of David Your anointed; and upon the great and holy House upon which Your name is called. Our God, our Father, Our Shepherd, nourish us, provide for us, sustain us, and relieve us; and grant us relief, Lord, our God, speedily, from all our troubles. And please make us not dependent, Lord, our God, upon the gifts of mortal men nor upon their loans; but rather only upon Your full, open, holy and generous hand; that we may neither be shamed nor disgraced, forever.

---

6 Devarim 8:10.

On Shabbat add:

רְצֵה וְהַחֲלִיצֵנוּ, יי אֱלֹהֵינוּ, בְּמִצְוֹתֶיךָ וּבְמִצְוַת יוֹם הַשְּׁבִיעִי, הַשַּׁבָּת הַגָּדוֹל וְהַקָּדוֹשׁ הַזֶּה. כִּי יוֹם זֶה גָּדוֹל וְקָדוֹשׁ הוּא לְפָנֶיךָ, לִשְׁבָּת בּוֹ וְלָנוּחַ בּוֹ בְּאַהֲבָה כְּמִצְוַת רְצוֹנֶךָ. וּבִרְצוֹנְךָ הָנִיחַ לָנוּ, יי אֱלֹהֵינוּ, שֶׁלֹּא תְהֵא צָרָה וְיָגוֹן וַאֲנָחָה בְּיוֹם מְנוּחָתֵנוּ. וְהַרְאֵנוּ, יי אֱלֹהֵינוּ, בְּנֶחָמַת צִיּוֹן עִירֶךָ, וּבְבִנְיַן יְרוּשָׁלַיִם עִיר קָדְשֶׁךָ, כִּי אַתָּה הוּא בַּעַל הַיְשׁוּעוֹת וּבַעַל הַנֶּחָמוֹת.

Favor and strengthen us, Lord, our God, through Your commandments, and through the commandment of the seventh day, this great and holy Sabbath. For this day is great and holy before You, [upon which we are enjoined] to refrain from work and to rest thereon with love, in accordance with the precept of Your will. And through Your will grant us, Lord, our God, that there be no trouble, sadness or grief on the day of our rest. And allow us, Lord, our God, to witness the consolation of Zion Your city; and the rebuilding of Jerusalem Your holy city, for You are the Master of salvations and the Master of consolations.

אֱלֹהֵינוּ וֵאלֹהֵי אֲבוֹתֵינוּ, יַעֲלֶה, וְיָבֹא, וְיַגִּיעַ, וְיֵרָאֶה, וְיֵרָצֶה, וְיִשָּׁמַע, וְיִפָּקֵד, וְיִזָּכֵר זִכְרוֹנֵנוּ וּפִקְדוֹנֵנוּ, וְזִכְרוֹן אֲבוֹתֵינוּ, וְזִכְרוֹן מָשִׁיחַ בֶּן דָּוִד עַבְדֶּךָ, וְזִכְרוֹן יְרוּשָׁלַיִם עִיר קָדְשֶׁךָ, וְזִכְרוֹן כָּל עַמְּךָ בֵּית יִשְׂרָאֵל לְפָנֶיךָ לִפְלֵיטָה, לְטוֹבָה, לְחֵן וּלְחֶסֶד וּלְרַחֲמִים, לְחַיִּים וּלְשָׁלוֹם, בְּיוֹם חַג הַמַּצּוֹת הַזֶּה. זָכְרֵנוּ יי אֱלֹהֵינוּ בּוֹ לְטוֹבָה, וּפָקְדֵנוּ בוֹ לִבְרָכָה, וְהוֹשִׁיעֵנוּ בוֹ לְחַיִּים.וּבִדְבַר יְשׁוּעָה וְרַחֲמִים, חוּס וְחָנֵּנוּ וְרַחֵם עָלֵינוּ וְהוֹשִׁיעֵנוּ, כִּי אֵלֶיךָ עֵינֵינוּ, כִּי אֵל מֶלֶךְ חַנּוּן וְרַחוּם אָתָּה.

Our God and God of our fathers, may there ascend, and come, and reach, and be seen, and be accepted, and be heard, and be recalled, and be remembered before You the remembrance and recollection of us, and the remembrance of our fathers, and the remembrance of the Messiah the son of David Your servant, and the remembrance of Jerusalem Your holy city, and the remembrance of all Your people the House of Israel, for deliverance, for well-being, for grace and for kindness and for mercy, for life and for peace, on this day of the festival of matzot. Remember us on this [day], Lord, our God, for good; and recollect us on this [day] for blessing; and preserve us on this [day] for life. And with Your word of salvation and mercy, be gracious and compassionate with us; and have mercy upon us and deliver us; for our eyes are turned to You; for You are a gracious and merciful God and King.

וּבְנֵה יְרוּשָׁלַיִם עִיר הַקֹּדֶשׁ בִּמְהֵרָה בְיָמֵינוּ. בָּרוּךְ אַתָּה יי, בּוֹנֵה בְרַחֲמָיו יְרוּשָׁלָיִם. אָמֵן.

Rebuild Jerusalem the holy city speedily in our days. Blessed are You, Lord, Who in His mercy rebuilds Jerusalem. Amen.

בָּרוּךְ אַתָּה יי אֱלֹהֵינוּ מֶלֶךְ הָעוֹלָם, הָאֵל אָבִינוּ, מַלְכֵּנוּ, אַדִּירֵנוּ, בּוֹרְאֵנוּ, גּוֹאֲלֵנוּ, יוֹצְרֵנוּ, קְדוֹשֵׁנוּ, קְדוֹשׁ יַעֲקֹב, רוֹעֵנוּ רוֹעֵה יִשְׂרָאֵל, הַמֶּלֶךְ הַטּוֹב וְהַמֵּטִיב לַכֹּל. שֶׁבְּכָל יוֹם וָיוֹם הוּא הֵטִיב, הוּא מֵטִיב, הוּא יֵיטִיב לָנוּ. הוּא גְמָלָנוּ, הוּא גוֹמְלֵנוּ, הוּא יִגְמְלֵנוּ לָעַד, לְחֵן, וּלְחֶסֶד, וּלְרַחֲמִים, וּלְרֶוַח, הַצָּלָה וְהַצְלָחָה, בְּרָכָה, וִישׁוּעָה, נֶחָמָה, פַּרְנָסָה, וְכַלְכָּלָה, וְרַחֲמִים, וְחַיִּים, וְשָׁלוֹם, וְכָל טוֹב, וּמִכָּל טוּב לְעוֹלָם אַל יְחַסְּרֵנוּ.

Blessed are You, Lord, our God, King of the universe, God, our Father, our King, our Might, our Creator, our Redeemer, our Maker, our Holy One, the Holy One of Jacob, our Shepherd, the Shepherd of Israel, the King Who is good and does good to all. For each and every day He has done good for us, He does good for us and He will do good for us; He has bestowed, He bestows and He will forever bestow upon us grace, kindness, and mercy, relief, salvation, and success, blessing, and help, consolation, sustenance, and nourishment, compassion, life, peace and all goodness; and may He never cause us to lack any good.

הָרַחֲמָן הוּא יִמְלוֹךְ עָלֵינוּ לְעוֹלָם וָעֶד.

The Merciful One! May He reign over us forever and ever.

הָרַחֲמָן הוּא יִתְבָּרֵךְ בַּשָּׁמַיִם וּבָאָרֶץ.

The Merciful One! May He be blessed in heaven and on earth.

הָרַחֲמָן הוּא יִשְׁתַּבַּח לְדוֹר דּוֹרִים, וְיִתְפָּאַר בָּנוּ לָעַד וּלְנֵצַח נְצָחִים, וְיִתְהַדַּר בָּנוּ לָעַד וּלְעוֹלְמֵי עוֹלָמִים.

The Merciful One! May He be praised for all generations, and be glorified through us forever and for all eternity, and honored through us forever and ever.

הָרַחֲמָן הוּא יְפַרְנְסֵנוּ בְּכָבוֹד.

The Merciful One! May He sustain us with honor.

הָרַחֲמָן הוּא יִשְׁבּוֹר עֻלֵּנוּ מֵעַל צַוָּארֵנוּ וְהוּא יוֹלִיכֵנוּ קוֹמְמִיּוּת לְאַרְצֵנוּ.

The Merciful One! May He break the yoke from our necks and may He lead us upright to our land.

הָרַחֲמָן הוּא יִשְׁלַח לָנוּ בְּרָכָה מְרֻבָּה בַּבַּיִת הַזֶּה, וְעַל שֻׁלְחָן זֶה שֶׁאָכַלְנוּ עָלָיו.

The Merciful One! May He send us abundant blessing into this house and upon this table at which we have eaten.

הָרַחֲמָן הוּא יִשְׁלַח לָנוּ אֶת אֵלִיָּהוּ הַנָּבִיא, זָכוּר לַטּוֹב, וִיבַשֶּׂר לָנוּ בְּשׂוֹרוֹת טוֹבוֹת יְשׁוּעוֹת וְנֶחָמוֹת.

The Merciful One! May he send us Elijah the Prophet – may he be remembered for good – that he may bring us good tidings, salvation and consolation.

Continue by selecting the appropriate formula below.

An individual eating in his own home recites:

הָרַחֲמָן, הוּא יְבָרֵךְ אוֹתִי (וְאֶת אִשְׁתִּי/ בַּעֲלִי, וְאֶת זַרְעִי, וְאֶת כָּל אֲשֶׁר לִי),

The Merciful One! May He bless me (and my wife/my husband and my children) and all that is mine (ours),

An individual eating in his parents' home recites:

הָרַחֲמָן, הוּא יְבָרֵךְ אֶת אָבִי מוֹרִי, בַּעַל הַבַּיִת הַזֶּה; וְאֶת אִמִּי מוֹרָתִי, בַּעֲלַת הַבַּיִת הַזֶּה; אוֹתָם,

168

וְאֶת בֵּיתָם, וְאֶת זַרְעָם, וְאֶת כָּל אֲשֶׁר לָהֶם,

The Merciful One! May He bless my father, my teacher, master of this house; and my mother, my teacher, mistress of this house; them, and their household, and their children and all that is theirs,

A guest eating in the home of another recites:

הָרַחֲמָן, הוּא יְבָרֵךְ אֶת בַּעַל הַבַּיִת הַזֶּה (וְאֶת אִשְׁתּוֹ, בַּעֲלַת הַבַּיִת הַזֶּה), אוֹתוֹ, וְאֶת בֵּיתוֹ (אוֹתָם, וְאֶת בֵּיתָם, וְאֶת זַרְעָם), וְאֶת כָּל אֲשֶׁר לוֹ (לָהֶם)

The Merciful One! May He bless the master of this house, (and his wife, mistress of this house/and his children), him and his household (them, and their household, and their children), and all that is his (theirs),

All continue:

אוֹתָנוּ וְאֶת כָּל אֲשֶׁר לָנוּ, כְּמוֹ שֶׁנִּתְבָּרְכוּ אֲבוֹתֵינוּ, אַבְרָהָם, יִצְחָק וְיַעֲקֹב בַּכֹּל מִכֹּל כֹּל, כֵּן יְבָרֵךְ אוֹתָנוּ כֻּלָּנוּ יַחַד, בִּבְרָכָה שְׁלֵמָה, וְנֹאמַר אָמֵן.

...us, and all that is ours. Just as He blessed our forefathers, Abraham, Isaac and Jacob, "in everything," "from everything," with "everything," so may He bless all of us together with a perfect blessing, and let us say, Amen.

בַּמָּרוֹם יְלַמְּדוּ עֲלֵיהֶם וְעָלֵינוּ זְכוּת, שֶׁתְּהֵא לְמִשְׁמֶרֶת שָׁלוֹם. וְנִשָּׂא בְרָכָה מֵאֵת יי וּצְדָקָה מֵאֱלֹהֵי יִשְׁעֵנוּ, וְנִמְצָא חֵן וְשֵׂכֶל טוֹב בְּעֵינֵי אֱלֹהִים וְאָדָם.

May those on high advocate on behalf of their merits (those of our forefathers) and ours, giving rise to a safeguarding of peace. And may we receive blessing from the Lord and just reward from the God of our salvation, and may we find grace and good favor in the eyes of God and man.

(הָרַחֲמָן, הוּא יַנְחִילֵנוּ יוֹם שֶׁכֻּלּוֹ שַׁבָּת וּמְנוּחָה לְחַיֵּי הָעוֹלָמִים.)

The Merciful One! May He cause us to inherit a day that is wholly Sabbath and repose for life everlasting.

הוּא יַנְחִילֵנוּ יוֹם שֶׁכֻּלּוֹ טוֹב (יֵשׁ מוֹסִיפִים: יוֹם שֶׁכֻּלּוֹ אָרֵךְ, יוֹם שֶׁצַּדִּיקִים יוֹשְׁבִים וְעַטְרוֹתֵיהֶם בְּרָאשֵׁיהֶם וְנֶהֱנִים מִזִּיו הַשְּׁכִינָה, וִיהִי חֶלְקֵנוּ עִמָּהֶם).

The Merciful One! May He cause us to inherit a day that is all good (*some add*: a day that is everlasting; a day when the righteous will sit with crowns on their heads, rejoicing in the radiance of the Divine Presence, and may our portion be with them).

הָרַחֲמָן הוּא יְזַכֵּנוּ לִימוֹת הַמָּשִׁיחַ וּלְחַיֵּי הָעוֹלָם הַבָּא. מִגְדּוֹל יְשׁוּעוֹת מַלְכּוֹ, וְעֹשֶׂה חֶסֶד לִמְשִׁיחוֹ, לְדָוִד וּלְזַרְעוֹ עַד עוֹלָם. עֹשֶׂה שָׁלוֹם בִּמְרוֹמָיו, הוּא יַעֲשֶׂה שָׁלוֹם עָלֵינוּ וְעַל כָּל יִשְׂרָאֵל, וְאִמְרוּ אָמֵן.

The Merciful One! May He grant that we be worthy of reaching the days of the Messiah and the life of the world to come. He is a tower of salvation to His king, and bestows kindness upon His anointed, to David and his descendants forever. He who makes peace in His heights, may He make peace for us and for all Israel; and say, Amen.

יְראוּ אֶת יי קְדֹשָׁיו, כִּי אֵין מַחְסוֹר לִירֵאָיו. כְּפִירִים רָשׁוּ וְרָעֵבוּ, וְדוֹרְשֵׁי יי לֹא יַחְסְרוּ כָל טוֹב. הוֹדוּ לַיי כִּי טוֹב, כִּי לְעוֹלָם חַסְדּוֹ. פּוֹתֵחַ אֶת יָדֶךָ, וּמַשְׂבִּיעַ לְכָל חַי רָצוֹן. בָּרוּךְ הַגֶּבֶר אֲשֶׁר יִבְטַח בַּיי, וְהָיָה יי מִבְטַחוֹ. נַעַר הָיִיתִי גַּם זָקַנְתִּי וְלֹא רָאִיתִי צַדִּיק נֶעֱזָב, וְזַרְעוֹ מְבַקֶּשׁ לָחֶם. יי עֹז לְעַמּוֹ יִתֵּן, יי יְבָרֵךְ אֶת עַמּוֹ בַשָּׁלוֹם.

Fear the Lord, you His holy ones, for there is no lack for those who fear Him. Young lions are in need and go hungry, but those who seek the Lord shall not lack any good. Give thanks to the Lord, for He is good; for His loving-kindness endures forever. You open Your hand and satisfy the desire of every living thing. Blessed is the man who trusts in the Lord, and whose trust is in the Lord alone. I was a youth, I have also aged; and I have not seen a righteous man forsaken and his children begging for bread. The Lord will give His people strength; the Lord will bless His people with peace.

בָּרוּךְ אַתָּה יי אֱלֹהֵינוּ מֶלֶךְ הָעוֹלָם, בּוֹרֵא פְּרִי הַגָּפֶן.

Blessed are You, Lord, our God, King of the universe, Who creates the fruit of the vine.

The third cup of wine is consumed, while leaning to the left.

Food for Thought

A. As was the case with the recitation of Kiddush (see p. 40), the inclusion of Birkat Hamazon in the Pesach Seder invests a familiar year-round ritual with new layers of significance. The wine over which the Birkat Hamazon is recited serves as the Seder's third cup of wine, and our thanks for sustenance is heightened by the general sense of gratitude that pervades the Seder evening.

On a deeper level, however, the Birkat Hamazon can be seen as advancing one of the fundamental lessons of the Seder.

B. Aside from Birkat Kohanim, the public Priestly Blessing, Birkat Hamazon is the only blessing of uncontested biblical origin in Jewish tradition. The obligation to bless God after meals is directly derived by the rabbis from the verse in Devarim, "And you

will eat, and you will be satisfied, *and you will bless* the Lord your God, concerning the good land that He has given you."[7]

At first glance, however, this halachic derivation seems somewhat strained. The phrase "and you will bless" is arguably descriptive in nature, part and parcel of Moshe's prediction concerning the nation's eventual reaction to the bounty of the land. What compels the Talmudic authorities to interpret the phrase "and you will bless" as an imperative, mandating the biblical obligation of Birkat Hamazon?

C. A rereading of the biblical verse in context may help us understand the rabbis' motivation. This sentence is part of a carefully structured presentation in which Moshe, shortly before his death, describes

---

7 Devarim 8:10.

to his people the potential benefits and dangers of the abundant land that they are about to enter. *The very bounty meant to sustain you*, Moshe warns the Israelites, *could well prove to be your undoing*.

The paragraph pivots on an apparent "cause-and-effect" structure established by the transition between three sentences:

> A land where you will eat bread without scarceness; you will lack nothing within it; a land whose stones are iron and from whose mountains you will mine copper.
>
> And you will eat, and you will be satisfied, and you will bless the Lord your God upon the good land that He has given you.
>
> Take care lest you forget the Lord your God by not observing His commandments, His laws and His statutes, which I command you today.[8]

Sated and satisfied by the wondrous natural wealth of the land, and filled with pride over your own accomplishments, Moshe warns, *you could easily forget your dependence upon God for the countless gifts that you have received*.

A problem, however, emerges from the text. One phrase does not fit the otherwise seamless "cause-and-effect" structure presented by Moshe. The insertion of the words "and you will bless the Lord your God" in the second sentence strikes an incongruous note. Blessing God can hardly be seen as a step along the path toward abandonment of our dependence upon Him. In fact, the opposite would seem to be true. If upon reaching a point of comfort and satiation, we bless God for the bounty that we have received, we will be *less likely* to forget His role in our good fortune.

Perhaps that is why the rabbis assert that, "and you shall bless the Lord your God" cannot be understood as part of Moshe's description of the potential problem facing the nation, but instead must be seen *as a corrective for that problem*. In the words of the Meshech Chochma, "When one eats and is satisfied, one is likely to rebel. God, therefore, commands the nation to recall His name and to bless Him, specifically at the point of satiation, and to remember that He is the One Who gives man power to succeed."[9] Precisely because of the context in which it is found, the rabbis interpret the phrase "and you shall bless the Lord your God" as a commandment.

D. How seamlessly, then, does Birkat Hamazon fit into the entire Seder structure! Over and over again, the Haggada has taught us that our remembrances of the Exodus are incomplete unless those remembrances lead us to a state of gratitude for all that we have received.

Birkat Hamazon takes this lesson one significant step further. Lack of *hakarat hatov* (recognition of goodness bestowed), the Torah warns us, is not only ungracious, but dangerous. An absence of gratitude to God inexorably leads to a loss of our own footing, as beings defined by the delicate balance between personal independence and continued dependence upon God. And when we lose our footing, the Torah testifies, the consequences can be devastating.

---

8   Devarim 8:9–11.
9   *Meshech Chochma* 8:10.

Turning the Page
Kos Eliyahu and Shfoch Chamatcha

The fourth cup of wine is poured, as well as a special cup for the prophet Eliyahu (according to another custom, only Eliyahu's cup is poured at this point, while the fourth cup of wine is poured immediately before recitation of the second section of Hallel; see below).

The door to the house is opened and the following paragraph is recited:

שְׁפֹךְ חֲמָתְךָ אֶל הַגּוֹיִם אֲשֶׁר לֹא יְדָעוּךָ, וְעַל מַמְלָכוֹת אֲשֶׁר בְּשִׁמְךָ לֹא קָרָאוּ. כִּי אָכַל אֶת יַעֲקֹב, וְאֶת נָוֵהוּ הֵשַׁמּוּ. שְׁפָךְ עֲלֵיהֶם זַעְמֶךָ, וַחֲרוֹן אַפְּךָ יַשִּׂיגֵם. תִּרְדֹּף בְּאַף וְתַשְׁמִידֵם מִתַּחַת שְׁמֵי יי.

Pour out Your wrath upon the nations who know You not, and upon the kingdoms who do not call upon Your name. For they have devoured Jacob and laid waste his habitation. Pour out Your fury upon them, and let the fierceness of Your anger overtake them. Pursue them with anger, and destroy them from beneath the heavens of the Lord.

Food for Thought

A. In many homes, the greeting of the prophet Eliyahu is one of the warmest, most memorable moments of the Seder. A special cup of wine is poured in the prophet's honor, the door of the house is opened and all gaze expectantly as we welcome the harbinger of the redemption[10] to our Seder table.

I remember thinking as a child: *Who knows? Perhaps this year will be different. Perhaps this year Eliyahu will be here in body, as well as in spirit. This could be, after all, the year of our ultimate redemption.*

And while the level of my expectations may have shifted a bit with the passage of time, I must admit that I still secretly find myself looking outside with the opening of the door, hoping against hope to see a man with a long white beard standing at our doorstep.

I would wager that I am not the only one who quietly harbors that hope...

B. Suddenly, however, the warmth of the moment collides with the text of the moment, as we recite a paragraph that seems out of place – not only at this juncture, but within the Seder as a whole.

"Shfoch chamatcha... Pour out Your wrath upon the nations who know You not... Pour out Your fury upon them, and let the fierceness of Your anger overtake them... Pursue them with anger, and destroy them from beneath the heavens of the Lord." What place

---

10 Malachi 3:23.

is there in the Seder liturgy for this apparent call for vengeance? Throughout the evening we have focused primarily on ourselves, our history, our struggles, our accomplishments, our gratitude, our mistakes, our responsibilities. Why now the need to turn against others? What has changed? If we were able to empathize with the pain of the Egyptians during the recitation of the ten plagues, can't we show compassion and forgiveness for other nations now?

C. These questions can all be answered, I believe, if we consider the pivotal juncture of the Seder at which we now stand. At this moment, we are about to turn away from the past and present, toward the future. Before we do so, however, the Seder reminds us that a critical step must first be taken. *There can be no successful move to the future*, the Haggada indicates, *without a real reckoning with the past.*

D. A refrain often heard in our post-Holocaust era: Why can't you let it go, already? Why do you insist on bringing up your people's past suffering, more than seventy years after the fact? Move on... Our wordless response can be found in the terrifying sweep of anti-Semitism across the face of Europe today; in the unbounded global hatred directed against the small State of Israel; in the glaring hypocrisy of the United Nations as it ignores the human rights violations of country after country, while continually singling out the State of Israel for condemnation; in the Holocaust deniers and in their brazen lies. Clearly, this is what happens when you try to "move on" toward the future, without reckoning with the past.

E. Cognizant of this very danger, the Torah weaves a warning into the biblical law that most directly deals with the eradication of evil. "Remember that which Amalek did to you, on the way as you left Egypt.... And it will be, when the Lord your God gives you rest from all your enemies round about, in the land the Lord your God gives you as an inheritance to possess it, you shall erase the remembrance of Amalek from under the heavens; you shall not forget!"[11]

At first glance, the Torah's instructions concerning the Jewish nation's dealings with its archenemy, Amalek, seem contradictory and self-defeating. God enjoins us to "remember" for the purpose of "erasing the remembrance," and then the Torah repeats, "You shall not forget!" Which is it? Does God want Amalek to be remembered or forgotten? Should the memory of this nation and its evil be preserved or erased?

And yet, upon consideration, the Torah's powerful message becomes abundantly clear. God wants us to recognize that *there is a fundamental difference between forgetting and erasing.* When you forget a problem, the problem remains. It may be out of sight, lurking in the shadows, but it continues to exist, poised to reassert itself, full force, at a moment's notice. In contrast, when you erase a problem, the problem is gone. The issues have been dealt with head on; no vestige of the problem remains.

Thus, the Torah issues its warning. *You may wish to forget Amalek and the evil he*

---

11 Devarim 25:17–19.

represents; you may wish to avoid the pain of confrontation and seek comfort in indifference. By doing so, however, you only ensure Amalek' survival. The ultimate erasure of Amalek's memory will be achieved solely through your continued remembrance of his malevolence and through your vigilant efforts toward its complete eradication.

F. And thus, at this point in the Seder, we deliver our message to the nations of the world. *Shfoch chamatcha...* We cannot move on to the future without reckoning with the past. Only if evil is confronted head on, only if its underlying causes are dealt with, only if all vestiges of that evil are erased from our hearts and from the hearts of those around us can we – and all the citizens of the world – ultimately hope to be safe.

G. Against this backdrop, the welcoming of the prophet Eliyahu and the pouring of his cup of wine become even more meaningfully symbolic. A review of Eliyahu's life and career finds this prophet to be a zealous defender of God's will in the face of the unremitting evil of the Northern Kingdom of Israel, its monarchs and its idolatrous priests.[12] The Midrash goes so far as to associate Eliyahu with the biblical figure Pinchas, the prototype of the righteous zealot in the Torah.[13] God's choice of Eliyahu as the harbinger of the final redemption, referenced in a prophetic paragraph read each year on the Shabbat before

Pesach,[14] thus sends a powerful message to the Jewish nation: *The path toward redemption will not be easy. Eliyahu must be your paradigm as you set the stage for the final act of your historical journey. His zeal and his passion must characterize your battle against evil, if you are to successfully move forward to a glorious future.*

H. And Eliyahu's cup of wine? Powerfully symbolic, as well... As noted earlier, a well-known tradition[15] connects the Seder's four cups of wine to the "four redemptions" referenced by God in his prediction of the impending Exodus[16] (see pp. 41–43). A rereading of the text, however, reveals a "fifth redemption," mentioned in the biblical text as well: *"v'heveti etchem el ha'aretz"* (and I will bring you to the land).[17] Where then is the cup for this "fifth redemption"? Why don't we drink five cups of wine at the Seder, instead of four?

According to many authorities, the fifth cup is present at the Seder, as Eliyahu's cup. The last redemption mentioned in the biblical passage is redemption in potential, to be realized only through the ingathering of the exiles at the end of days. To acknowledge the work yet to be done in order to reach our nation's ultimate goals, we do not drink the fifth cup of wine. We instead reserve it for Eliyahu, the harbinger of the final redemption.

---

12 I Melachim 17–II Melachim 2.
13 *Pirkei D'Rabi Eliezer* 45:5; *Zohar*, Ki Tisa 190a.
14 Haftarat Shabbat Hagadol, Malachi 3:23.
15 Talmud Yerushalmi Pesachim 10:1.
16 Shmot 6:6–7.
17 Shmot 6:8.

I. For further discussion: from testimony to memory.

As I write these words, the Jewish nation stands on the brink of a sad and inexorable historical transition. One by one, the last survivors of the Holocaust are passing from our midst, carrying with them the final eyewitness accounts of the most horrific genocide in the history of humankind.

What will the world be like when testimony is gone and only memory remains?

If Holocaust denial can exist in the presence of living eyewitnesses, how powerfully will that pathology proliferate when the eyewitnesses are gone?

If we are today witnessing a sweep of open anti-Semitism across the globe, unprecedented since the Shoah, what will greet our eyes tomorrow?

What can each of us do to ensure that the powerful lessons of the Holocaust will not be lost, as the opportunity for testimony fades and we all become the caretakers of memory?

Seder Unit IV – The Future

Seder Sections Hallel, Nirtza

Having shared a journey through our people's past and present, we now stand poised to enter the fourth and last unit of the Seder evening, in which we turn our attention toward the future.

We close the formal Seder proceedings through the recitation of the second section of Hallel, reflecting our yearning for and our anticipation of the ultimate redemption.

The evening finally ends with Nirtza, a series of liturgical poems that have been added over the ages as an epilogue to the Seder.

Seder Section 13 • HALLEL
Psalms of Praise

The Seder participants join together in joyous song and praise as the second section of Hallel is now recited (see pp. 183–84 for more on Hallel). This section consists of the remaining passages of Hallel Hamitzri (Psalms 115–118), Hallel Hagadol (Psalm 136), and specific closing passages.

If possible, the four stanzas of the paragraph beginning with *"Hodu la'Shem ki tov"* (Give thanks to the Lord, for He is good) and the four stanzas of the paragraph beginning with *"Ana, Hashem, hoshiya na"* (O' Lord, please help us) should be recited responsively.[1]

Those who have not yet poured the fourth cup of wine do so now.

לֹא לָנוּ, יי, לֹא לָנוּ, כִּי לְשִׁמְךָ תֵּן כָּבוֹד, עַל חַסְדְּךָ עַל אֲמִתֶּךָ. לָמָּה יֹאמְרוּ הַגּוֹיִם, אַיֵּה נָא אֱלֹהֵיהֶם? וֵאלֹהֵינוּ בַשָּׁמָיִם כֹּל אֲשֶׁר חָפֵץ עָשָׂה. עֲצַבֵּיהֶם כֶּסֶף וְזָהָב, מַעֲשֵׂה יְדֵי אָדָם. פֶּה לָהֶם וְלֹא יְדַבֵּרוּ, עֵינַיִם לָהֶם וְלֹא יִרְאוּ, אָזְנַיִם לָהֶם וְלֹא יִשְׁמָעוּ, אַף לָהֶם וְלֹא יְרִיחוּן. יְדֵיהֶם וְלֹא יְמִישׁוּן, רַגְלֵיהֶם וְלֹא יְהַלֵּכוּ, לֹא יֶהְגּוּ בִּגְרוֹנָם. כְּמוֹהֶם יִהְיוּ עֹשֵׂיהֶם, כֹּל אֲשֶׁר בֹּטֵחַ בָּהֶם. יִשְׂרָאֵל בְּטַח בַּיי. עֶזְרָם וּמָגִנָּם הוּא. בֵּית אַהֲרֹן בִּטְחוּ בַיי, עֶזְרָם וּמָגִנָּם הוּא. יִרְאֵי יי בִּטְחוּ בַיי. עֶזְרָם וּמָגִנָּם הוּא.

Not to us, Lord, not to us, but to Your name give honor, for Your kindness and Your truth. Why should the nations say, "Where, now, is their God?" Our God is in heaven, whatever He wills, He does. Their idols are of silver and gold, the product of human hands. They have mouths, but cannot speak; they have eyes, but cannot see; they have ears, but cannot hear; they have noses, but cannot smell. Their hands cannot feel; their feet cannot walk; they can make no sound with their throats. Like them should be their makers, everyone who trusts in them. Israel, trust in the Lord! He is their help and their shield. House of Aaron, trust in the Lord! He is their help and their shield. You who fear the Lord, trust in the Lord! He is their help and their shield.

יי זְכָרָנוּ יְבָרֵךְ. יְבָרֵךְ אֶת בֵּית יִשְׂרָאֵל, יְבָרֵךְ אֶת בֵּית אַהֲרֹן, יְבָרֵךְ יִרְאֵי יי, הַקְּטַנִּים עִם הַגְּדֹלִים. יֹסֵף יי עֲלֵיכֶם, עֲלֵיכֶם וְעַל בְּנֵיכֶם. בְּרוּכִים אַתֶּם לַיי, עֹשֵׂה שָׁמַיִם וָאָרֶץ. הַשָּׁמַיִם שָׁמַיִם לַיי, וְהָאָרֶץ נָתַן לִבְנֵי אָדָם. לֹא הַמֵּתִים יְהַלְלוּ יָהּ, וְלֹא כָּל יֹרְדֵי דוּמָה. וַאֲנַחְנוּ נְבָרֵךְ יָהּ, מֵעַתָּה וְעַד עוֹלָם, הַלְלוּיָהּ.

The Lord, Who has remembered us, will bless. He will bless the House of Israel; He will bless the House of Aaron; He will bless those who fear the Lord, the small with the great. May the Lord grant you increase, you and your children. You are blessed

---

1 *Shulchan Aruch*, Orach Chaim 479:1; Rema, ibid.

unto the Lord, the Maker of heaven and earth. The heavens are the heavens of the Lord, but the earth He has given to mankind. The dead praise not the Lord, nor do any who go down into the silence [of the grave]. But we will bless the Lord, from now to eternity. Praise the Lord!

אָהַבְתִּי כִּי יִשְׁמַע יי אֶת קוֹלִי, תַּחֲנוּנָי. כִּי הִטָּה אָזְנוֹ לִי וּבְיָמַי אֶקְרָא.
אֲפָפוּנִי חֶבְלֵי מָוֶת, וּמְצָרֵי שְׁאוֹל מְצָאוּנִי, צָרָה וְיָגוֹן אֶמְצָא, וּבְשֵׁם יי אֶקְרָא:
אָנָּה יי מַלְּטָה נַפְשִׁי. חַנּוּן יי וְצַדִּיק, וֵאלֹהֵינוּ מְרַחֵם. שֹׁמֵר פְּתָאִים יי, דַּלּוֹתִי
וְלִי יְהוֹשִׁיעַ. שׁוּבִי נַפְשִׁי לִמְנוּחָיְכִי, כִּי יי גָּמַל עָלָיְכִי. כִּי חִלַּצְתָּ נַפְשִׁי מִמָּוֶת,
אֶת עֵינִי מִן דִּמְעָה, אֶת רַגְלִי מִדֶּחִי. אֶתְהַלֵּךְ לִפְנֵי יי בְּאַרְצוֹת הַחַיִּים.
הֶאֱמַנְתִּי כִּי אֲדַבֵּר, אֲנִי עָנִיתִי מְאֹד. אֲנִי אָמַרְתִּי בְחָפְזִי כָּל הָאָדָם כֹּזֵב.

I love [Him], because the Lord hears my voice, my supplications. For He turned His ear to me; and I will call [upon Him] all my days. The pangs of death encompassed me, and the confines of the grave have found me; trouble and sorrow did I encounter, and I called upon the name of the Lord: "I beseech You, Lord, deliver my soul!" Gracious is the Lord and just; our God is compassionate. The Lord preserves the simple; I was brought low, and He saved me. Return, my soul, to your rest; for the Lord has dealt bountifully with you. For You have delivered my soul from death, my eyes from tears, my foot from stumbling. I will walk before the Lord in the lands of the living. I had faith even when I spoke of how I am greatly afflicted, [even when] I said in my haste, "All men are deceitful."

מָה אָשִׁיב לַיי, כָּל תַּגְמוּלוֹהִי עָלָי. כּוֹס יְשׁוּעוֹת אֶשָּׂא, וּבְשֵׁם יי אֶקְרָא. נְדָרַי
לַיי אֲשַׁלֵּם, נֶגְדָה נָא לְכָל עַמּוֹ. יָקָר בְּעֵינֵי יי הַמָּוְתָה לַחֲסִידָיו. אָנָּה יי כִּי אֲנִי
עַבְדֶּךָ, אֲנִי עַבְדְּךָ בֶּן אֲמָתֶךָ, פִּתַּחְתָּ לְמוֹסֵרָי. לְךָ אֶזְבַּח זֶבַח תּוֹדָה וּבְשֵׁם יי
אֶקְרָא. נְדָרַי לַיי אֲשַׁלֵּם נֶגְדָה נָא לְכָל עַמּוֹ. בְּחַצְרוֹת בֵּית יי, בְּתוֹכֵכִי יְרוּשָׁלַיִם,
הַלְלוּיָהּ.

How can I repay the Lord for all His bountiful dealings toward me? The cup of salvation will I raise and upon the the name of the Lord will I call. My vows to the Lord I will fulfill, in the presence of all His people. Costly in the eyes of the Lord is the death of His pious ones. I beseech you, Lord, for I am Your servant. I am Your servant the son of Your handmaid; You have released my bonds. To You I will offer a thanksgiving offering, and I will call upon the name of the Lord. My vows to the Lord I will fulfill, in the presence of all His people, in the courtyards of the House of the Lord, in your midst, Jerusalem. Praise the Lord!

הַלְלוּ אֶת יי כָּל גּוֹיִם. שַׁבְּחוּהוּ כָּל הָאֻמִּים.
כִּי גָבַר עָלֵינוּ חַסְדּוֹ, וֶאֱמֶת יי לְעוֹלָם, הַלְלוּיָהּ.

Praise the Lord, all nations! Extol Him, all peoples! For His kindness has overwhelmed us, and the truth of the Lord endures forever. Praise the Lord!

הוֹדוּ לַיי כִּי טוֹב, כִּי לְעוֹלָם חַסְדּוֹ.

יֹאמַר נָא יִשְׂרָאֵל: כִּי לְעוֹלָם חַסְדּוֹ.

יֹאמְרוּ נָא בֵית אַהֲרֹן: כִּי לְעוֹלָם חַסְדּוֹ.

יֹאמְרוּ נָא יִרְאֵי יי: כִּי לְעוֹלָם חַסְדּוֹ.

Give thanks to the Lord, for He is good; for His loving-kindness endures forever!
Let Israel now say: "For His loving-kindness endures forever!"
Let the House of Aaron now say: "For His loving-kindness endures forever!"
Let those who fear the Lord now say: "For His loving-kindness endures forever!"

מִן הַמֵּצַר קָרָאתִי יָּה, עָנָנִי בַמֶּרְחָב יָהּ. יי לִי לֹא אִירָא, מַה יַּעֲשֶׂה לִי אָדָם? יי לִי בְּעֹזְרָי, וַאֲנִי אֶרְאֶה בְשֹׂנְאָי. טוֹב לַחֲסוֹת בַּיי, מִבְּטֹחַ בָּאָדָם. טוֹב לַחֲסוֹת בַּיי, מִבְּטֹחַ בִּנְדִיבִים. כָּל גּוֹיִם סְבָבוּנִי, בְּשֵׁם יי כִּי אֲמִילַם. סַבּוּנִי גַם סְבָבוּנִי, בְּשֵׁם יי כִּי אֲמִילַם. סַבּוּנִי כִדְבֹרִים דֹּעֲכוּ כְּאֵשׁ קוֹצִים, בְּשֵׁם יי כִּי אֲמִילַם. דָּחֹה דְחִיתַנִי לִנְפֹּל וַיי עֲזָרָנִי. עָזִּי וְזִמְרָת יָהּ, וַיְהִי לִי לִישׁוּעָה. קוֹל רִנָּה וִישׁוּעָה בְּאָהֳלֵי צַדִּיקִים: יְמִין יי עֹשָׂה חָיִל. יְמִין יי רוֹמֵמָה, יְמִין יי עֹשָׂה חָיִל! לֹא אָמוּת כִּי אֶחְיֶה, וַאֲסַפֵּר מַעֲשֵׂי יָהּ. יַסֹּר יִסְּרַנִי יָּהּ, וְלַמָּוֶת לֹא נְתָנָנִי. פִּתְחוּ לִי שַׁעֲרֵי צֶדֶק, אָבֹא בָם אוֹדֶה יָהּ. זֶה הַשַּׁעַר לַיי, צַדִּיקִים יָבֹאוּ בוֹ.

Out of narrow confines I called to God; God answered me with expansive relief. The Lord is for me, I will not fear: What can man do to me? The Lord is for me as an aid, and I can face my enemies. It is better to take refuge in the Lord than to trust in man. It is better to take refuge in the Lord than to trust in princes. All nations surround me; in the name of the Lord, I cut them down. They surround me, they encircle me; in the name of the Lord, I cut them down. They encircle me like bees, yet they are extinguished [quickly] like a fire [consuming] thorns; in the name of the Lord, I cut them down. You [my foes] pushed me repeatedly that I might fall; but the Lord helped me. My strength and song is the Lord, and [He] has been my salvation. The sound of joyous song and salvation is in the tents of the righteous: "The right hand of the Lord performs deeds of valor. The right hand of the Lord is exalted; the right hand of the Lord performs deeds of valor!" I shall not die, for I shall live and relate the deeds of God. God has tried me sorely, but to death He has not relinquished me. Open for me the gates of righteousness; I will enter them and give thanks to the Lord. This is the gateway to the Lord; the righteous will enter it.

אוֹדְךָ כִּי עֲנִיתָנִי, וַתְּהִי לִי לִישׁוּעָה. אוֹדְךָ כִּי עֲנִיתָנִי, וַתְּהִי לִי לִישׁוּעָה.

אֶבֶן מָאֲסוּ הַבּוֹנִים, הָיְתָה לְרֹאשׁ פִּנָּה. אֶבֶן מָאֲסוּ הַבּוֹנִים, הָיְתָה לְרֹאשׁ פִּנָּה.

מֵאֵת יי הָיְתָה זֹּאת, הִיא נִפְלָאת בְּעֵינֵינוּ. מֵאֵת יי הָיְתָה זֹּאת, הִיא נִפְלָאת בְּעֵינֵינוּ.

זֶה הַיּוֹם עָשָׂה יי, נָגִילָה וְנִשְׂמְחָה בוֹ. זֶה הַיּוֹם עָשָׂה יי, נָגִילָה וְנִשְׂמְחָה בוֹ.

I will give thanks to You, for You have answered me and have become my salvation.
I will give thanks to You, for You have answered me and have become my salvation.
The stone scorned by the builders has become the main cornerstone.
The stone scorned by the builders has become the main cornerstone.
From the Lord has this sprung; it is wondrous in our eyes.
From the Lord has this sprung; it is wondrous in our eyes.
This is the day the Lord has made; let us rejoice and be glad on it.
This is the day the Lord has made; let us rejoice and be glad on it.

אָנָּא, יי, הוֹשִׁיעָה נָּא.
אָנָּא, יי, הוֹשִׁיעָה נָּא.
אָנָּא, יי, הַצְלִיחָה נָּא.
אָנָּא, יי, הַצְלִיחָה נָּא.

We beseech You, Lord, please save [us]!
We beseech You, Lord, please save [us]!
We beseech You, Lord, please grant us success!
We beseech You, Lord, please grant us success!

בָּרוּךְ הַבָּא בְּשֵׁם יי, בֵּרַכְנוּכֶם מִבֵּית יי.
בָּרוּךְ הַבָּא בְּשֵׁם יי, בֵּרַכְנוּכֶם מִבֵּית יי.
אֵל יי וַיָּאֶר לָנוּ, אִסְרוּ חַג בַּעֲבֹתִים עַד קַרְנוֹת הַמִּזְבֵּחַ.
אֵל יי וַיָּאֶר לָנוּ, אִסְרוּ חַג בַּעֲבֹתִים עַד קַרְנוֹת הַמִּזְבֵּחַ.
אֵלִי אַתָּה וְאוֹדֶךָּ, אֱלֹהַי אֲרוֹמְמֶךָּ.
אֵלִי אַתָּה וְאוֹדֶךָּ, אֱלֹהַי אֲרוֹמְמֶךָּ.
הוֹדוּ לַיי כִּי טוֹב, כִּי לְעוֹלָם חַסְדּוֹ.
הוֹדוּ לַיי כִּי טוֹב, כִּי לְעוֹלָם חַסְדּוֹ.

Blessed is he who comes in the name of the Lord;
we bless you from the House of the Lord.
Blessed is he who comes in the name of the Lord;
we bless you from the House of the Lord.
The Lord is God, He has given us light; bind the festival offering with thick cords
until [you bring it to] the horns of the altar.
The Lord is God, He has given us light; bind the festival offering with thick cords
until [you bring it to] the horns of the altar.
You are my God and I will thank You; my God, I will exalt You.
You are my God and I will thank You; my God, I will exalt You.
Give thanks to the Lord, for He is good; for His loving-kindness endures forever!
Give thanks to the Lord, for He is good; for His loving-kindness endures forever!

Food for Thought

A. As noted above, Hallel is divided into two sections on the Seder night. The first section, recited prior to the meal, focuses on the past and is considered by many authorities to be an integral component in the retelling of the Exodus narrative.

The second section, recited at this point in the Seder, is anticipatory in character, focusing on the ultimate redemption toward which all of Jewish history leads.

B. The thematic distinction between these two sections is reflected in a clear change in tone...

Hallel's purpose before the meal was to express our gratitude to God for past kindnesses. The passages included at that point in the Seder were therefore limited to the first two paragraphs of Hallel Hamitzri, consisting entirely of praise.

As we now turn our attention to the second recitation of Hallel, however, our task is different. We are no longer looking backward with gratitude, but forward with a mixture of hope and apprehension.

The Hallel we recite at this point in the Seder, therefore, consists of the remaining passages of Hallel Hamitzri, which are marked by both praise and plea. We rejoice in the certainty of eventual redemption, yet reflect insecurity over the challenges that still lie ahead. A palpable journey of spiritual and emotional conflict is reflected in the text: from the joyous declaration "To You I will offer a thanksgiving offering, and I will call upon the name of the Lord" to the impassioned supplication "Out of narrow confines I called to God"; from the confident exclamation "Give thanks to the Lord, for He is good" to the heartfelt cry "We beseech You, Lord, please save [us]!"[2]

C. This section of Hallel thus captures the essential dialectic at the core of the Jewish people's approach to history. We recognize that, while our nation's ultimate destiny may be clear, the parameters of the journey toward that destiny are not.

That the Mashiach will arrive is certain. *When* he will arrive, however, *how* he will arrive, and, most importantly, *who among us* or among our children will be there to greet him upon his arrival – all these variables are in our hands.

As we contemplate our future, the Hallel we recite is complex. We praise God with a deep sense of confidence in our ultimate redemption, even as we pray to Him that we be personally worthy of that redemption.

---

2   A number of ideas expressed in these paragraphs are based on the comments of Rabbi Joseph Soloveitchik on this section of the Haggada. See Genack, *The Seder Night: An Exalted Evening*, pp. 140–41.

The Primary Mitzvot of the Seder
HALLEL: Psalms of Praise

A. Psalms 113 to 118, collectively traditionally known as Hallel, or more specifically, Hallel Hamitzri,[3] are designated for recitation at specific festive points of the Jewish calendar year or in response to particular events.

B. The source of the obligation to recite Hallel is the subject of rabbinic debate. Some authorities maintain that the obligation is biblical in nature, based on any one of a number of possible sources in the Torah.[4] Other scholars view the requirement as rabbinic in origin.[5] Yet other authorities distinguish between varying occasions and circumstances, maintaining that at times, the obligation to recite Hallel is of biblical origin, and at other times, of rabbinic derivation.[6]

C. An additional layer of complexity is added when we consider the recitation of Hallel at the Seder. Some authorities argue that even those who consider Hallel to be of rabbinic origin year-round view its inclusion in the Seder as biblically mandated, either as part of the retelling of the Exodus story or as a natural response to the experience of personal redemption felt during the Seder service.[7]

D. Numerous details distinguish the recitation of Hallel on the Seder night from its recitation during the rest of the year, including the following:

1. A blessing introduces Hallel year-round. The rabbis debate whether such a blessing should be included on the Seder night. In practice, no blessing is recited.[8]

2. Year-round, Hallel is recited while standing. On the Seder night, we remain seated during its recitation.[9]

3. During the year, Hallel is said during the day.[10] During the Seder. it is recited at night.

4. Women are generally exempt from the recitation of Hallel throughout the year. They are obligated, however, to recite Hallel at the Seder.[11]

E. Numerous explanations are offered by the scholars for the features that distinguish

---

3 These passages are designated by this title because of references to the Exodus contained within them.

4 Ba'al Halachot Gedolot, *minyan hamitzvot*; *Sefer Yere'im* 262; *Sefer Mitzvot Ketanot* 146.

5 Rambam, *Mishneh Torah*, Hilchot Chanuka 3:6.

6 Ramban, *Sefer Hamitzvot*, shoresh 1; Chatam Sofer, Yoreh Deah 233.

7 *Mishnat Ya'abetz* 18, 19; Rabbi Joseph Soloveitchik maintains that although the Rambam views the year-round recitation of Hallel as a rabbinical mandate, he considers the obligation on the Seder night to be of biblical origin – an essential component in the mitzva of *sippur Yetziat Mitzrayim*. Genack, *The Seder Night: An Exalted Evening*, p. 104.

8 *Mishna Berura* 480:1.

9 Ibid.

10 Mishna Megilla 2:5; Talmud Bavli Megilla 20b.

11 Tosafot, Sukka 38a; *Shulchan Aruch*, Orach Chaim 472:14.

the Seder-night Hallel. One global approach, emerging from the Geonic period, becomes the foundation for the thoughts of many scholars who follow. The towering tenth- to eleventh-century halachic authority Rav Hai Gaon suggests that, on the Seder night, Hallel is uniquely offered in the form of *shira* (song).[12] Later scholars explain this to mean that while at other calendar junctures, Hallel is recited to commemorate past events or to mark special festive occasions, the Hallel of the Seder night is recited in response to immediately occurring events.[13]

As we have repeatedly noted, the entire Seder evening is constructed to make each participant feel *"as if he personally came out from Egypt."* As a spontaneous outpouring of gratitude for that which is *happening to us now*, the Seder evening Hallel, therefore, requires no blessing; is offered by all who are touched by the events, male and female; is not considered "testimony" and can therefore be offered while seated; and is offered at the time of experience, day or night.

F. As previously noted, Hallel is divided into two sections on the Seder night. The first section, recited prior to the meal, is limited to the first two passages of Hallel Hamitzri (Psalms 113–114) which focus on the past. This recitation is considered by many authorities to be an integral component in the retelling of the Exodus narrative. The second section, consisting of the remaining passages of Hallel Hamitzri (Psalms 115–118), is anticipatory in character and focuses on the future ultimate redemption. The recitation of this latter section may well rise out of the general obligation – considered by many authorities to be rabbinically derived – to praise God for the goodness that He provides throughout our lives.[14]

G. In our Haggadot, the recitation of the second section of Hallel is augmented by the addition of Psalm 136, known as Hallel Hagadol (the Great Hallel), and specific closing prayers.

H. Hallel should be recited aloud – slowly, clearly and with deep intent – by all present. In many homes, this recitation is enhanced as those assembled join in song. The sections that are recited responsively throughout the year should, if possible, be recited responsively at the Seder, as well.

---

12 Rabbeinu Nissim, Pesachim 118a.

13 Gerlitz, *Haggada shel Pesach Mi'beit Halevi*, p. 195.

14 Genack, *The Seder Night: An Exalted Evening*, p. 105. We have noted that the second section of Hallel actually mirrors both praise and apprehension in its consideration of the future. The existence of this internal dialectic, however, does not necessarily contradict the contention that the obligation to recite this section rises out of the general obligation to praise God. Rooted in reality, Judaism recognizes and accepts the vast range of conflicting emotions that can and do accompany the execution of any significant human enterprise.

A Contested Closing?

The following paragraph, *Yehallelucha*, is recited year-round at the close of Hallel Hamitzri. Its placement in the Seder proceedings, however, has become the subject of rabbinic debate across the centuries.

Over time, two major traditions have developed...

The generally accepted Ashkenazic practice is to recite this paragraph here, at the close of the normative sections of Hallel Hamitzri. According to this custom, however, the paragraph is recited without the usual closing blessing.

The generally accepted Sephardic custom is to reserve the recitation of *Yehallelucha* until later in the Seder, after the various additions to Hallel have been recited (see p. 193).

An outline of other variations between these two customs and a discussion of the reasons for the differing traditions will be offered at the conclusion of Hallel (see pp. 194–96).

יְהַלְלוּךָ יי אֱלֹהֵינוּ כָּל מַעֲשֶׂיךָ, וַחֲסִידֶיךָ צַדִּיקִים עוֹשֵׂי רְצוֹנֶךָ, וְכָל עַמְּךָ בֵּית יִשְׂרָאֵל בְּרִנָּה יוֹדוּ וִיבָרְכוּ, וִישַׁבְּחוּ, וִיפָאֲרוּ, וִירוֹמְמוּ, וְיַעֲרִיצוּ, וְיַקְדִּישׁוּ, וְיַמְלִיכוּ אֶת שִׁמְךָ מַלְכֵּנוּ. כִּי לְךָ טוֹב לְהוֹדוֹת, וּלְשִׁמְךָ נָאֶה לְזַמֵּר, כִּי מֵעוֹלָם וְעַד עוֹלָם אַתָּה אֵל.

All Your works shall praise You, Lord, our God; and Your pious ones, the righteous who do Your will, and all Your people, the House of Israel, with joyous song will thank and bless and praise and glorify and exalt and revere and sanctify and proclaim the sovereignty of Your name, our King. For to You it is good to offer thanks, and to Your name it is fitting to offer song; for from the remotest past unto eternity, You are God.

Additions to Hallel at the Seder 1
Hallel Hagadol

Having concluded Hallel Hamitzri, the normative year-round Hallel, we now
recite Psalm 136, known as Hallel Hagadol (the Great Hallel).

הוֹדוּ לַיי כִּי טוֹב, כִּי לְעוֹלָם חַסְדּוֹ.

הוֹדוּ לֵאלֹהֵי הָאֱלֹהִים, כִּי לְעוֹלָם חַסְדּוֹ.

הוֹדוּ לַאֲדֹנֵי הָאֲדֹנִים, כִּי לְעוֹלָם חַסְדּוֹ.

לְעֹשֵׂה נִפְלָאוֹת גְּדֹלוֹת לְבַדּוֹ, כִּי לְעוֹלָם חַסְדּוֹ.

לְעֹשֵׂה הַשָּׁמַיִם בִּתְבוּנָה, כִּי לְעוֹלָם חַסְדּוֹ.

לְרוֹקַע הָאָרֶץ עַל הַמָּיִם, כִּי לְעוֹלָם חַסְדּוֹ.

לְעֹשֵׂה אוֹרִים גְּדֹלִים, כִּי לְעוֹלָם חַסְדּוֹ.

אֶת הַשֶּׁמֶשׁ לְמֶמְשֶׁלֶת בַּיּוֹם, כִּי לְעוֹלָם חַסְדּוֹ.

אֶת הַיָּרֵחַ וְכוֹכָבִים לְמֶמְשְׁלוֹת בַּלָּיְלָה, כִּי לְעוֹלָם חַסְדּוֹ.

לְמַכֵּה מִצְרַיִם בִּבְכוֹרֵיהֶם, כִּי לְעוֹלָם חַסְדּוֹ.

וַיּוֹצֵא יִשְׂרָאֵל מִתּוֹכָם, כִּי לְעוֹלָם חַסְדּוֹ.

בְּיָד חֲזָקָה וּבִזְרוֹעַ נְטוּיָה, כִּי לְעוֹלָם חַסְדּוֹ.

לְגֹזֵר יַם סוּף לִגְזָרִים, כִּי לְעוֹלָם חַסְדּוֹ.

וְהֶעֱבִיר יִשְׂרָאֵל בְּתוֹכוֹ, כִּי לְעוֹלָם חַסְדּוֹ.

וְנִעֵר פַּרְעֹה וְחֵילוֹ בְיַם סוּף, כִּי לְעוֹלָם חַסְדּוֹ.

לְמוֹלִיךְ עַמּוֹ בַּמִּדְבָּר, כִּי לְעוֹלָם חַסְדּוֹ.

לְמַכֵּה מְלָכִים גְּדֹלִים, כִּי לְעוֹלָם חַסְדּוֹ.

וַיַּהֲרֹג מְלָכִים אַדִּירִים, כִּי לְעוֹלָם חַסְדּוֹ.

לְסִיחוֹן מֶלֶךְ הָאֱמֹרִי, כִּי לְעוֹלָם חַסְדּוֹ.

וּלְעוֹג מֶלֶךְ הַבָּשָׁן, כִּי לְעוֹלָם חַסְדּוֹ.

וְנָתַן אַרְצָם לְנַחֲלָה, כִּי לְעוֹלָם חַסְדּוֹ.

נַחֲלָה לְיִשְׂרָאֵל עַבְדּוֹ, כִּי לְעוֹלָם חַסְדּוֹ.

שֶׁבְּשִׁפְלֵנוּ זָכַר לָנוּ, כִּי לְעוֹלָם חַסְדּוֹ.

וַיִּפְרְקֵנוּ מִצָּרֵינוּ, כִּי לְעוֹלָם חַסְדּוֹ.

נוֹתֵן לֶחֶם לְכָל בָּשָׂר, כִּי לְעוֹלָם חַסְדּוֹ.

הוֹדוּ לְאֵל הַשָּׁמָיִם, כִּי לְעוֹלָם חַסְדּוֹ.

Give thanks to the Lord, for He is good; for His loving-kindness endures forever.

Give thanks to the God of gods; for His loving-kindness endures forever.

Give thanks to the Master of masters; for His loving-kindness endures forever.

To Him Who alone does great wonders; for His loving-kindness endures forever.

To Him Who with understanding made the heavens; for His loving-kindness endures forever.

To Him Who spread forth the earth above the waters; for His loving-kindness endures forever.

To Him Who made the great lights; for His loving-kindness endures forever;

The sun, to rule by day; for His loving-kindness endures forever;

The moon and stars, to rule by night; for His loving-kindness endures forever.

To Him Who smote Egypt through their firstborn; for His loving-kindness endures forever;

And brought Israel out from among them; for His loving-kindness endures forever;

With a strong hand and with an outstretched arm; for His loving-kindness endures forever.

To Him who split the Reed Sea into sections; for His loving-kindness endures forever;

And made Israel pass through the midst of it; for His loving-kindness endures forever;

And overthrew Pharaoh and his host in the Reed Sea; for His loving-kindness endures forever.

To Him Who led His people through the wilderness; for His loving-kindness endures forever.

To Him Who smote great kings; for His loving-kindness endures forever;

And slew mighty kings; for His loving-kindness endures forever;

Sichon, king of the Amorites; for His loving-kindness endures forever;

And Og, king of Bashan; for His loving-kindness endures forever;

And gave their land as a heritage; for His loving-kindness endures forever;

A heritage to Israel, His servant; for His loving-kindness endures forever.

Who, in our lowliness, remembered us; for His loving-kindness endures forever;

And delivered us from our oppressors; for His loving-kindness endures forever.

Who gives food to all flesh; for His loving-kindness endures forever.

Give thanks to the God of heaven; for His loving-kindness endures forever.

Food for Thought

A. Hallel Hagadol (the Great Hallel) is added to the Seder service at the suggestion of the Mishnaic sage Rabbi Tarfon.[15] While debate unfolds among later Talmudic authorities as to the exact parameters of Rabbi Tarfon's proposal,[16] accepted practice identifies Hallel Hagadol with Psalm 136.[17]

Logic would dictate that this psalm is referred to as the "Great Hallel" because of its numerous powerful themes. A puzzling alternative explanation, however, is offered by the major Talmudic sage Rabbi Yochanan: "And why is [Psalm 136] referred to as Hallel Hagadol? Rabbi Yochanan stated, 'Because [this passage chronicles how] the Holy One Blessed Be He sits in the heights of the universe and distributes food to all creatures.'"[18]

B. Of the many possible reasons that could be cited for the designation of the content of Psalm 136 as "great," Rabbi Yochanan's explanation seems the least intuitive. This passage cites such miraculous divine deeds as the creation of the world, the Exodus from Egypt, the parting of the Reed Sea, and more. Why choose what seems to be the least dramatic of the cited phenomena, God's continuing sustenance of the world, as the reason for the designation of this passage as the "Great Hallel"?

And yet, perhaps, our question actually highlights Rabbi Yochanan's point... While other observers might be drawn to the unusual and dramatic, Rabbi Yochanan maintains that the most powerful phenomenon cited in Psalm 136 is not one of its many listed one-time events. In this scholar's eyes, God's ongoing sustenance of the intricate world around us constitutes His greatest miracle – and represents the greatest level of His devotion to us.

C. Rabbi Yochanan's suggestion is supported by a powerful pattern rooted in the Torah's description of God's creation of the world.

The creation narrative is periodically punctuated with the phrase "And God saw that it [His creation] was good."[19] At face value, this statement seems difficult to understand. Mortal man must wait until the completion of a project in order to determine its full value. A perfect, all-knowing God, however, cannot make mistakes. He knows the completed nature of His creation from the outset. Why then does the Torah describe God as creating and only afterwards determining that His creations are "good"?

In a brilliant stroke, the Ramban answers this question by distinguishing between two different actions attributed to God throughout the creation narrative. The Torah tells us that God "spoke" (e.g., "and God said let there be light") and that God "saw" ("and God saw that it was good").

When God "speaks" during the story of creation, says the Ramban, He brings

---

15 Talmud Bavli Pesachim 118a.
16 Ibid.
17 Tosefta, Ta'anit 2:17.
18 Talmud Bavli Pesachim 118a.
19 Bereishit 1:4, 10, 12, 18, 21, 25.

something into being; He *creates*. When God "sees," on the other hand, He moves from the realm of creating to the realm of *sustaining*. This transition is marked by the phrase "and God saw that it was good." The phrase appears when God has completed an element of creation and desires to maintain its existence.

The Ramban, however, goes much further. He emphasizes that God continues to sustain each element of creation eternally. Were God to withdraw for even a moment of time, all would revert to nothingness.[20] The phrase "and God saw that it was good" conveys the concept of God's continued involvement in the world. Through this eternal involvement, the process of creation continues until the end of days.

Millennia later, the rabbis reflect this idea in the blessings before the Shma, with their authorship of the phrase "You renew in your goodness, each day, constantly, the works of creation."[21]

God's active sustenance of the world is essential for its continued existence. Rabbi Yochanan, therefore, views that ongoing sustenance as the greatest of the miracles cited in Psalm 136 and the apparent reason for this psalm's designation as the Great Hallel. We should never lose sight, this towering sage reminds us, of the continuing extraordinary miracles that surround us each day.

D. For further discussion.

Over the course of my rabbinic career I have observed that communities often excel at acute care, yet somehow fail at chronic care. We rally at times of crisis, when the need is clear and dramatic. When others truly need us most, however, in the continuing, quiet aftermath of difficult events, we frequently fail to notice.

Rabbi Yochanan's explanation for the title of Hallel Hagadol contains a moral lesson, not only concerning God's actions, but also concerning our own. We meet our greatest interpersonal challenges when our physical and spiritual sustenance of those around us is ongoing, not transitory.

---

20 Ramban, Bereishit 1:4.
21 Morning prayers.

Additions to Hallel at the Seder 2
Nishmat/Yishtabach (*Yehallelucha*)

Hallel at the Seder concludes with the recitation of the Nishmat/Yishtabach prayer
and a closing blessing. This blessing will vary according to tradition (see below).

נִשְׁמַת כָּל חַי תְּבָרֵךְ אֶת שִׁמְךָ, יי אֱלֹהֵינוּ. וְרוּחַ כָּל בָּשָׂר תְּפָאֵר וּתְרוֹמֵם
זִכְרְךָ, מַלְכֵּנוּ, תָּמִיד. מִן הָעוֹלָם וְעַד הָעוֹלָם אַתָּה אֵל, וּמִבַּלְעָדֶיךָ אֵין לָנוּ מֶלֶךְ
גּוֹאֵל וּמוֹשִׁיעַ, פּוֹדֶה וּמַצִּיל, וּמְפַרְנֵס, וּמְרַחֵם, בְּכָל עֵת צָרָה וְצוּקָה. אֵין לָנוּ
מֶלֶךְ אֶלָּא אָתָּה.

אֱלֹהֵי הָרִאשׁוֹנִים וְהָאַחֲרוֹנִים, אֱלוֹהַּ כָּל בְּרִיּוֹת, אֲדוֹן כָּל תּוֹלָדוֹת, הַמְהֻלָּל
בְּרֹב הַתִּשְׁבָּחוֹת, הַמְנַהֵג עוֹלָמוֹ בְּחֶסֶד, וּבְרִיּוֹתָיו בְּרַחֲמִים. וַיי לֹא יָנוּם וְלֹא
יִישָׁן. הַמְעוֹרֵר יְשֵׁנִים וְהַמֵּקִיץ נִרְדָּמִים, וְהַמֵּשִׂיחַ אִלְּמִים, וְהַמַּתִּיר אֲסוּרִים,
וְהַסּוֹמֵךְ נוֹפְלִים, וְהַזּוֹקֵף כְּפוּפִים, לְךָ לְבַדְּךָ אֲנַחְנוּ מוֹדִים.

אִלּוּ פִינוּ מָלֵא שִׁירָה כַּיָּם, וּלְשׁוֹנֵנוּ רִנָּה כַּהֲמוֹן גַּלָּיו, וְשִׂפְתוֹתֵינוּ שֶׁבַח
כְּמֶרְחֲבֵי רָקִיעַ, וְעֵינֵינוּ מְאִירוֹת כַּשֶּׁמֶשׁ וְכַיָּרֵחַ, וְיָדֵינוּ פְרוּשׂוֹת כְּנִשְׁרֵי שָׁמַיִם,
וְרַגְלֵינוּ קַלּוֹת כָּאַיָּלוֹת, אֵין אֲנַחְנוּ מַסְפִּיקִים לְהוֹדוֹת לְךָ, יי, אֱלֹהֵינוּ וֵאלֹהֵי
אֲבוֹתֵינוּ, וּלְבָרֵךְ אֶת שְׁמֶךָ עַל אַחַת מֵאֶלֶף אַלְפֵי אֲלָפִים, וְרִבֵּי רְבָבוֹת פְּעָמִים,
הַטּוֹבוֹת שֶׁעָשִׂיתָ עִם אֲבוֹתֵינוּ וְעִמָּנוּ.

מִמִּצְרַיִם גְּאַלְתָּנוּ, יי אֱלֹהֵינוּ, וּמִבֵּית עֲבָדִים פְּדִיתָנוּ, בְּרָעָב זַנְתָּנוּ וּבְשָׂבָע
כִּלְכַּלְתָּנוּ, מֵחֶרֶב הִצַּלְתָּנוּ וּמִדֶּבֶר מִלַּטְתָּנוּ, וּמֵחֳלָיִם רָעִים וְנֶאֱמָנִים דִּלִּיתָנוּ.
עַד הֵנָּה עֲזָרוּנוּ רַחֲמֶיךָ וְלֹא עֲזָבוּנוּ חֲסָדֶיךָ, וְאַל תִּטְּשֵׁנוּ יי אֱלֹהֵינוּ לָנֶצַח.
עַל כֵּן אֵבָרִים שֶׁפִּלַּגְתָּ בָּנוּ, וְרוּחַ וּנְשָׁמָה שֶׁנָּפַחְתָּ בְּאַפֵּינוּ, וְלָשׁוֹן אֲשֶׁר שַׂמְתָּ
בְּפִינוּ, הֵן הֵם יוֹדוּ, וִיבָרְכוּ, וִישַׁבְּחוּ, וִיפָאֲרוּ, וִירוֹמְמוּ, וְיַעֲרִיצוּ, וְיַקְדִּישׁוּ,
וְיַמְלִיכוּ אֶת שִׁמְךָ מַלְכֵּנוּ.

כִּי כָל פֶּה לְךָ יוֹדֶה, וְכָל לָשׁוֹן לְךָ תִשָּׁבַע, וְכָל בֶּרֶךְ לְךָ תִכְרַע, וְכָל קוֹמָה
לְפָנֶיךָ תִשְׁתַּחֲוֶה, וְכָל לְבָבוֹת יִירָאוּךָ, וְכָל קֶרֶב וּכְלָיוֹת יְזַמְּרוּ לִשְׁמֶךָ. כַּדָּבָר
שֶׁכָּתוּב, כָּל עַצְמוֹתַי תֹּאמַרְנָה, יי מִי כָמוֹךָ, מַצִּיל עָנִי מֵחָזָק מִמֶּנּוּ, וְעָנִי
וְאֶבְיוֹן מִגֹּזְלוֹ?

מִי יִדְמֶה לָּךְ, וּמִי יִשְׁוֶה לָּךְ, וּמִי יַעֲרָךְ לָךְ? הָאֵל הַגָּדוֹל הַגִּבּוֹר וְהַנּוֹרָא, אֵל
עֶלְיוֹן, קֹנֵה שָׁמַיִם וָאָרֶץ. נְהַלֶּלְךָ וּנְשַׁבֵּחֲךָ וּנְפָאֶרְךָ וּנְבָרֵךְ אֶת שֵׁם קָדְשֶׁךָ,
כָּאָמוּר: לְדָוִד, בָּרְכִי נַפְשִׁי אֶת יי, וְכָל קְרָבַי אֶת שֵׁם קָדְשׁוֹ.

הָאֵל בְּתַעֲצֻמוֹת עֻזֶּךָ, הַגָּדוֹל בִּכְבוֹד שְׁמֶךָ, הַגִּבּוֹר לָנֶצַח וְהַנּוֹרָא בְּנוֹרְאוֹתֶיךָ,
הַמֶּלֶךְ הַיּוֹשֵׁב עַל כִּסֵּא רָם וְנִשָּׂא.

שׁוֹכֵן עַד, מָרוֹם וְקָדוֹשׁ שְׁמוֹ. וְכָתוּב: רַנְּנוּ צַדִּיקִים בַּיי, לַיְשָׁרִים נָאוָה תְהִלָּה.

The soul of every living being shall bless Your name, Lord, our God; and the spirit of all flesh shall continually glorify and exalt Your remembrance, our King. From the remotest past to eternity You are God; and other than You we have no King, Redeemer and Savior, Who liberates, and rescues, and sustains, and shows mercy in every time of trouble and distress. We have no King but You.

God of the first and of the last [generations], God of all creatures, Master of all generations, Who is extolled through a multitude of praises, Who guides His world with loving-kindness and His creatures with mercy. And the Lord neither slumbers nor sleeps. He arouses the sleepers and awakens the slumberous, and makes the mute speak, and releases the bound, and supports the falling, and raises the bowed. To You alone we give thanks:

Even if our mouths were filled with song as the sea, and our tongues with joyous singing as its myriad waves, and our lips with praise as the expanse of the firmament, and our eyes shone with light like the sun and the moon, and our hands spread forth like the eagles of heaven, and our feet were as swift as deer, we would still be unable to thank You sufficiently, Lord, our God and God of our fathers, and to bless Your name, for even one of the thousand thousand, thousands of thousands, and myriads of myriad instances of favor that you have done for our forefathers and for us.

You have redeemed us from Egypt, Lord, our God; and from the house of bondage you have freed us; in famine You have nourished us and in plenty sustained us; from the sword You have saved us and from pestilence rescued us; and from sore and lasting maladies you have delivered us. Heretofore, Your mercies have helped us, and Your loving-kindness has not forsaken us. And do not abandon us, Lord, our God, forever! Therefore, the limbs that You arranged within us, and the spirit and soul that You breathed into our nostrils, and the tongue that You placed in our mouths; indeed, they shall thank, and bless, and praise, and glorify, and exalt, and revere, and sanctify, and proclaim the sovereignty of Your name, our King.

For every mouth shall give thanks to You, and every tongue shall swear to You, and every knee shall bend to You, and all the erect shall bow down before You, and all hearts shall fear You, and all innermost parts and organs shall sing praise to Your name, as it is written: "All my bones will say, 'Lord, who is like You? [You] Who rescues the poor from one stronger than he, the poor and the destitute from one who would rob him!'"[22]

Who is like You? Who is equal to You? Who can be compared to You? The God, great, mighty and awesome; God most high; Possessor of heaven and earth! We will laud You, and praise You, and glorify You, and bless Your holy name, as it is said: "[A Psalm] of David. Bless the Lord, my soul; and all that is within me, bless His holy name."[23]

The God in the power of Your strength; the Great in the glory of Your name; the Mighty forever, and the awe-inspiring through Your awesome deeds; the King Who sits upon a high and lofty throne.

He who inhabits eternity, exalted and holy is His name. And it is written: "Exult, righteous ones, in the Lord; for the upright [the offering of] praise is fitting."[24]

---

22 Tehillim 35:10.
23 Tehillim 103:1.
24 Tehillim 33:1.

By the mouth of the upright, You shall be praised.
By the words of the righteous, You shall be blessed.
By the tongues of the pious, You shall be extolled.
And amid the holy, You shall be sanctified.

בְּפִי יְשָׁרִים תִּתְהַלָּל,
וּבְדִבְרֵי צַדִּיקִים תִּתְבָּרַךְ,
וּבִלְשׁוֹן חֲסִידִים תִּתְרוֹמָם,
וּבְקֶרֶב קְדוֹשִׁים תִּתְקַדָּשׁ.

And in the assemblies of the myriads of Your
people, the House of Israel, through joyous song
shall Your name, our King, be glorified in each
and every generation. For such is the obligation
of all creatures before You, Lord, our God and
God of our fathers, to thank, to laud, to praise,
to glorify, to exalt, to adore, to bless, to elevate
and to acclaim You, even surpassing all the
words of song and praise of David, son of Yishai,
Your anointed servant.

וּבְמַקְהֲלוֹת רִבְבוֹת
עַמְּךָ בֵּית יִשְׂרָאֵל בְּרִנָּה
יִתְפָּאֵר שִׁמְךָ מַלְכֵּנוּ בְּכָל
דּוֹר וָדוֹר, שֶׁכֵּן חוֹבַת כָּל
הַיְצוּרִים לְפָנֶיךָ, יי אֱלֹהֵינוּ
וֵאלֹהֵי אֲבוֹתֵינוּ, לְהוֹדוֹת,
לְהַלֵּל, לְשַׁבֵּחַ, לְפָאֵר,
לְרוֹמֵם, לְהַדֵּר, לְבָרֵךְ, לְעַלֵּה
וּלְקַלֵּס, עַל כָּל דִּבְרֵי שִׁירוֹת
וְתִשְׁבְּחוֹת דָּוִד בֶּן יִשַׁי,
עַבְדְּךָ מְשִׁיחֶךָ.

Praised be Your name forever, the God, our King,
the Great and Holy in heaven and on earth. For
to You, Lord, our God and God of our fathers,
are befitting song and praise, laud and hymn,
strength and dominion, victory, greatness
and might, renown and glory, holiness and
sovereignty, blessings and thanksgivings from
henceforth and unto eternity.

יִשְׁתַּבַּח שִׁמְךָ לָעַד מַלְכֵּנוּ,
הָאֵל הַמֶּלֶךְ הַגָּדוֹל וְהַקָּדוֹשׁ
בַּשָּׁמַיִם וּבָאָרֶץ, כִּי לְךָ נָאֶה,
יי אֱלֹהֵינוּ וֵאלֹהֵי אֲבוֹתֵינוּ,
שִׁיר וּשְׁבָחָה, הַלֵּל וְזִמְרָה,
עֹז וּמֶמְשָׁלָה, נֶצַח, גְּדֻלָּה
וּגְבוּרָה, תְּהִלָּה וְתִפְאֶרֶת,
קְדֻשָּׁה וּמַלְכוּת, בְּרָכוֹת
וְהוֹדָאוֹת מֵעַתָּה וְעַד עוֹלָם.

Those who recited the paragraph of *Yehallelucha* earlier in the Seder (see p. 185) do not repeat it here, but conclude Hallel with the following blessing (Yishtabach's usual concluding blessing):

בָּרוּךְ אַתָּה יי, אֵל, מֶלֶךְ, גָּדוֹל בַּתִּשְׁבָּחוֹת, אֵל הַהוֹדָאוֹת, אֲדוֹן הַנִּפְלָאוֹת,
הַבּוֹחֵר בְּשִׁירֵי זִמְרָה, מֶלֶךְ, אֵל חֵי הָעוֹלָמִים.

Blessed are You, Lord, Almighty God, King, great and extolled in praises, God of
thanksgivings, Lord of wonders, Who takes pleasure in songs of praise; King, the
Life of all worlds.

Those who have not yet recited the paragraph of *Yehallelucha* omit Yishtabach's concluding blessing above and end Hallel with the paragraph of *Yehallelucha* below, including the concluding blessing that usually follows *Yehallelucha* (see explanation for these options below).

יְהַלְלוּךָ יי אֱלֹהֵינוּ כָּל מַעֲשֶׂיךָ, וַחֲסִידֶיךָ צַדִּיקִים עוֹשֵׂי רְצוֹנֶךָ, וְכָל עַמְּךָ בֵּית יִשְׂרָאֵל בְּרִנָּה יוֹדוּ, וִיבָרְכוּ, וִישַׁבְּחוּ, וִיפָאֲרוּ, וִירוֹמְמוּ, וְיַעֲרִיצוּ, וְיַקְדִּישׁוּ, וְיַמְלִיכוּ, אֶת שִׁמְךָ, מַלְכֵּנוּ. כִּי לְךָ טוֹב לְהוֹדוֹת וּלְשִׁמְךָ נָאֶה לְזַמֵּר, כִּי מֵעוֹלָם וְעַד עוֹלָם אַתָּה אֵל. בָּרוּךְ אַתָּה יי, מֶלֶךְ מְהֻלָּל בַּתִּשְׁבָּחוֹת.

All Your works shall praise You, Lord, our God; and Your pious ones, the righteous who do Your will, and all Your people, the House of Israel, with joyous song will thank and bless and praise and glorify and exalt and revere and sanctify and proclaim the sovereignty of Your name, our King. For to You it is good to offer thanks, and to Your name it is fitting to offer song; for from the remotest past unto eternity, You are God. Blessed are You, Lord, King Who is extolled with praises.

Food for Thought

A. The differing customs surrounding the text at this juncture of the Seder rise out of an enigmatic Mishnaic directive instructing the Seder participants to conclude Hallel and recite Birchat Hashir (the Blessing of Song) over the fourth cup of wine.

Exactly what, ask the rabbis in subsequent generations, *is the Blessing of Song?*

Two opinions are offered in the Talmud. Rabbi Yehuda identifies this blessing with the paragraph *Yehallelucha*, recited year-round at the close of Hallel Hamitzri. In contrast, Rabbi Yochanan insists that the Blessing of Song is the Nishmat prayer, regularly recited year-round in the Shabbat and festival morning services.[25] Nishmat concludes with Yishtabach, a paragraph that on Shabbat and festivals forms the last paragraph of Nishmat, but during the daily morning services serves as a complete prayer on its own.

The Talmudic debate between Rabbi Yehuda and Rabbi Yochanan engenders further disagreement among later classical commentaries. Their disagreement gives rise, in turn, to varying traditions concerning the textual flow at this juncture of the Seder.

B. Some authorities, based on Rabbi Yehuda's identification of *Yehallelucha* as the Blessing of Song, end Hallel earlier, with this standard closing. These authorities limit the recitation of Hallel at the Seder to the passages of Hallel Hamitzri and completely omit Hallel Hagadol and Nishmat/Yishtabach from their Haggadot.[26]

Other scholars, accepting Rabbi Yochanan's choice of Nishmat as law, omit the paragraph of *Yehallelucha* entirely from their Haggada texts, in favor of the inclusion of Nishmat/Yishtabach.[27]

Finally, a third set of scholars argues that Rabbi Yochanan never intended to reject the inclusion of the paragraph of *Yehallelucha* in the Seder. He simply insists that Nishmat/Yishtabach should be recited, as well. The Haggadot of these scholars, therefore, include both suggested closing passages.[28]

C. On a practical level, two commonly accepted customs have developed over time, incorporating both *Yehallelucha* and Nishmat/Yishtabach in the proceedings.

Most individuals who pray according to Nusach Ashkenaz, the Ashkenazic rite, recite the paragraph of *Yehallelucha* earlier in the Seder (see p. 185), but omit this paragraph's usual concluding blessing. They then continue with Hallel Hagadol (Psalm 136) and the prayers of Nishmat/Yishtabach. According to this custom, Nishmat/Yishtabach serves as the closing for the entire recitation of Hallel at the Seder, and the blessing that generally concludes Yishtabach in the morning prayers is therefore recited.

In contrast, the majority of those individuals who practice the Sephardic rite

---

25 Talmud Bavli Pesachim 118a.

26 *Haggadat Rav Amram Gaon*; Rambam, *Mishneh Torah,* Hilchot Chametz U'matza 8:10; Rambam, Nusach Hahaggada.

27 Haggadat Hagra, p. 121.

28 Rashbam, Pesachim 118a.

recite the paragraph of *Yehallelucha* at this point in the Seder, after the recitation of Hallel Hagadol and Nishmat/Yishtabach. According to this tradition, *Yehallelucha* replaces Yishtabach as the prayer that concludes Hallel at the Seder. The usual closing blessing for *Yehallelucha* is therefore recited, while the usual closing blessing associated with Yishtabach is omitted (see instructions on p. 193).

D. Sound complicated? It certainly does! Which raises the obvious questions...

Why do the rabbis invest so much energy debating the inclusion, exclusion and/or placement of the paragraphs of *Yehallelucha* and Nishmat/Yishtabach in the Haggada? Why does it matter which of these passages closes the recitation of Hallel on the Seder evening? What motivates the seminal Talmudic dispute between Rabbi Yehuda and Rabbi Yochanan concerning the definition of the "Blessing of Song"? What is the basis for the various practices in the centuries that follow?

E. A brief review of the paragraphs involved reveals that this rabbinic dialogue, spanning centuries, is far from arbitrary. The rabbis are actually debating the tone that should be struck as the formal Seder proceedings draw to a close. The two potential prayers that they suggest for Hallel's conclusion, *Yehallelucha* and Nishmat/Yishtabach, reflect two very different approaches to our relationship with God.

Nishmat, while a prayer of praise, speaks of man's fundamental inability to properly extol God...

"Even if our mouths were filled with song as the sea, and our tongues with joyous singing as its myriad waves, and our lips with praise as the expanse of the firmament, and our eyes shone with light like the sun and the moon, and our hands spread forth like the eagles of heaven, and our feet were as swift as deer, *we would still be unable to thank You sufficiently, Lord, our God and God of our fathers, and to bless Your name,* for even one of the thousand thousand, thousands of thousands, and myriads of myriad instances of favor that you have done for our forefathers and for us."

To the anonymous author of Nishmat,[29] the vast chasm separating an unlimited God from limited man renders man unable to even begin to comprehend, much less describe, the true character of the Divine. Words are all we have – and words are clearly inadequate.

In contrast, the authors of *Yehallelucha* reflect no such discomfort...

"All Your works shall praise You, Lord, our God; and Your pious ones, the righteous who do Your will, and all Your people, the House of Israel, with joyous song will thank and bless and praise and glorify and exalt and revere and sanctify and proclaim the sovereignty of Your name, our King. For to You it is good to offer thanks, and to Your name it is fitting to offer song..."

Which shall it be? the rabbis argue. *Are we to close our praise at the Seder with Nishmat/Yishtabach emphasizing our distance from an unfathomable God, or should we close with Yehallelucha, underscoring our deep desire to somehow comprehend and connect with the Divine?*

---

29 One of the most ancient of Jewish prayers, Nishmat's actual authorship remains shrouded in mystery.

F. Ultimately, the decision is made in the breach. In spite of variations, the accepted Ashkenazic and Sephardic rites determine to include both *Yehallelucha* and Nishmat in the Haggada. In doing so, toward the end of the Seder, the rabbis capture the fundamental tension that shapes a Jew's approach to God, in prayer and beyond.

On the one hand, Jewish thought clearly underscores the mystery of the Divine. Source after source in the Torah and beyond testifies to God's transcendence over the physical world and to the noncorporeal nature of His existence. God remains distant, well beyond the understanding of mortal man.

"Kadosh, Kadosh, Kadosh Hashem Tzevakot" (Holy, Holy, Holy is the Lord of Hosts...), the prophet Yeshayahu hears the celestial hosts proclaiming, in a vision that is eventually incorporated into the key Jewish prayer called Kedusha.[30]

The threefold repetition of God's holiness in this prophecy is particularly telling. To be holy in Jewish thought means to be separate, distinct. A threefold repetition in Jewish law establishes a *chazaka*, a full reality. As his vision opens, Yeshayahu perceives God as completely apart, totally distant from man and man's cognition...

On the other hand, in the very next breath, the celestial beings in Yeshayahu's vision continue: *"...melo chol ha'aretz kevodo"* (the whole world is filled with His glory).[31]

The distant God is, at once, suddenly accessible, clearly visible to man in all of man's surroundings. One need only look at a blossoming flower, at the intricate workings of the human brain, at the spark in the eye of a recipient of kindness, to perceive God's presence in our lives each day.

G. Here then, is the concrete resolution of the rabbinic struggle at this point of the Seder evening. As Hallel, the ultimate expression of gratitude to God in the Haggada, reaches its conclusion, *both Yehallelucha and Nishmat/Yishtabach must be recited.*

We prepare to reenter our worlds fully aware of the dialectic that fashions our relationship with God. Distant and accessible, beyond our understanding yet present in our hearts, God invites us to pierce the cloud of mystery surrounding the Divine. While that cloud will never dissipate, each of us can find a place of light within it – our own personal place of communion with our Creator.

---

30 Yeshayahu 6:3.
31 Ibid.

The Fourth Cup of Wine and Blessing after Wine

Upon the conclusion of Hallel, we complete another Seder mitzva with the consumption of the fourth and last cup of wine.

The familiar year-round blessing following the consumption of wine is then recited. On Shabbat, add the words in parentheses.

בָּרוּךְ אַתָּה יי אֱלֹהֵינוּ מֶלֶךְ הָעוֹלָם, בּוֹרֵא פְּרִי הַגָּפֶן.

Blessed are You, Lord, our God, King of the universe, Who creates the fruit of the vine.

The wine is consumed while leaning to the left.

בָּרוּךְ אַתָּה יי אֱלֹהֵינוּ מֶלֶךְ הָעוֹלָם, עַל הַגֶּפֶן וְעַל פְּרִי הַגֶּפֶן, וְעַל תְּנוּבַת הַשָּׂדֶה, וְעַל אֶרֶץ חֶמְדָּה טוֹבָה וּרְחָבָה, שֶׁרָצִיתָ וְהִנְחַלְתָּ לַאֲבוֹתֵינוּ, לֶאֱכוֹל מִפִּרְיָהּ וְלִשְׂבּוֹעַ מִטּוּבָהּ. רַחֵם נָא, יי אֱלֹהֵינוּ, עַל יִשְׂרָאֵל עַמֶּךָ, וְעַל יְרוּשָׁלַיִם עִירֶךָ, וְעַל צִיּוֹן מִשְׁכַּן כְּבוֹדֶךָ, וְעַל מִזְבְּחֶךָ וְעַל הֵיכָלֶךָ. וּבְנֵה יְרוּשָׁלַיִם עִיר הַקֹּדֶשׁ בִּמְהֵרָה בְיָמֵינוּ, וְהַעֲלֵנוּ לְתוֹכָהּ וְשַׂמְּחֵנוּ בְּבִנְיָנָהּ, וְנֹאכַל מִפִּרְיָהּ, וְנִשְׂבַּע מִטּוּבָהּ, וּנְבָרֶכְךָ עָלֶיהָ בִּקְדֻשָּׁה וּבְטָהֳרָה, (וּרְצֵה וְהַחֲלִיצֵנוּ בְּיוֹם הַשַּׁבָּת הַזֶּה.) וְשַׂמְּחֵנוּ בְּיוֹם חַג הַמַּצּוֹת הַזֶּה, כִּי אַתָּה יי טוֹב וּמֵטִיב לַכֹּל, וְנוֹדֶה לְּךָ עַל הָאָרֶץ וְעַל פְּרִי הַגֶּפֶן (בארץ ישראל: פְּרִי גַּפְנָהּ). בָּרוּךְ אַתָּה יי, עַל הָאָרֶץ וְעַל פְּרִי הַגֶּפֶן (בארץ ישראל: פְּרִי גַּפְנָהּ).

Blessed are You, Lord, our God, King of the universe, for the vine and the fruit of the vine; for the produce of the field; and for the desirable good and spacious land that You were pleased to give as a heritage to our fathers, that they might eat of its fruit and be satisfied with its goodness. Please have mercy, Lord, our God, on Israel, Your people; and on Jerusalem, Your city; and on Zion, the abode of Your glory; and on Your altar; and on Your Temple. Rebuild Jerusalem, the holy city, speedily in our days, and bring us up into it, and make us rejoice in its rebuilding; that we may eat of its fruit, and be satisfied with its goodness, and bless You upon it in holiness and purity. (And favor us and strengthen us on this Shabbat day.) And gladden us on this day of the festival of matzot. For You, Lord, are good and do good to all, and we give thanks to You for the land and for the fruit of the vine (in Israel substitute: the fruit of its vine). Blessed are You, Lord, for the land and for the fruit of the vine (in Israel substitute: the fruit of its vine).

The consumption of the fourth cup of wine marks the conclusion of the formal Seder service and the fulfillment of all the obligatory mitzvot of the evening: the retelling of the Exodus story, the eating of the matza, the eating of the *maror*, the consumption of the four cups of wine, the recitation of Hallel, reclining (and, according to some authorities, the consumption of *charoset*).

What follows is epilogue...

Seder Section 14 • NIRTZA
The Conclusion of the Seder

The formal Seder service finally concluded, the evening's ritual continues with a series of *piyutim* (liturgical poems or songs) that have been added to the Haggada over the ages.

These poems are not found in the early Haggadot of the Geonic period, but first begin to appear during the Middle Ages in the Haggadot of Chachmei Ashkenaz, the classical sages of the geographical area that is now Germany.

As we will see, the *piyutim* of Nirtza are originally composed by disparate authors for use on occasions unconnected to the Seder evening, and are subsequently incorporated into the Haggada by later authorities. Eventually, a total of seven *piyutim* are added to the Ashkenazic Haggada. Some of these poems make their way into the Sephardic text, as well.

The title of this section of song, Nirtza, contains a subliminal reference to the Seder's roots as the anniversary of the first Korban Pesach. As we have noted (see "Making Sense of the Seder II: A Historical Perspective," pp. 5–11), the Korban Pesach was essentially a shared family meal. Nonetheless, this offering also marked the birth of Jewish national ritual worship through the mandated sacrificial rite. The root word of the title Nirtza – *ratzon* (acceptance) – appears repeatedly from this point on, in variant forms, in conjunction with the Torah's description of the sacrifices. Ritual alone, the Torah testifies, has no intrinsic value. Only those offerings marked by proper intent and meaningful performance are ultimately acceptable to God.

Reflecting back on the Seder, Nirtza thus underscores both the limitations and the power of ritual as a whole. When symbolic worship is turned into superstition, its performance actually undermines our relationship with God. Ritual is meant to be meaningful, to teach and shape the character of those who perform it. God desires our personal refinement through the mitzvot, as Jews and as human beings. Only service that moves us toward that goal is ultimately deemed "acceptable."

Having completed the Seder, we now pray that the ceremonies we have performed, when seen within the context of our general relationship with God, will prove pleasing to Him. During Nirtza we express the hope that our Seder will have found *ratzon*, acceptance before God's Heavenly Throne.

Finally, it is particularly fitting that Nirtza closes the Seder through song. With voices raised in unison at the Seder table, year after year, countless families develop their own Nirtza traditions. Age-old melodies are shared, new tunes introduced, harmonies developed, on-key and off-key riffs produced, all to be embellished upon at the next Seder.

The Seder thus ends with a highly individualized experience, as each family makes its own unique contribution to this evening of history, and, in the process, produces new memories that will last for generations.

Nirtza *Piyut* 1: Chassal Siddur Pesach

חֲסַל סִדּוּר פֶּסַח כְּהִלְכָתוֹ, כְּכָל מִשְׁפָּטוֹ וְחֻקָתוֹ. כַּאֲשֶׁר זָכִינוּ לְסַדֵּר אוֹתוֹ, כֵּן נִזְכֶּה לַעֲשׂוֹתוֹ. זָךְ שׁוֹכֵן מְעוֹנָה, קוֹמֵם קְהַל עֲדַת מִי מָנָה. בְּקָרוֹב נַהֵל נִטְעֵי כַנָּה, פְּדוּיִם לְצִיּוֹן בְּרִנָּה. לְשָׁנָה הַבָּאָה בִּירוּשָׁלָיִם!

The order of the Pesach Service is now complete in accordance with its laws; [in compliance] with all of its regulations and statutes. As we have been privileged to arrange it, so may we merit its [full] performance [in the messianic era]. O Pure One, Who dwells on high, raise up the assembled congregation [of whom it was said], "Who can count them?" Speedily lead the offshoots of Your plants, redeemed, to Zion with joyful song.

לְשָׁנָה הַבָּאָה בִּירוּשָׁלָיִם!
Next year in Jerusalem!

Food for Thought

A. The eleventh-century French scholar Rabbi Yom Tov Ellem composed a lengthy *piyut* for the morning prayers on Shabbat Hagadol, the Shabbat before Pesach. This poem includes a review of the practical laws of the Pesach festival and closes with a paragraph that begins with the words *"Chassal siddur Pesach k'hilchato"* (The order of the Pesach service is now completed in accordance with all its laws).

In its original context on Shabbat Hagadol, this paragraph apparently was an entreaty that one should merit, on the Seder night, to fulfill the Seder laws just reviewed.

B. By the fourteenth century, however, this poignant paragraph begins to appear in the Haggada itself, immediately after the close of the formal Seder proceedings, transforming it into a coda for the entire Seder service.

We have completed the obligations of the Pesach Seder, we proclaim to God, *in accordance with all of their laws, ordinances and statutes. Just as*

we have merited their performance this evening, so may we merit the full performance of all the Pesach rituals, next year in Yerushalayim.

The first of the Nirtza poems thus serves as a bridge between the formal Seder proceedings and the passages that follow.

C. At the conclusion of Chassal Siddur Pesach we loudly proclaim *"L'shana haba'a bi'rushalayim"* (Next year in Yerushalayim).

This proclamation is universally issued on two occasions during the Jewish year: at the close of the Seder and at the close of Yom Kippur, marking the two months of the year when, according to Talmudic authorities, the final redemption is most clearly expected: the month of Nissan and the month of Tishrei.[1]

Our Seder journey has come full circle. We opened Maggid with the statement "This year we are here; next year may we be in the Land of Israel." We close the Seder with the statement "Next year in Yerushalayim."

---

1 Talmud Bavli Rosh Hashana 11a; Tosafot, Rosh Hashana 27a.

An Obligatory Interlude: Sefirat Ha'omer

The Torah commands the verbal counting of forty-nine days, from the second day of Pesach until the festival of Shavuot.

While originally associated with the Temple service, the obligation of Sefirat Ha'omer (the counting of the Omer) continues in force to this day – according to some authorities in continuing fulfillment of the biblical mandate,[2] according to other scholars as a rabbinic mitzva performed in remembrance of the Temple.[3]

During the second Seder observed outside the Land of Israel, therefore, we pause to allow those who have not yet begun to fulfill this mitzva to do so now.

Logic would have dictated that the Omer be counted immediately upon the close of the formal Seder proceedings, before Nirtza begins. The performance of this mitzva is, however, delayed until after the recitation of the first Nirtza *piyut*, Chassal Siddur Pesach. This delay underscores the aforementioned role of Chassal Siddur Pesach as a bridge between the Seder and the songs that follow.

During the second Seder observed outside the Land of Israel, those who have not yet begun to count the Omer recite aloud the following blessing, first-day count and one-line petition.

בָּרוּךְ אַתָּה יי אֱלֹהֵינוּ מֶלֶךְ הָעוֹלָם, אֲשֶׁר קִדְּשָׁנוּ בְּמִצְוֹתָיו וְצִוָּנוּ עַל סְפִירַת הָעֹמֶר. הַיּוֹם יוֹם אֶחָד לָעֹמֶר.

הָרַחֲמָן הוּא יַחֲזִיר לָנוּ עֲבוֹדַת בֵּית הַמִּקְדָּשׁ לִמְקוֹמָהּ, בִּמְהֵרָה בְיָמֵינוּ, אָמֵן סֶלָה

Blessed are You, Lord, our God, Who has sanctified us with his commandments and commanded us concerning the counting of the Omer.

Today is the first day of the Omer.

The Merciful One! May He return for us the service of the Holy Temple to its place, speedily in our days, amen selah.

---

2   Rambam, *Mishneh Torah*, Hilchot Temidin U'musafin 7:22; *Sefer Hachinuch*, mitzva 306.
3   *Shulchan Aruch*, Orach Chaim 489:2; *Mishna Berura* 489:14 (in the name of the majority of halachic decisors).

Food for Thought

A. While the Torah provides no clear rationale for the mitzva of Sefirat Ha'omer, classical and contemporary scholars offer a wide variety of approaches toward an understanding of the obligation.

B. Most obviously, Sefirat Ha'omer is perceived by many scholars a linkage between the two holidays that border the mitzva, Pesach and Shavuot. Through the act of counting, we testify that the Revelation at Sinai (commemorated on Shavuot) was the goal and purpose of the Exodus from Egypt (commemorated on Pesach).[4] This relationship is established at the outset when God informs Moshe at the burning bush: "And this is your sign that I have sent you: when you take the people out of Egypt, you shall serve God on this mountain."[5]

On a deeper level, our counting consequently affirms that the physical freedom of the Exodus is incomplete without the spiritual freedom granted by God's law, a truth mirrored in the famous rabbinic dictum "No one is truly free other than he who is involved in the study of Torah."[6] By counting the days between Pesach and Shavuot, many scholars continue, we also are meant to reexperience the sense of excitement and anticipation that marked this period for the Israelites, newly redeemed from Egypt.[7] Just as we would "count the remaining days" toward an extraordinary event in our personal lives, so too we should feel a real sense of anticipation each year as we again approach the holiday marking the Revelation at Sinai.

C. Other authorities choose to view these days primarily as a period of "purification from" rather than "anticipation toward."

By the time of the Exodus, the Israelites have been defiled from centuries of immersion in Egyptian society and culture. Numerous sources, in fact, maintain that they have descended to the forty-ninth of fifty possible stages of defilement and are on the verge of becoming irredeemable.[8]

With haste,[9] at the last moment, God pulls the nation back from the brink. The newly freed slaves, however, must now undergo a process of purification before they can encounter God and receive the Torah at Sinai. Forty-nine days – one to counter each level of defilement experienced – must elapse before Revelation can take place.

By counting the days between Pesach and Shavuot each year, we remember and mark this refining journey.

Based on this approach, the Ohr Hachaim explains why Sefirat Ha'omer begins each year on the *second* day of Pesach, rather than on the *first*. The Exodus, he observes, occurs on the first day of the festival. For a portion of that day, therefore, the Israelites yet remain in Egypt, and the journey of purification cannot yet begin.[10]

---

4   *Sefer Hachinuch*, mitzva 273.
5   Shmot 3:12.
6   Pirkei Avot 6:2.
7   *Sefer Hachinuch*, mitzva 273.
8   Shla Hakadosh, commentary on the Haggada, s.v. "Matza zu."
9   Shmot 12:12.
10 Ohr Hachaim, Vayikra 23:15.

D. In stark contrast to the opinions cited above, a number of scholars emphasize the agricultural, rather than the historical, dimension of the Omer period. Opening the yearly harvest season, these days stretch from the beginning of the barley harvest (marked on the holiday of Pesach) to the beginning of the wheat harvest (marked on the holiday of Shavuot).[11]

As the weather conditions over this period are critical determinants of the success or failure of the entire harvest, the Sforno perceives the associated rituals to be expressions of thanksgiving and prayer. The Omer offering itself, he says, was brought in thanks for the barley harvest. An accompanying *korban*[12] served as a prayer for future success. Sefirat Ha'omer represents the daily prayers during this period, while the holiday of Shavuot is celebrated, in part, as an expression of thanks for the grain harvest.[13]

Choosing an eminently practical path, the Abudarham maintains that Sefirat Ha'omer was meant to counteract a farmer's inevitable preoccupation with his harvest. Counting the days to Shavuot would ensure that he would not forget his obligation to travel to Jerusalem to celebrate the holiday.[14]

Finally, the Maharal finds reference to the global connection between the physical and spiritual dimensions of our lives within the ritual of Sefirat Ha'omer. This scholar maintains that we are enjoined to number the days toward Revelation specifically as the harvest season begins, in order to underscore the well-known rabbinic maxim "Where there is no flour, there is no Torah."[15] Proper Torah study can only take place against the backdrop of a healthy, well-nourished lifestyle.[16]

E. Rabbi Joseph Soloveitchik perceives yet another lesson embedded in the act of Sefirat Ha'omer. The Rav suggests that, in Jewish experience, an individual can perform an act of counting within two realms: the realm of Sefira and the realm of minyan (the root of each of these terms means "to count").

When you count in the realm of minyan, the Rav explains, all that matters is the attainment of the ultimate goal, the endpoint of your counting. Nine upstanding, righteous men can assemble for a prayer service, but without a tenth, there is no minyan.

When you count in the realm of Sefira, however, things are different. Although you still count toward a goal, each individual unit within the calculation becomes an independent goal, as well. Someone counting precious diamonds, for example, is certainly interested in the total number of diamonds possessed, but also pauses and holds each gem up to the rays of the sun, admiring and appreciating its unique facets, color and shape. The act of Sefirat Ha'omer teaches us to count our days in the realm of Sefira – that is, to see each day as a goal unto itself.

Too often, we live exclusively goal-oriented lives, moving from accomplishment to accomplishment, from milestone to milestone,

---

11 Ramban, Vayikra 23:15.
12 Vayikra 23:12.
13 Sforno, Vayikra 23:10.
14 *Sefer Abudarham*, Sefirat Ha'omer.
15 Pirkei Avot 3:21.
16 *Sefer Drashot Maharal Mi'Prague*, Drush al HaTorah.

rarely stopping to appreciate the significance of each passing day. And yet, when all is said and done, it is the quality of the journey that, in large measure, defines our lives. The ordinary moments spent with family and friends are as significant as – if not more significant than – the milestones themselves.

The Rav's observation may also be mirrored in two versions of the verbal formula for Sefirat Ha'omer that have developed over the years. Some communities recite, "Today is the [first, second, third, etc.] day *la'Omer*" (literally "to the Omer"), while others count *"ba'Omer"* (literally "in the midst of the Omer"). Taken together, these two versions form the balance that should mark our approach to life. On the one hand, without goals our lives are aimless. We therefore count *la'Omer*, toward the endpoint of the Omer count. On the other hand, never losing sight of the journey's value, we also count *ba'Omer*, in the midst of the Omer.

F. A historical overlay, emerging from the first to second centuries CE, dramatically transforms the days of the Omer from a time of anticipation and celebration to a period of sorrow and mourning. The Talmud relates: "Rabbi Akiva had twelve thousand pairs of students...and all of them died in one period because they failed to treat each other with respect.... They all died during the period between Pesach and Shavuot."[17]

In commemoration of this tragedy, the rabbis ordained that a portion of the Omer period be circumscribed by laws of mourning. Marriages and other festive celebrations as well as haircuts are prohibited during the restricted period, the exact computation of which varies according to custom, from community to community.[18]

At first glance, the powerful reaction of Jewish law to the death of Rabbi Akiva's students seems strange. Jewish history is sorely marked by myriad that do not result in similar halachic commemorations. What makes this event different?

The Talmud explains that the death of these sages, tragic as it was in and of itself, actually resulted in a greater calamity. At a critical juncture of Jewish history, during the vulnerable period following the destruction of the Second Temple, the loss of Rabbi Akiva's students left the world "desolate" through loss of Torah study.[19] Their death represented a break in the chain of oral tradition at a time when such a rupture threatened the very survival of the Jewish nation. Only Rabbi Akiva's success in finding and teaching new students "in the South" ultimately mitigated the calamitous effects of this tragedy.[20]

This historical overlay placed upon the days of the Omer is clearly neither arbitrary nor coincidental. Both the potential effects of the death of Rabbi Akiva's students and the fundamental cause of their demise connect directly to the period leading to Sinai.

Revelation marks not only the communication of the Written Law, but the launching of the Oral Law, as well. The rupture in the transmission of that oral tradition, created by the loss of Rabbi Akiva's students, threatens the very legacy of Sinai.

---

17 Talmud Bavli Yevamot 62b.
18 *Shulchan Aruch*, Orach Chaim 493; *Mishna Berura*, ibid.
19 Talmud Bavli Yevamot 62b; Rashi, ibid.
20 Talmud Bavli Yevamot 62b.

Concerning the relationship between the cause of the tragedy and the Omer period, one need look no further than the teachings of Rabbi Akiva himself. Rabbi Akiva famously considers *"V'ahavta l'reiacha kamocha"* (Love your fellow as yourself) to be the most important principle of the Torah.[21] By negating that very principle through their behavior, the students of this great sage contradict the very Torah to which they have otherwise dedicated their lives.

G. For further discussion.

A powerfully perplexing mystery arises from the Omer period.

As noted above, Rabbi Akiva emphatically identifies love for your fellow as for yourself as the most important principle of the Torah. Yet his students perish because they fail to treat each other with respect.

Can it be that one of our greatest sages fails to impart his core belief to his students? The problem would be less glaring had Rabbi Akiva's students perished as a result of any other sin. But to transgress the very precept that serves as the core of their mentor's beliefs and practices... How can it be?

Perhaps chronology is the issue. We do not know when Rabbi Akiva determines the centrality of the mitzva of *V'ahavta*. Perhaps this realization arises only in sorrowful retrospect, as a result of the tragic loss of his students. Perhaps it is precisely their death that leads their mentor to recognize the emptiness of Torah observance absent a foundation of interpersonal respect.

Or perhaps our tradition is referencing an entirely different life lesson through this tragedy – a lesson of overarching significance for us all. The stark inconsistency between Rabbi Akiva's core belief and the actions of his students may reflect the universal challenge of intergenerational transmission.

We often make the mistake of assuming that just because something is vital to us, it will automatically be of importance to our children – that the ideas and beliefs that lie at the heart of our worldview are so obvious, they need not be openly stated and taught.

Nothing could be further from the truth.

Our children grow up in worlds different from our own, and within those worlds they form their own personal convictions. The basic foundations that we consider central to our lives are not automatically "givens" within theirs. The deep connection, for example, that we feel toward the State of Israel – in large measure a product of our own life experiences and the experiences of our parents – will not automatically develop in the hearts of our progeny, who are more temporally and emotionally removed than we are from the creation of the State.

As we strive to convey critical ideas and principles to future generations, we can make no assumptions of prior knowledge and conviction. We must consciously and actively teach each and every one of the ideas and principles we feel important, through open discussion and deed.

Perhaps Rabbi Akiva fails to teach his students the central value of his worldview precisely because he considers it self-evident. And just perhaps, across the centuries, he teaches us not to make the same mistake.

---

21 Talmud Yerushalmi Nedarim 9:4.

Nirtza *Piyut* 2: Az Rov Nissim

Outside of Israel, this *piyut* is recited only on the first Seder night.

וּבְכֵן, וַיְהִי בַּחֲצִי הַלַּיְלָה

And thus, it came to pass at midnight.

אָז רוֹב נִסִּים הִפְלֵאתָ בַּלַּיְלָה,

בְּרֹאשׁ אַשְׁמוּרוֹת זֶה הַלַּיְלָה,

גֵּר צֶדֶק נִצַּחְתּוֹ כְּנֶחֱלַק לוֹ לַיְלָה,

וַיְהִי בַּחֲצִי הַלַּיְלָה.

Then [in times of old] did you perform many miracles at night,
In the beginning of the first watch of this night,
You granted the righteous convert [Abraham] victory when he divided his men
at night,[22] And it came to pass at midnight.

דַּנְתָּ מֶלֶךְ גְּרָר בַּחֲלוֹם הַלַּיְלָה,

הִפְחַדְתָּ אֲרַמִּי בְּאֶמֶשׁ לַיְלָה,

וַיָּשַׂר יִשְׂרָאֵל לְמַלְאָךְ וַיּוּכַל לוֹ לַיְלָה,

וַיְהִי בַּחֲצִי הַלַּיְלָה.

You judged the King of Gerar [Avimelech] in a dream at night,[23]
You frightened the Aramean [Laban] in the darkness of night,[24]
Israel [Jacob] wrestled with an angel and overcame him at night,[25]
And it came to pass at midnight.

זֶרַע בְּכוֹרֵי פַתְרוֹס מָחַצְתָּ בַּחֲצִי הַלַּיְלָה,

חֵילָם לֹא מָצְאוּ בְּקוּמָם בַּלַּיְלָה,

טִיסַת נְגִיד חֲרֹשֶׁת סִלִּיתָ בְּכוֹכְבֵי לַיְלָה,

וַיְהִי בַּחֲצִי הַלַּיְלָה.

The firstborn of Patros [Egypt] You did crush at midnight,[26]
Their wealth they could not find when they awoke at night,[27]
The army of the prince of Charosheth [Sisera] you swept away with the the stars
of the night,[28]
And it came to pass at midnight

---

22 A reference to Avraham's excursion to rescue his nephew, Lot, patriarchal period, Bereishit 14:15.

23 A reference to God's warning to the Philistine king, Avimelech, concerning the welfare of the matriarch Sara, patriarchal period, Bereishit 20:3.

24 A reference to God's warning to Lavan concerning the welfare of his nephew, the patriarch Yaakov, patriarchal period, Bereishit 31:24.

25 A reference to the patriarch Yaakov's struggle with an angel on the eve of his reunion with his brother Esav, patriarchal period, Bereishit 32:23–27.

26 A reference to the plague of the firstborn, Shmot 12:29.

27 A reference to the Egyptian wealth taken by the Israelites during the Exodus, Shmot 12:36.

28 A reference to a passage in the Song of Devora following the Israelites' defeat of the Canaanite army, led by the general Sisera, period of the Judges, Shoftim 5:20.

יָעַץ מְחָרֵף לְנוֹפֵף אִוּוּי, הוֹבַשְׁתָּ פְגָרָיו בַּלַּיְלָה,
כָּרַע בֵּל וּמַצָּבוֹ בְּאִישׁוֹן לַיְלָה,
לְאִישׁ חֲמוּדוֹת נִגְלָה רָז חֲזוֹת לַיְלָה,   וַיְהִי בַּחֲצִי הַלַּיְלָה.

The blasphemer [Senacherib] had planned to raise his hand against the desired place [Jerusalem], but You turned him into dry corpses in the night,[29]
The idol Bel and its pedestal were overthrown in the darkness of the night,[30]
To the beloved man [Daniel] was revealed the secret vision at night,[31]
And it came to pass at midnight.

מִשְׁתַּכֵּר בִּכְלֵי קֹדֶשׁ נֶהֱרַג בּוֹ בַּלַּיְלָה,
נוֹשַׁע מִבּוֹר אֲרָיוֹת פּוֹתֵר בְּעִתּוּתֵי לַיְלָה,
שִׂנְאָה נָטַר אֲגָגִי וְכָתַב סְפָרִים לַיְלָה,   וַיְהִי בַּחֲצִי הַלַּיְלָה.

He who became drunk [Belshazar] by drinking from the holy vessels was killed that very night,[32] saved from the lions' den, he [Daniel] interpreted the dreadful dreams of the night,[33] great hatred the Agagite [Haman] cherished, and he wrote edicts by night,[34]
And it came to pass at midnight.

עוֹרַרְתָּ נִצְחֲךָ עָלָיו בְּנֶדֶד שְׁנַת לַיְלָה,
פּוּרָה תִדְרוֹךְ לְשׁוֹמֵר מַה מִּלַּיְלָה,
צָרַח כַּשֹּׁמֵר וְשָׂח אָתָא בֹקֶר וְגַם לַיְלָה,   וַיְהִי בַּחֲצִי הַלַּיְלָה.

You launched Your victory over him [Haman] by disturbing sleep at night,[35]
You will trample the winepress on behalf of those who ask the watchmen, "What of the night?"[36]
He [God] shall answer like a watchman and say, "The morning [redemption] is coming as well as the night,"[37]

---

29 A reference to the miraculous decimation of the Assyrian army during its siege of Jerusalem. First Temple period, II Melachim 19:35.
30 A reference to the destruction of the idol Bel, in a dream dreamt by the Babylonian king, Nebuchadnezzar, and interpreted by the prophet Daniel, period of Babylonian exile, Daniel 2:34.
31 A reference to God's revelations to the prophet Daniel, period of Babylonian exile, Daniel 2:19.
32 A reference to the defiling actions of the Babylonian king, Belshazar, and to his immediate demise, period of Babylonian exile, Daniel 5.
33 A reference to the prophet Daniel's miraculous rescue from the lion's den and his subsequent prophecies, period of Babylonian exile, Daniel 5:17–24.
34 A reference to the machinations of Haman against the Jews during the Purim story, end of Babylonian exile to beginning of Second Temple period, Esther 3.
35 A reference to the turning point of the Purim story, when the sleep of the Persian King Achashverosh is disturbed in the middle of the night, end of Babylonian exile to beginning of Second Temple period, Esther 6:1.
36 A reference to the prophecy of the prophet Yeshayahu, in which the Jews call out to their "Watchman," God, because of the oppression of exile ("the night"), First Temple period, Yeshayahu 21:11.
37 A reference to the continuation of Yeshayahu's prophecy, in which God promises "morning," deliverance for the deserving, Yeshayahu 21:12.

And it came to pass at midnight.

קָרֵב יוֹם אֲשֶׁר הוּא לֹא יוֹם וְלֹא לַיְלָה,

רָם הוֹדַע כִּי לְךָ הַיּוֹם אַף לְךָ הַלַּיְלָה,

שׁוֹמְרִים הַפְקֵד לְעִירְךָ כָּל הַיּוֹם וְכָל הַלַּיְלָה,

תָּאִיר כְּאוֹר יוֹם חֶשְׁכַּת לַיְלָה,   וַיְהִי בַּחֲצִי הַלַּיְלָה:

Draw near the day that is neither day nor night [the day of redemption],[38]
Most High, make it known that Yours is the day as well as the night,
Appoint watchmen for Your City [Jerusalem] all day and all night,
Make bright, like the very day, the darkness of the night,
And it came to pass at midnight.

Food for Thought

A. Composed circa the sixth century CE by Yannai, one of the earliest authors of Jewish liturgical poetry, Az Rov Nissim is based upon a midrashic source claiming that "All miracles performed for Israel, within which evildoers were punished, took place at night."[39]

Written in the form of an alphabetical acrostic, the poem lists a series of such nighttime events (see explanatory footnotes), including the final plague meted out against the Egyptians, the plague of the firstborn. Originally composed for recitation on the Shabbat when the Exodus narrative was read in the Torah cycle, Az Rov Nissim became part of the Shabbat Hagadol liturgy in some communities before making its way into the Seder service.

B. In order to more closely connect the *piyut* to the themes of the evening, the phrase *"Va'yehi ba'chatzi halaila"* (And it came to pass at midnight) is repeated as a refrain with each stanza of the poem. This phrase is quoted from the Torah's introduction to the plague of the firstborn.[40]

After reviewing miracles of the past, Az Rov Nissim turns toward the future with a closing prayer evoking the ultimate redemption: "Draw near the day that is neither day nor night.... Make bright, like the very day, the darkness of the night!"

---

38 A reference to the prophecy of the prophet Zecharya, describing the day of deliverance as a day that will be "neither day nor night," period of Babylonian exile, Zecharya 14:7.

39 Midrash Rabba Bamidbar 20:11.

40 Shmot 12:29.

Nirtza *Piyut* 3: Ometz Gevurotecha

Outside of Israel, this *piyut* is recited only on the second Seder night.

וּבְכֵן, וַאֲמַרְתֶּם זֶבַח פֶּסַח

And therefore you shall say, "This is the Pesach offering."

אֹמֶץ גְּבוּרוֹתֶיךָ הִפְלֵאתָ בַּפֶּסַח,
בְּרֹאשׁ כָּל מוֹעֲדוֹת נִשֵּׂאתָ פֶּסַח,
גִּלִּיתָ לָאֶזְרָחִי חֲצוֹת לֵיל פֶּסַח,
וַאֲמַרְתֶּם זֶבַח פֶּסַח.

The power of Your might did You wondrously demonstrate on Pesach,
At the head of all appointed times did You raise [the festival of] Pesach,[41]
You revealed to the Ezrachite [Abraham] what would happen at midnight on Pesach,[42]
And you shall say, "This is the Pesach offering."

דְּלָתָיו דָּפַקְתָּ כְּחֹם הַיּוֹם בַּפֶּסַח,
הִסְעִיד נוֹצְצִים עֻגוֹת מַצּוֹת בַּפֶּסַח,
וְאֶל הַבָּקָר רָץ זֵכֶר לְשׁוֹר עֵרֶךְ פֶּסַח,
וַאֲמַרְתֶּם זֶבַח פֶּסַח.

You knocked on his [Abraham's] door in the midday heat on Pesach,[43]
He provided the angels with matzot on which to dine during Pesach,[44]
And he ran to the cattle,[45] foreshadowing the festive offering of Pesach,
And you shall say, "This is the Pesach offering."

זֹעֲמוּ סְדוֹמִים וְלֹהֲטוּ בָּאֵשׁ בַּפֶּסַח,
חֻלַּץ לוֹט מֵהֶם, וּמַצּוֹת אָפָה בְּקֵץ פֶּסַח,
טִאטֵאתָ אַדְמַת מֹף וְנֹף בְּעָבְרְךָ בַּפֶּסַח,
וַאֲמַרְתֶּם זֶבַח פֶּסַח.

The Sodomites angered [God] and were consumed by fire[46] on Pesach,
Lot was rescued from them[47] and he baked matzot at the end of Pesach,
You swept clean the land of Moph and Noph [Egypt] when you passed
through on Pesach,
And you shall say, "This is the Pesach offering."

---

41 A reference to God's designation of the month of Nissan, the month containing Pesach, as the beginning of the calendar year, Shmot 12:1.

42 A reference to the Covenant between the Pieces, during which God infoms the patriarch Avraham of the future servitude and ultimate redemption of his descendants, patriarchal period, Bereishit 15:9–21.

43 A reference to God's appearance to the patriarch Avraham as he sits at the entrance to his tent in the heat of the day, patriarchal period, Bereishit 18:1.

44 A reference to the visit of the three angels to Avraham on that same occasion, patriarchal period, Bereishit 18:6.

45 A continuing reference to the visit of the three angels to Avraham, patriarchal period, Bereishit 18:7.

46 A reference to the destruction of the sinful cities of Sodom and Amora, patriarchal period, Bereishit 19:24–25.

47 A reference to the sparing of Avraham's nephew, Lot, from the conflagration that destroys Sodom, patriarchal period, Bereishit 19:16.

יָהּ, רֹאשׁ כָּל אוֹן מָחַצְתָּ בְּלֵיל שִׁמּוּר פֶּסַח,

כַּבִּיר, עַל בֵּן בְּכוֹר פָּסַחְתָּ בְּדַם פֶּסַח,

לְבִלְתִּי תֵּת מַשְׁחִית לָבֹא בִּפְתָחַי בַּפֶּסַח,

וַאֲמַרְתֶּם זֶבַח פֶּסַח.

Lord, You struck the head of every firstborn [in Egypt] on the watchful night of Pesach,[48]
Almighty, You passed over Your firstborn [the children of Israel] because of the blood-mark of Pesach,[49] not allowing the destroyer to enter my doors on Pesach,
And you shall say, "This is the Pesach offering."

מְסֻגֶּרֶת סֻגְּרָה בְּעִתּוֹתֵי פֶּסַח,

נִשְׁמְדָה מִדְיָן בִּצְלִיל שְׂעוֹרֵי עֹמֶר פֶּסַח,

שֹׂרְפוּ מִשְׁמַנֵּי פּוּל וְלוּד בִּיקַד יְקוֹד פֶּסַח,

וַאֲמַרְתֶּם זֶבַח פֶּסַח.

The sealed city [Jericho] fell in the season of Pesach,[50] Midian was destroyed by [a dream of] the barley cake, the Omer offering brought on Pesach,[51]
The mighty captains of Pul and Lud [Assyria] were consumed in a great conflagration on Pesach,[52]
And you shall say, "This is the Pesach offering."

עוֹד הַיּוֹם בְּנֹב לַעֲמוֹד, עַד גָּעָה עוֹנַת פֶּסַח,

פַּס יָד כָּתְבָה לְקַעֲקֵעַ צוּל בַּפֶּסַח,

צָפֹה הַצָּפִית עָרוֹךְ הַשֻּׁלְחָן, בַּפֶּסַח,

וַאֲמַרְתֶּם זֶבַח פֶּסַח.

The day he [Senacherib] halted at Nob was before the advent of Pesach,[53]
A hand wrote of the doom of Zul [Babylonia] on a wall on Pesach,[54]
The watch was set, the table [the downfall of Babylon] spread on Pesach,[55]
And you shall say, "This is the Pesach offering."

קָהָל כִּנְּסָה הֲדַסָּה צוֹם לְשַׁלֵּשׁ בַּפֶּסַח,

רֹאשׁ מִבֵּית רָשָׁע מָחַצְתָּ בְּעֵץ חֲמִשִּׁים בַּפֶּסַח,

שְׁתֵּי אֵלֶּה רֶגַע, תָּבִיא לְעוּצִית בַּפֶּסַח,

תָּעֹז יָדְךָ וְתָרוּם יְמִינְךָ, כְּלֵיל הִתְקַדֶּשׁ חַג פֶּסַח,

וַאֲמַרְתֶּם זֶבַח פֶּסַח.

---

48 A reference to the plague of the firstborn, Shmot 12:29.

49 A reference to the protection of the Israelites from the plague of the firstborn, Shmot 12:22–23.

50 A reference to the conquest of the city of Yericho, period of the conquest of Canaan, Yehoshua 4:19.

51 A reference to Gideon's dream of a rolling barley cake striking the encampment of the marauding Midianite army, period of the Judges, Shoftim 7:13. The Midrash explains that the barley cake represented the Israelites' Omer offering, in the merit of which the Midianites were subdued. Midrash Rabba Vayikra 28.

52 A reference to the prophet Yeshayahu's prophecy concerning the punishment of the princes of Assyria, First Temple period, Yeshayahu 10:16.

53 A reference to the delay experienced by the Assyrian armies upon their arrival at Nob, First Temple period, Yeshayahu 10:32.

54 A reference to the inscription on the wall of the palace of the Babylonian king, Belshazar, by a miraculous hand. The inscription was interpreted by the prophet Daniel as predicting Belshazar's fall, period of Babylonian exile, Daniel 5.

55 A reference to Belshazar's appointment of guards and preparations for a feast in his mistaken expectation of military victory, period of Babylonian exile, Yeshayahu 21:5.

Hadassah [Esther] assembled the congregation for a three-day fast on Pesach,[56]

The chief of the wicked clan [Haman] You crushed, with a gallows of fifty cubits on Pesach,[57]

A double punishment will You suddenly bring on the Utzites [Edom] on Pesach,[58]

Let Your hand be strengthened and Your right hand raised as on the night of the consecration of the festival of Pesach,

And you shall say, "This is the Pesach offering."

Food for Thought

A. The author of Ometz Gevurotecha, Rabbi Elazar Hakalir (circa sixth to seventh centuries CE), is one of the greatest and most prolific of the Jewish liturgical poets. His extensive works populate Jewish prayer across the calendar year.

In this *piyut*, Hakalir outlines the many historical events, from patriarchal times onward, that occur on the dates that coincide with the Pesach festival (see explanatory footnotes).

B. Like Az Rov Nissim, Ometz Gevurotecha is fashioned in a series of stanzas forming an alphabetical acrostic, with a one-line refrain introducing each stanza. In this case, the refrain consists of the phrase *"Va'amartem zevach Pesach"* (And you shall say: This is the feast of Pesach), a phrase that appears in the Torah in a section of instruction to children concerning the Pesach rituals.[59]

---

56 A reference to Esther's call upon the Persian Jewish community to pray and fast for her protection, end of Babylonian exile to beginning of Second Temple period, Esther 4:16; Talmud Bavli Megilla 15a.

57 A reference to the execution of Haman, the villain of the Purim story, end of Babylonian exile to beginning of Second Temple period, Esther 7:9–10; Talmud Bavli Megilla 16a.

58 A prayer that the dual woes of child loss and widowhood, prophetically predicted against the Babylonians (Yeshayahu 47:9), should now strike the nation of Edom (Rome and its spiritual descendants).

59 Shmot 12:27.

Nirtza *Piyut* 4: Ki Lo Na'eh, Ki Lo Ya'eh

כִּי לוֹ נָאֶה, כִּי לוֹ יָאֶה.

To Him [praise is] becoming, to Him [praise is] fitting.

אַדִּיר בִּמְלוּכָה, בָּחוּר כַּהֲלָכָה, גְּדוּדָיו יֹאמְרוּ לוֹ:
לְךָ וּלְךָ;לְךָ כִּי לְךָ; לְךָ אַף לְךָ; לְךָ, יי הַמַּמְלָכָה.   כִּי לוֹ נָאֶה, כִּי לוֹ יָאֶה.

Powerful in kingship, perfectly chosen; His legions [angels] say to Him: "To You and to You; to You; indeed to You; to You, only to You; to You, Lord, is the sovereignty." For to Him [praise is] becoming, for to Him [praise is] fitting.

דָּגוּל בִּמְלוּכָה, הָדוּר כַּהֲלָכָה, וְתִיקָיו יֹאמְרוּ לוֹ:
לְךָ וּלְךָ;לְךָ כִּי לְךָ; לְךָ אַף לְךָ; לְךָ, יי הַמַּמְלָכָה.   כִּי לוֹ נָאֶה, כִּי לוֹ יָאֶה.

Renowned in kingship, perfectly glorious; His faithful [Israel] say to Him: "To You and to You; to You, indeed to You; to You, only to You; to You, Lord, is the sovereignty." For to Him [praise is] becoming, for to Him [praise is] fitting.

זַכַּאי בִּמְלוּכָה, חָסִין כַּהֲלָכָה, טַפְסְרָיו יֹאמְרוּ לוֹ:
לְךָ וּלְךָ;לְךָ כִּי לְךָ; לְךָ אַף לְךָ; לְךָ, יי הַמַּמְלָכָה.   כִּי לוֹ נָאֶה, כִּי לוֹ יָאֶה.

Worthy in kingship, perfectly immutable; His officers [angels] say to Him: "To You and to You; to You; indeed to You; to You, only to You; to You, Lord, is the sovereignty." For to Him [praise is] becoming, for to Him [praise is] fitting.

יָחִיד בִּמְלוּכָה, כַּבִּיר כַּהֲלָכָה, לִמּוּדָיו יֹאמְרוּ לוֹ:
לְךָ וּלְךָ;לְךָ כִּי לְךָ; לְךָ אַף לְךָ; לְךָ, יי הַמַּמְלָכָה.   כִּי לוֹ נָאֶה, כִּי לוֹ יָאֶה.

Unique in kingship, perfectly powerful; His learned ones [Israel] say unto Him: "To You and to You; to You, indeed to You; to You, only to You; to You, Lord, is the sovereignty." For to Him [praise is] becoming, for to Him [praise is] fitting.

מוֹשֵׁל בִּמְלוּכָה, נוֹרָא כַּהֲלָכָה, סְבִיבָיו יֹאמְרוּ לוֹ:
לְךָ וּלְךָ;לְךָ כִּי לְךָ; לְךָ אַף לְךָ; לְךָ, יי הַמַּמְלָכָה.   כִּי לוֹ נָאֶה, כִּי לוֹ יָאֶה.

Commanding in kingship, perfectly awe-inspiring; His surrounding ones [angels] say unto Him: "To You and to You; to You, indeed to You; to You, only to You; to You, Lord, is the sovereignty." For to Him [praise is] becoming, for to Him [praise is] fitting.

עָנָו בִּמְלוּכָה, פּוֹדֶה כַּהֲלָכָה, צַדִּיקָיו יֹאמְרוּ לוֹ:
לְךָ וּלְךָ;לְךָ כִּי לְךָ; לְךָ אַף לְךָ; לְךָ, יי הַמַּמְלָכָה.   כִּי לוֹ נָאֶה, כִּי לוֹ יָאֶה.

Humble in kingship, perfectly redeeming; His righteous ones [Israel] say unto Him: "To You and to You; to You, indeed to You; to You, only to You; to You, Lord, is the sovereignty." For to Him [praise is] becoming, for to Him [praise is] fitting.

קָדוֹשׁ בִּמְלוּכָה, רַחוּם כַּהֲלָכָה, שִׁנְאַנָּיו יֹאמְרוּ לוֹ:
לְךָ וּלְךָ;לְךָ כִּי לְךָ; לְךָ אַף לְךָ; לְךָ, יי הַמַּמְלָכָה.
כִּי לוֹ נָאֶה, כִּי לוֹ יָאֶה.

Holy in kingship, perfectly merciful; His ministers [angels] say unto Him: "To You and to You; to You, indeed to You; to You, only to You; to You, Lord, is the sovereignty." For to Him [praise is] becoming, for to Him [praise is] fitting.

תַּקִּיף בִּמְלוּכָה, תּוֹמֵךְ כַּהֲלָכָה, תְּמִימָיו יֹאמְרוּ לוֹ:
לְךָ וּלְךָ;לְךָ כִּי לְךָ; לְךָ אַף לְךָ; לְךָ, יי הַמַּמְלָכָה.
כִּי לוֹ נָאֶה, כִּי לוֹ יָאֶה.

Almighty in kingship, perfectly supportive; His innocent ones [Israel] say unto Him: "To You and to You; to You, indeed to You; to You, only to You; to You, Lord, is the sovereignty." For to Him [praise is] becoming, for to Him [praise is] fitting.

Food for Thought

A. Of unknown authorship, Ki Lo Na'eh, Ki Lo Ya'eh was recited at the Seder tables of numerous classical authorities, including the towering thirteenth-century German scholar Rabbi Meir ben Baruch, the Maharam of Rothenberg.[60]

The poem consists of eight stanzas, each of which is divided into three parts. The first two of these parts reflect praises of God, while the third part enumerates the various heavenly and earthly hosts who praise Him. The stanzas, which unfold as an alphabetical acrostic, each close with the declaration "Ki Lo na'eh, ki Lo ya'eh" (For to Him [praise is] becoming, for to Him [praise is] fitting).

B. The tribute offered by the various groups praising God in this poem is particularly puzzling: "Lecha u'Lecha; Lecha ki Lecha; Lecha af Lecha; Lecha Hashem hamamlacha" (To You and to You; to You, indeed to You; to You, only to You; to You, Lord, is the sovereignty).

Some authorities explain this phrase as poetic shorthand, referencing numerous scriptural verses in which the word Lecha (to You) is applied to God.[61] Other scholars suggest that the sevenfold repetition of the word lecha hints at phenomena based on the number seven, such as seven days of the week and seven firmaments between heaven and earth.

---

60 Kasher, *Haggada Shleima*, p. 189.
61 Rabbi Elyakim Shatz, Seder Hatefillot Amsterdam, quoted in Kasher, *Haggada Shleima*.

Nirtza *Piyut* 5: Adir Hu

אַדִּיר הוּא, יִבְנֶה בֵּיתוֹ בְּקָרוֹב; בִּמְהֵרָה בִּמְהֵרָה, בְּיָמֵינוּ בְּקָרוֹב. אֵל בְּנֵה, אֵל בְּנֵה, בְּנֵה בֵּיתְךָ בְּקָרוֹב!

Mighty is He, may He soon rebuild His House; speedily, speedily, soon in our days. God rebuild, God rebuild, rebuild Your House soon!

בָּחוּר הוּא, גָּדוֹל הוּא, דָּגוּל הוּא, יִבְנֶה בֵּיתוֹ בְּקָרוֹב; בִּמְהֵרָה בִּמְהֵרָה, בְּיָמֵינוּ בְּקָרוֹב. אֵל בְּנֵה, אֵל בְּנֵה, בְּנֵה בֵּיתְךָ בְּקָרוֹב!

Chosen is He, Great is He, Renowned is He, may He soon rebuild His House; speedily, speedily, soon in our days. God rebuild, God rebuild, rebuild Your House soon!

הָדוּר הוּא, וָתִיק הוּא, זַכַּאי הוּא, חָסִיד הוּא, יִבְנֶה בֵּיתוֹ בְּקָרוֹב; בִּמְהֵרָה בִּמְהֵרָה, בְּיָמֵינוּ בְּקָרוֹב. אֵל בְּנֵה, אֵל בְּנֵה, בְּנֵה בֵּיתְךָ בְּקָרוֹב!

Glorious is He, Faithful is He, Worthy is He, Righteous is He; may He soon rebuild His House; speedily, speedily, soon in our days. God rebuild, God rebuild, rebuild Your House soon!

טָהוֹר הוּא, יָחִיד הוּא, כַּבִּיר הוּא, לָמוּד הוּא, מֶלֶךְ הוּא, נוֹרָא הוּא, סַגִּיב הוּא, עִזּוּז הוּא, פּוֹדֶה הוּא, צַדִּיק הוּא, יִבְנֶה בֵּיתוֹ בְּקָרוֹב; בִּמְהֵרָה בִּמְהֵרָה, בְּיָמֵינוּ בְּקָרוֹב. אֵל בְּנֵה, אֵל בְּנֵה, בְּנֵה בֵּיתְךָ בְּקָרוֹב!

Pure is He, Unique is He, Commanding is He, Wise is He, Regal is He, Awe-inspiring is He, Exalted is He, Powerful is He, Redeeming is He, Just is He, may He soon rebuild His House; speedily, speedily, soon in our days. God rebuild, God rebuild, rebuild Your House soon!

קָדוֹשׁ הוּא, רַחוּם הוּא, שַׁדַּי הוּא, תַּקִּיף הוּא, יִבְנֶה בֵּיתוֹ בְּקָרוֹב; בִּמְהֵרָה בִּמְהֵרָה, בְּיָמֵינוּ בְּקָרוֹב. אֵל בְּנֵה, אֵל בְּנֵה, בְּנֵה בֵּיתְךָ בְּקָרוֹב!

Holy is He, Merciful is He, Almighty is He, Dominant is He, may He soon rebuild His House; speedily, speedily, soon in our days. God rebuild, God rebuild, rebuild Your House soon!

Food for Thought

A. Another *piyut* of unknown authorship, Adir Hu differs from the previous *piyut*, Ki Lo Na'eh, Ki Lo Ya'eh, in a significant way. While both of these poems are replete with praises of God, Adir Hu adds a powerful repeated request for the divine rebuilding of the Temple. The appropriateness of this request on the Seder evening again traces to the Talmudic assertion that the month of Nissan is one of the two calendar points when the final redemption can be most clearly expected to occur.

B. The verses of Adir Hu, like those of previous *piyutim*, unfold in the form of an alphabetical acrostic.

Nirtza *Piyut* 6: Echad Mi Yode'a

אֶחָד מִי יוֹדֵעַ? אֶחָד אֲנִי יוֹדֵעַ: אֶחָד אֱלֹהֵינוּ שֶׁבַּשָּׁמַיִם וּבָאָרֶץ.

Who knows one? I know one: One [is] our God, in heaven and on earth.

שְׁנַיִם מִי יוֹדֵעַ? שְׁנַיִם אֲנִי יוֹדֵעַ: שְׁנֵי לֻחוֹת הַבְּרִית, אֶחָד אֱלֹהֵינוּ שֶׁבַּשָּׁמַיִם וּבָאָרֶץ.

Who knows two? I know two: two [are the] tablets of the Covenant; One [is] our God, in heaven and on earth.

שְׁלֹשָׁה מִי יוֹדֵעַ? שְׁלֹשָׁה אֲנִי יוֹדֵעַ: שְׁלֹשָׁה אָבוֹת, שְׁנֵי לֻחוֹת הַבְּרִית, אֶחָד אֱלֹהֵינוּ שֶׁבַּשָּׁמַיִם וּבָאָרֶץ.

Who knows three? I know three: three [are the] patriarchs; two [are the] tablets of the Covenant; One [is] our God, in heaven and on earth.

אַרְבַּע מִי יוֹדֵעַ? אַרְבַּע אֲנִי יוֹדֵעַ: אַרְבַּע אִמָּהוֹת, שְׁלֹשָׁה אָבוֹת, שְׁנֵי לֻחוֹת הַבְּרִית, אֶחָד אֱלֹהֵינוּ שֶׁבַּשָּׁמַיִם וּבָאָרֶץ.

Who knows four? I know four: four [are the] matriarchs; three [are the] patriarchs; two [are the] tablets of the Covenant; One [is] our God, in heaven and on earth.

חֲמִשָּׁה מִי יוֹדֵעַ? חֲמִשָּׁה אֲנִי יוֹדֵעַ: חֲמִשָּׁה חוּמְשֵׁי תוֹרָה, אַרְבַּע אִמָּהוֹת, שְׁלֹשָׁה אָבוֹת, שְׁנֵי לֻחוֹת הַבְּרִית, אֶחָד אֱלֹהֵינוּ שֶׁבַּשָּׁמַיִם וּבָאָרֶץ.

Who knows five? I know five: five [are the] books of the Torah; four [are the] matriarchs; three [are the] patriarchs; two [are the] tablets of the Covenant; One [is] our God, in heaven and on earth.

שִׁשָּׁה מִי יוֹדֵעַ? שִׁשָּׁה אֲנִי יוֹדֵעַ: שִׁשָּׁה סִדְרֵי מִשְׁנָה, חֲמִשָּׁה חוּמְשֵׁי תוֹרָה, אַרְבַּע אִמָּהוֹת, שְׁלֹשָׁה אָבוֹת, שְׁנֵי לֻחוֹת הַבְּרִית, אֶחָד אֱלֹהֵינוּ שֶׁבַּשָּׁמַיִם וּבָאָרֶץ.

Who knows six? I know six: six [are the] orders of the Mishna, five [are the] books of the Torah; four [are the] matriarchs; three [are the] patriarchs; two [are the] tablets of the Covenant; One [is] our God, in heaven and on earth.

שִׁבְעָה מִי יוֹדֵעַ? שִׁבְעָה אֲנִי יוֹדֵעַ: שִׁבְעָה יְמֵי שַׁבַּתָּא, שִׁשָּׁה סִדְרֵי מִשְׁנָה, חֲמִשָּׁה חוּמְשֵׁי תוֹרָה, אַרְבַּע אִמָּהוֹת, שְׁלֹשָׁה אָבוֹת, שְׁנֵי לֻחוֹת הַבְּרִית, אֶחָד אֱלֹהֵינוּ שֶׁבַּשָּׁמַיִם וּבָאָרֶץ.

Who knows seven? I know seven: seven [are the] days of the week; six [are the] orders of the Mishna, five [are the] books of the Torah; four [are the] matriarchs; three [are the] patriarchs; two [are the] tablets of the Covenant; One [is] our God, in heaven and on earth.

שְׁמוֹנָה מִי יוֹדֵעַ? שְׁמוֹנָה אֲנִי יוֹדֵעַ: שְׁמוֹנָה יְמֵי מִילָה, שִׁבְעָה יְמֵי שַׁבַּתָּא, שִׁשָּׁה סִדְרֵי מִשְׁנָה, חֲמִשָּׁה חוּמְשֵׁי תוֹרָה, אַרְבַּע אִמָּהוֹת, שְׁלֹשָׁה אָבוֹת, שְׁנֵי לֻחוֹת הַבְּרִית, אֶחָד אֱלֹהֵינוּ שֶׁבַּשָּׁמַיִם וּבָאָרֶץ.

Who knows eight? I know eight: eight [are the] days to circumcision; seven [are the] days of the week; six [are the] orders of the Mishna, five [are the] books of the Torah; four [are the] matriarchs; three [are the] patriarchs; two [are the] tablets of the Covenant; One [is] our God, in heaven and on earth.

תִּשְׁעָה מִי יוֹדֵעַ? תִּשְׁעָה אֲנִי יוֹדֵעַ: תִּשְׁעָה יַרְחֵי לֵדָה, שְׁמוֹנָה יְמֵי מִילָה, שִׁבְעָה יְמֵי שַׁבַּתָּא, שִׁשָּׁה סִדְרֵי מִשְׁנָה, חֲמִשָּׁה חוּמְשֵׁי תוֹרָה, אַרְבַּע אִמָּהוֹת, שְׁלֹשָׁה אָבוֹת, שְׁנֵי לֻחוֹת הַבְּרִית, אֶחָד אֱלֹהֵינוּ שֶׁבַּשָּׁמַיִם וּבָאָרֶץ.

Who knows nine? I know nine: nine [are the] months of pregnancy; eight [are the] days to circumcision; seven [are the] days of the week; six [are the] orders of the Mishna, five [are the] books of the Torah; four [are the] matriarchs; three [are the] patriarchs; two [are the] tablets of the Covenant; One [is] our God, in heaven and on earth.

עֲשָׂרָה מִי יוֹדֵעַ? עֲשָׂרָה אֲנִי יוֹדֵעַ: עֲשָׂרָה דִבְּרַיָּא, תִּשְׁעָה יַרְחֵי לֵדָה, שְׁמוֹנָה יְמֵי מִילָה, שִׁבְעָה יְמֵי שַׁבַּתָּא, שִׁשָּׁה סִדְרֵי מִשְׁנָה, חֲמִשָּׁה חוּמְשֵׁי תוֹרָה, אַרְבַּע אִמָּהוֹת, שְׁלֹשָׁה אָבוֹת, שְׁנֵי לֻחוֹת הַבְּרִית, אֶחָד אֱלֹהֵינוּ שֶׁבַּשָּׁמַיִם וּבָאָרֶץ.

Who knows ten? I know ten: ten [are the] Ten Declarations; nine [are the] months of pregnancy; eight [are the] days to circumcision; seven [are the] days of the week; six [are the] orders of the Mishna, five [are the] books of the Torah; four [are the] matriarchs; three [are the] patriarchs; two [are the] tablets of the Covenant; One [is] our God, in heaven and on earth.

אַחַד עָשָׂר מִי יוֹדֵעַ? אַחַד עָשָׂר אֲנִי יוֹדֵעַ: אַחַד עָשָׂר כּוֹכְבַיָּא, עֲשָׂרָה דִבְּרַיָּא, תִּשְׁעָה יַרְחֵי לֵדָה, שְׁמוֹנָה יְמֵי מִילָה, שִׁבְעָה יְמֵי שַׁבַּתָּא, שִׁשָּׁה סִדְרֵי מִשְׁנָה, חֲמִשָּׁה חוּמְשֵׁי תוֹרָה, אַרְבַּע אִמָּהוֹת, שְׁלֹשָׁה אָבוֹת, שְׁנֵי לֻחוֹת הַבְּרִית, אֶחָד אֱלֹהֵינוּ שֶׁבַּשָּׁמַיִם וּבָאָרֶץ.

Who knows eleven? I know eleven: eleven [are the] stars [of Joseph's dream]; ten [are the] Ten Declarations; nine [are the] months of pregnancy; eight [are the] days to circumcision; seven [are the] days of the week; six [are the] orders of the Mishna, five [are the] books of the Torah; four [are the] matriarchs; three [are the] patriarchs; two [are the] tablets of the Covenant; One [is] our God, in heaven and on earth.

שְׁנֵים עָשָׂר מִי יוֹדֵעַ? שְׁנֵים עָשָׂר אֲנִי יוֹדֵעַ: שְׁנֵים עָשָׂר שִׁבְטַיָּא, אַחַד עָשָׂר כּוֹכְבַיָּא, עֲשָׂרָה דִבְּרַיָּא, תִּשְׁעָה יַרְחֵי לֵדָה, שְׁמוֹנָה יְמֵי מִילָה, שִׁבְעָה יְמֵי

שַׁבַּתָּא, שִׁשָּׁה סִדְרֵי מִשְׁנָה, חֲמִשָּׁה חוּמְשֵׁי תוֹרָה, אַרְבַּע אִמָּהוֹת, שְׁלֹשָׁה אָבוֹת, שְׁנֵי לֻחוֹת הַבְּרִית, אֶחָד אֱלֹהֵינוּ שֶׁבַּשָּׁמַיִם וּבָאָרֶץ.

Who knows twelve? I know twelve: twelve [are the] tribes [of Israel]; eleven [are the] stars [of Joseph's dream]; ten [are the] Ten Declarations; nine [are the] months of pregnancy; eight [are the] days to circumcision; seven [are the] days of the week; six [are the] orders of the Mishna, five [are the] books of the Torah; four [are the] matriarchs; three [are the] patriarchs; two [are the] tablets of the Covenant; One [is] our God, in heaven and on earth.

שְׁלֹשָׁה עָשָׂר מִי יוֹדֵעַ? שְׁלֹשָׁה עָשָׂר אֲנִי יוֹדֵעַ: שְׁלֹשָׁה עָשָׂר מִדַּיָּא, שְׁנֵים עָשָׂר שִׁבְטַיָּא, אַחַד עָשָׂר כּוֹכְבַיָּא, עֲשָׂרָה דִבְּרַיָּא, תִּשְׁעָה יַרְחֵי לֵדָה, שְׁמוֹנָה יְמֵי מִילָה, שִׁבְעָה יְמֵי שַׁבַּתָּא, שִׁשָּׁה סִדְרֵי מִשְׁנָה, חֲמִשָּׁה חוּמְשֵׁי תוֹרָה, אַרְבַּע אִמָּהוֹת, שְׁלֹשָׁה אָבוֹת, שְׁנֵי לֻחוֹת הַבְּרִית, אֶחָד אֱלֹהֵינוּ שֶׁבַּשָּׁמַיִם וּבָאָרֶץ.

Who knows thirteen? I know thirteen: thirteen [are the] Attributes [of God's mercy]; twelve [are the] tribes [of Israel]; eleven [are the] stars [of Joseph's dream]; ten [are the] Ten Declarations; nine [are the] months of pregnancy; eight [are the] days to circumcision; seven [are the] days of the week; six [are the] orders of the Mishna, five [are the] books of the Torah; four [are the] matriarchs; three [are the] patriarchs; two [are the] tablets of the Covenant; One [is] our God, in heaven and on earth.

Food for Thought

A. While the authorship of Echad Mi Yode'a is uncertain, tradition maintains that this *piyut* was displayed on a parchment hanging in the study of the Talmudist and mystic Rabbi Elazar of Worms, also known as Elazar Rokeach (1176–1238 CE).[62]

B. In spite of its early origins, however, Echad Mi Yode'a only begins to appear in the Haggadot of Ashkenaz in the sixteenth century.[63] A variant of Echad Mi Yode'a was traditionally recited in some communities on Shabbat during the seven days of celebration following a wedding.[64]

The question-and-answer format of this *piyut* certainly makes Echad Mi Yode'a an appropriate and valued addition to the Seder – an evening characterized by questions and answers.[65]

---

62 Kasher, *Haggada Shleima*, p. 190.
63 *Encyclopedia Judaica*.
64 Kasher, *Haggada Shleima*, p. 190.
65 *Seder Ha'aruch*, vol. 2, pp. 274–75.

Nirtza *Piyut* 7: Chad Gadya

חַד גַּדְיָא, חַד גַּדְיָא, דְּזַבִּין אַבָּא בִּתְרֵי זוּזֵי. חַד גַּדְיָא, חַד גַּדְיָא.

One little goat, one little goat that my father bought for two *zuzim*. One little goat, one little goat.

וְאָתָא שׁוּנְרָא, וְאָכְלָה לְגַּדְיָא, דְּזַבִּין אַבָּא בִּתְרֵי זוּזֵי. חַד גַּדְיָא, חַד גַּדְיָא.

And then came a cat and ate the goat that my father bought for two *zuzim*. One little goat, one little goat.

וְאָתָא כַלְבָּא, וְנָשַׁךְ לְשׁוּנְרָא, דְּאָכְלָה לְגַּדְיָא, דְּזַבִּין אַבָּא בִּתְרֵי זוּזֵי. חַד גַּדְיָא, חַד גַּדְיָא.

And then came a dog and bit the cat that ate the goat that my father bought for two *zuzim*. One little goat, one little goat.

וְאָתָא חוּטְרָא, וְהִכָּה לְכַלְבָּא, דְּנָשַׁךְ לְשׁוּנְרָא, דְּאָכְלָה לְגַּדְיָא, דְּזַבִּין אַבָּא בִּתְרֵי זוּזֵי. חַד גַּדְיָא, חַד גַּדְיָא.

And then came a stick and beat the dog that bit the cat that ate the goat that my father bought for two *zuzim*. One little goat, one little goat.

וְאָתָא נוּרָא, וְשָׂרַף לְחוּטְרָא, דְּהִכָּה לְכַלְבָּא, דְּנָשַׁךְ לְשׁוּנְרָא, דְּאָכְלָה לְגַּדְיָא, דְּזַבִּין אַבָּא בִּתְרֵי זוּזֵי. חַד גַּדְיָא, חַד גַּדְיָא.

And then came a fire and burned the stick that beat the dog that bit the cat that ate the goat that my father bought for two *zuzim*. One little goat, one little goat.

וְאָתָא מַיָּא, וְכָבָה לְנוּרָא, דְּשָׂרַף לְחוּטְרָא, דְּהִכָּה לְכַלְבָּא, דְּנָשַׁךְ לְשׁוּנְרָא, דְּאָכְלָה לְגַּדְיָא, דְּזַבִּין אַבָּא בִּתְרֵי זוּזֵי. חַד גַּדְיָא, חַד גַּדְיָא.

And then came water and quenched the fire that burned the stick that beat the dog that bit the cat that ate the goat that my father bought for two *zuzim*. One little goat, one little goat.

וְאָתָא תוֹרָא, וְשָׁתָא לְמַיָּא, דְּכָבָה לְנוּרָא, דְּשָׂרַף לְחוּטְרָא, דְּהִכָּה לְכַלְבָּא, דְּנָשַׁךְ לְשׁוּנְרָא, דְּאָכְלָה לְגַּדְיָא, דְּזַבִּין אַבָּא בִּתְרֵי זוּזֵי. חַד גַּדְיָא, חַד גַּדְיָא.

And then came an ox and drank the water that quenched the fire that burned the stick that beat the dog that bit the cat that ate the kid that my father bought for two *zuzim*. One little goat, one little goat.

וְאָתָא הַשּׁוֹחֵט, וְשָׁחַט לְתוֹרָא, דְּשָׁתָא לְמַיָּא, דְּכָבָה לְנוּרָא, דְּשָׂרַף לְחוּטְרָא,דְּהִכָּה לְכַלְבָּא, דְּנָשַׁךְ לְשׁוּנְרָא, דְּאָכְלָה לְגַּדְיָא, דְּזַבִּין אַבָּא בִּתְרֵי זוּזֵי. חַד גַּדְיָא, חַד גַּדְיָא.

And then came the slaughterer and slaughtered the ox that drank the water that quenched the fire that burned the stick that beat the dog that bit the cat that ate the goat that my father bought for two *zuzim*. One little goat, one little goat.

וְאָתָא מַלְאַךְ הַמָּוֶת, וְשָׁחַט לְשׁוֹחֵט, דְּשָׁחַט לְתוֹרָא, דְּשָׁתָא לְמַיָּא, דְּכָבָה לְנוּרָא, דְּשָׂרַף לְחוּטְרָא,דְּהִכָּה לְכַלְבָּא, דְּנָשַׁךְ לְשׁוּנְרָא, דְּאָכְלָה לְגַדְיָא, דְּזַבִּין אַבָּא בִּתְרֵי זוּזֵי. חַד גַּדְיָא, חַד גַּדְיָא.

And then came the Angel of Death and slaughtered the slaughterer, who slaughtered the ox that drank the water that quenched the fire that burned the stick that beat the dog that bit the cat that ate the goat that my father bought for two *zuzim*. One little goat, one little goat.

וְאָתָא הַקָּדוֹשׁ בָּרוּךְ הוּא, וְשָׁחַט לְמַלְאָךְ הַמָּוֶת, דְּשָׁחַט לְשׁוֹחֵט, דְּשָׁחַט לְתוֹרָא, דְּשָׁתָא לְמַיָּא, דְּכָבָה לְנוּרָא, דְּשָׂרַף לְחוּטְרָא, דְּהִכָּה לְכַלְבָּא, דְּנָשַׁךְ לְשׁוּנְרָא, דְּאָכְלָה לְגַדְיָא, דְּזַבִּין אַבָּא בִּתְרֵי זוּזֵי. חַד גַּדְיָא, חַד גַּדְיָא.

And then came the Holy One, Blessed Be He, and slaughtered the Angel of Death, who slaughtered the slaughterer, who slaughtered the ox that drank the water that quenched the fire that burned the stick that beat the dog that bit the cat that ate the goat that my father bought for two *zuzim*. One little goat, one little goat.

Food for Thought

A. The last *piyut* recited on the Seder night is the most well known of the Haggada's *piyutim*, yet also the most mysterious and obscure.

Chad Gadya is a poem of unknown authorship, but like Echad Mi Yode'a is reported to have been displayed in the study of Rabbi Elazar Rokeach in the early thirteenth century. This early sighting notwithstanding, Chad Gadya is the most recent of the Nirtza poems to be included at the Seder, making its first appearance in a printed Haggada in Prague in 1590.

B. After indicating that a solitary goat is bought by a father for two *zuzim* (a *zuz* being an ancient Judean coin), Chad Gadya outlines a series of nine violent attacks: by a cat upon the goat; by a dog upon the cat; by a stick upon the dog, and so forth, culminating in God's destruction of the Angel of Death. No reference is made to any subject associated with Pesach. In fact, no direct reference is made to any overriding religious theme at all.

The obvious question, therefore, must be raised: Why is Chad Gadya included in the Haggada, particularly as the culminating entry in the text?

C. A variety of answers have been suggested by the scholars.

Some scholars view Chad Gadya as an allegorical review of the turbulent historical passage of the Jewish people. The goat, these scholars maintain, symbolizes the Jewish nation, while the various "attackers" represent that nation's countless persecutors across the ages. The *piyut* ends on a positive note, with the ultimate redemption symbolized by God's slaying of the Angel of Death.

Other authorities offer vastly different interpretations for this poem, suggesting themes ranging from the spiritual challenges confronting individuals over the course of their lives to the steps of the Pesach ritual performed in Temple times.

D. Perhaps, however, another global interpretation can be offered for the strange inclusion of Chad Gadya in the Seder service.

Throughout the evening that now draws to a close, we have celebrated the "Seder," the divinely driven historical "order" that shapes our nation's journey (see p. 14). We have shared in a world in which everything makes sense, all questions have answers and God's presence is clearly evident in our national history from its earliest footfalls.

We now, however, prepare to leave the rarefied atmosphere of the Seder and reenter a world in which God's presence can be difficult to discern – where cats eat goats, dogs bite cats, sticks beat dogs with impunity; where the natural order continues around us, without apparent divine intervention. More significantly, we reemerge into a world that often does not make sense, in which questions don't always have answers and the righteous may well suffer while the wicked may well prosper.

As the Seder closes, Chad Gadya offers a nod to the world in which we daily live, *yet simultaneously offers a significant qualification.*

By weaving a tale in which seemingly random violence ultimately gives way to God's will, this *piyut* urges us not to be misled by "appearances" around us. God is present in our world, Chad Gadya declares, even when He is hidden; our lives are not governed by chance but by divine plans beyond our comprehension. We are traveling toward a day when all will become clear.

The Seder is designed to remain with us long after its conclusion; coloring our sometimes difficult days with a deep, abiding belief in God's guiding hand. Serving as the "airlock" through which we move from the Seder evening to the rest of our lives, Chad Gadya marks the first step in the application of the Seder's messages to a challenging, often bewildering world.

Afterword

And thus, as the Seder ends, we turn our attention to new beginnings.

Step by step, from Kiddush to Chad Gadya, the Haggada has led us along a transformative path designed to immerse us, as participants, in the flow of Jewish history. We have been challenged to connect with our past; to catch a glimpse of our future; and, above all, to energize our present efforts.

When all is said and done, however, this evening's carefully planned journey will find true significance only in its aftermath.

If, through our active participation, we have allowed the Seder to successfully work its magic; if the evening's lessons will resonate in our hearts and shape our actions during the days to come; then, who knows? Perhaps this year our nation will reach its goals. Perhaps our next Seder will be celebrated together with our entire people, in the shadow of a rebuilt Temple, in the holy city of Yerushalayim.

Rabbi Shmuel Goldin

Made in the USA
Las Vegas, NV
12 April 2024

88608335R10131